DISCRIMINATION LAUNDERING

While discrimination in the workplace is often perceived to be instigated by "rogue" employees acting against the better interest of their employers, the truth is often the opposite: organizations are inciting discrimination through the work environments that they create. Worse, the law increasingly ignores this reality and exacerbates the problem. In this groundbreaking book, *Discrimination Laundering*, Tristin K. Green describes the process of discrimination laundering, showing how judges are changing the law to protect employers, and why. By bringing organizations back into the discussion of discrimination, with real-world stories and extensive social-science research, Green shows how organizational and legal efforts to minimize discrimination – usually by policing individuals over broader organizational change – are taking us in the wrong direction, and how the law could do better by creating incentives for organizational efforts that are likely to minimize discrimination, instead of inciting it.

Tristin K. Green is a professor of law at the University of San Francisco and a member of the Law and Society Association. She has written extensively in the field of employment discrimination law, seeking to better understand how discrimination operates and how to better structure the law to incentivize meaningful change. She has co-authored an article with Alexandra Kalev, a sociologist, on the relational nature of discrimination, and co-authored a casebook edition with Herma Hill Kay entitled *Sex-Based Discrimination*.

Discrimination Laundering

THE RISE OF ORGANIZATIONAL INNOCENCE AND THE CRISIS OF EQUAL OPPORTUNITY LAW

TRISTIN K. GREEN

CAMBRIDGE
UNIVERSITY PRESS

CAMBRIDGE
UNIVERSITY PRESS

University Printing House, Cambridge CB2 8BS, United Kingdom
One Liberty Plaza, 20th Floor, New York, NY 10006, USA
477 Williamstown Road, Port Melbourne, VIC 3207, Australia
4843/24, 2nd Floor, Ansari Road, Daryaganj, Delhi – 110002, India
79 Anson Road, #06-04/06, Singapore 079906

Cambridge University Press is part of the University of Cambridge.

It furthers the University's mission by disseminating knowledge in the pursuit of
education, learning, and research at the highest international levels of excellence.

www.cambridge.org
Information on this title: www.cambridge.org/9781107142008
10.1017/9781316494158

First published 2017

Printed in the United Kingdom by Clays, St Ives plc

A catalog record for this publication is available from the British Library.

Library of Congress Cataloguing in Publication Data
Names: Green, Tristin K., author.
Title: Discrimination laundering : the rise of organizational innocence
and the crisis of equal opportunity law / Tristin K. Green.
Description: Cambridge [UK]; New York : Cambridge University Press, 2017. |
Includes bibliographical references and index.
Identifiers: LCCN 2016026405| ISBN 9781107142008 (hardback) |
ISBN 9781316506998 (paperback)
Subjects: LCSH: Discrimination in employment–Law and legislation. |
Labor laws and legislation. | BISAC: LAW / Labor & Employment.
Classification: LCC K1770 .G74 2017 | DDC 344.7301/133–dc23
LC record available at https://lccn.loc.gov/2016026405

ISBN 978-1-107-14200-8 Hardback
ISBN 978-1-316-50699-8 Paperback

Contents

Acknowledgments   *vii*

Introduction   1

1   The Threads of Organizational Innocence   20

PART I: DISCRIMINATION LAUNDERING

2   Individual Discrimination: The Emerging Law of
     Complaint and Response   45

3   Systemic Discrimination: Erasing the Aggregate and
     Entrenching a Law of Complaint and Response   66

4   Class, Culture, and Limiting the Purview of Title VII   85

PART II: WHAT IS WRONG WITH
DISCRIMINATION LAUNDERING

5   The Laundered Workplace   101

6   How Organizations Discriminate – and What They
     Can Do To Stop   116

PART III: REVERSING DISCRIMINATION
LAUNDERING

7   Reversing Discrimination Laundering   145

Notes   162
Index   199

Acknowledgments

I owe thanks to many people. Those whom I mention here went above and beyond, reading portions of the manuscript and in some cases, the full beast. To Catherine Albiston, Rachel Arnow-Richman, Camille Gear Rich, Orly Lobel, Leticia Saucedo, Michelle Travis, and Deborah Widiss for instrumental and collaborative brainstorming at early stages. To Kathy Abrams, Martha Chamallas, and Alexandra Kalev for their careful and thoughtful reads of several chapters, and to Thomas Healy, Solangel Maldonado, Michelle Travis, and Deborah Widiss, who took on the more herculean task of reading a full draft. Solangel and Deborah were extraordinarily generous with their time and comments on an early, still-forming version. And to Ellen Berrey and several anonymous reviewers for Cambridge who sharpened my thinking and provided insightful and constructive criticism at the proposal stage.

I also benefited from feedback on my presentation of the manuscript in various stages at faculty colloquia, including at the Seattle University School of Law and Drexel University Thomas R. Kline School of Law, and at conferences, and also from feedback over the years on my articles in which I explored similar themes and ideas.

Thanks also to Amy Wright, Co-Director of the Zief Law Library, for lightning-quick and helpful research and advice when my own research skills failed me.

To the many others with whom I had numerous conversations along the way, whose work I read and re-read, and also to those who shared with me stories of their working lives and experiences, for helping me think through these important issues. My goal is to be thoughtful, if not always right, and I could not have gotten even close without many conversations, both with people who agree with me and with many who do not.

Most of all, to Mark and Avery, the boys in my life who put up with the long process of my writing a first book – and with my constant remarking about racial and gender inequality as it unfolds in all aspects of our lives. And for supporting me always, my mother, Jo Green.

Introduction

Equal opportunity – an ideal that Americans agreed upon in the 1960s and have valued ever since – is under threat. Equal opportunity as equal treatment, pure and simple. A common commitment to a workplace where racial and gender stereotypes and biases will not infect employment decisions, will not determine worker success. The threat is playing out in the American courts as they shape employment discrimination law under Title VII of the Civil Rights Act, the principal federal statute prohibiting discrimination in the United States. Over the past several decades, the courts have driven the law in a dramatic turn toward protecting employers from liability for discrimination. The shift is pervasive and in forward motion. It is affecting all areas, from the law governing individual acts of discrimination and harassment to the law of systemic discrimination. Worse, hidden as it is behind talk of procedure, agency principles, and civility codes, the shift is going unnoticed.

The root of the threat lies not in outright judicial hostility to equal opportunity law or civil rights generally, although there is some of that, but in a deeper, more fundamental change in view about how discrimination operates within organizations. Employment discrimination is increasingly seen as a problem of low-level, rogue employees acting on biases that are socially constructed and carried out without the influence and against the interest of the organizations for which they work. Organizations are innocent under this view. They provide the venue, the neutral physical architecture for discrimination, but nothing more.

This book tells the story of discrimination laundering: the rise of organizational innocence in the courts' understanding of employment discrimination and the corresponding narrowing of employer liability in the law. We are used to thinking about laundering in the financial context as a process of taking dirty, illegal money, accumulated through racketeering, illegal drug sales, and gun deals, for example, and superficially cleansing it by running it through legitimate organizations. Discrimination laundering is a similar process, but it is a process of law, a process whereby the law cleanses the workplace of unlawful discrimination – not in reality, but in perception, by sleight of hand. Employment discrimination today is being recast as interpersonal conflict and not properly the subject of Title VII concern. And organizations are being recast as mere bystanders, even victims, of the discrimination that is recognized by law. Once recast, organizations are increasingly protected by the law from responsibility for their own role in inciting bias and discrimination within their walls.

Discrimination laundering falls squarely within the great American risk shift of the twenty-first century.[1] Employees bear more of their health and retirement costs than ever before. Organizations increasingly undertake routine mass layoffs, firing workers on an economic downturn or moving mammoth factories to areas with cheaper labor. They are hiring more part-time, contingent workers with hourly pay and variable schedules that can literally fluctuate with market demands.[2] Discrimination laundering similarly places the costs of discrimination principally on individual employees, both the victims and the perceived or potential discriminators, leaving employers with little responsibility.

Discrimination laundering also aligns with powerful ideological movements in American law, organizations, and society. Individuals and individual agency dominate an American discourse of liberal individualism. In so many ways we tend in American culture to emphasize individuals over all else, as causal actors and as victims, from the rhetoric of choice to that of civil rights. Neo-liberalism takes this emphasis on individuals even further to position the individuals as rational and empowered participants in an unfettered capitalist and increasingly globalized market.[3]

Post-racialism (and post-sexism) similarly permeates the social lens.[4] The idea here is that we as a society are past making race or sex matter in our policies. Inequalities experienced by members of racial groups in American society are seen as a product principally if not exclusively of individuals' bad choices rather than of discrimination, disadvantage, and group privilege. Post-racialism also translates today into a pervasive and growing sense among whites and men that race and sex are just not a big deal anymore, even when expressly encountered in day-to-day interactions. Under this view, race and sex are simply sidelines to interpersonal conflicts, preferences, and tensions that can occur in a variety of venues of our lives. Post-racialism wipes the slate clean, leaving us with no more reason to see racial or gender insult or discrimination than to see insult on some other basis, or no basis at all ("Those two just never got along.").

The rhetoric of diversity pervasive in the management profession, organizations, and broader society adds further fuel to the personalizing fire. "Managing diversity" describes a managerial as opposed to a legal obligation.[5] It emphasizes individual conduct in discrete interactions rather than change in the structural or cultural influences on those interactions, and it fosters mediation of personal conflict that can arise out of difference of all kinds, not just difference around categories like race and sex protected under Title VII. In this way, diversity and conflict around diversity are driven to the personal and business purview and severed from nondiscrimination goals.

Indeed, the personalizing of discrimination (so that much discrimination is rendered invisible to and not actionable by law, and so that organizations have narrow legal responsibility for the discrimination that remains) may be the single most dominant refrain in the rise of organizational innocence, the new frame for thinking about how discrimination operates, and in the narrowing of employer responsibility for inequality and discrimination in the law. Organizations are seen at worst to provide a physical venue for discrimination, just as neighborhoods provide geographic proximity for gangs or family-run picnics and schools maintain playgrounds where kids can play and also tease and bully their peers.

But the frame of organizational innocence is wrong. It misses the many ways in which organizations construct, leverage, and capitalize on race and sex today. Brands, sales forces, and advertising teams are designed to appeal to people along race and sex lines. Employees are matched to markets and sometimes even job categories according to their race and sex. And even when organizations do not formally sanction discrimination, they can incite discrimination through the structures, practices, and cultures that they create and maintain. Organizations actively shape their cultures using specific management tools, many of which are regularly outlined in the business literature, on the pages of the *Harvard Business Review* and similar publications. Organizations recruit and reward certain behavioral and appearance styles, encouraging a cultural "fit" with the industry and the organization. They structure account distribution, family accommodation policies, and pay, promotion, and discipline systems with employee behavior expressly in mind. These systems, practices, and cultures in turn affect the interactions, judgments, and decisions of the employees who operate within them on a daily basis.

Not only is the story of organizational innocence wrong; the practical effects of the discrimination laundering that it fuels are dire. The shift in law alters the legal pressure put on organizations so that in the laundered workplace, organizations have little antidiscrimination work to do. High-level executives must refrain from making comments that reflect bias in the process of making their policy decisions, and from instructing lower-level decision makers to discriminate. Beyond that, organizations can focus their nondiscrimination efforts almost exclusively on creating systems for individual complaint and on responding to complaints within those systems, investigating discrete incidents and delivering discipline, where appropriate. Organizations have no legal incentive to monitor for patterns of discrimination or to consider whether their structures, practices, or cultures are inciting biases and resulting in disparate outcomes for women and racial minorities.

And this is precisely how things are playing out in the field, as organizations focus on individuals over all else. Aside from formal nondiscrimination policies and grievance processes, diversity training is the most popular diversity measure adopted by organizations today, alongside measures designed to insulate managerial decisions from bias. These measures have been shown to be largely ineffective, even harmful. Complaints, investigations, and disciplinary actions result in individual policing without attention to broader structural causes. Under these measures, individual employees – including those who are perceived to have discriminated by making an insensitive remark or a decision tainted by racial or gender bias – take the brunt of nondiscrimination efforts while much of the discrimination that produces disparate outcomes in employment continues.

Yet stratification and segregation persist along race and sex lines both in the overall American workplace and in some industries and some organizations more than others. Just a quick glance at recent research tells us this much. Before the Civil Rights Act, black men, black women, and white women almost never held the same job in the same workplace as white men. That changed in the 1960s, when black men made strong gains in skilled blue-collar jobs and black women made gains in clerical work. But in 1980, occupational integration stalled, and since then in some cases has taken a step backward. Transportation services, media and motion pictures, construction, securities and commodities brokerages all reflect a trend toward re-segregation today.[6] Women of all races have also made inroads into men's jobs since the 1960s, but segregation and stratification persist. Half of women or men in this country would have to change occupations for there to be gender parity across occupations.[7] And segregation is directly related to the pay gap. Women's median earnings are less than men's in nearly all occupations, and occupations dominated by men tend to pay more than occupations that are female dominated.[8]

There are certainly many causes for the segregation and stratification that we see today in the American workforce and in American workplaces. Prison and criminal sentencing policies, health-care disparities, poverty, worker preferences, housing segregation, education, family responsibilities; the list goes on. The research nonetheless consistently points to discrimination – inequities in treatment in employment – as one cause. Simple test studies in which sets of black and white job candidates are paired, given equivalent credentials, and sent to apply for jobs show not only that black applicants are less likely to receive an interview than their white counterparts, but also that if they get an interview, they are likely to have a shorter interview and to encounter more negative remarks. They are more likely to be denied a job and steered to less desirable jobs.[9] One recent study found that white applicants are preferred by many hiring managers even when the white applicant has a criminal record and the black applicant does not.[10] Sophisticated statistical studies similarly show that discrimination is a likely explanation for at least some of the segregation and stratification along race, sex, and race-sex lines in position and pay in this country.[11]

What we need is more positive inter-group interactions at work, not fewer, and yet the policing mindset that discrimination laundering promotes entrenches segregation and raises social anxiety to make productive inter-group interactions less likely. We need the law to pressure organizations to pay more attention to their structures, systems, and work cultures – to the context of the workplace over which they already exert substantial control – than to individuals and discrete moments of interaction or decision. Research shows that organizational-level changes to things such as recruitment practices, accountability structures (including having leaders who take seriously non-discrimination as an institutional goal), and systems for organizing work and for determining merit can improve organizational conditions so that they are likely to minimize rather than incite bias in the workplace. There is no single answer for all organizations, but there is reason to be optimistic: organizations can and do influence whether interactions within their walls are likely to be bias reducing or bias producing. We need organizations to put nondiscrimination on the table, in their boardrooms and their executive suites, not just to mandate the latest version of "bias-busting" training for managers or to tamp down on individuals as a way of checking a compliance box.

This book calls for a renewed, open, and deliberative conversation about employer responsibility and the future of equal employment opportunity law based on a full picture of how discrimination operates in workplaces. Understanding the full picture – and that organizational innocence presents only part of the picture – does not resolve all of the difficult questions about what the law should look like. But it does alter our perspective. Bringing organizations back in, acknowledging that they play a role in how and to what extent discrimination operates within their walls, shows how important it is for the law to better see organizational sources of discrimination, to identify those organizations that are inciting bias and producing discrimination, and to incentivize organizational change that will actually avoid and reduce it.

The book makes several recommendations for how the law might do this. Most importantly, reversing discrimination laundering will require an acknowledgment of the limits of individual discrimination law and of the potential of systemic discrimination law. It will also require an openness to the law as a tool for change, including change of some of our longstanding work cultures, and steady resistance to the idea that organizations cannot effectively structure and manage their workforces in ways that minimize rather than incite discrimination.

THE BOOK'S APPROACH

This is a book primarily about the law, not as dry, abstract subject, but as ongoing influence on work organizations and in turn on people's everyday lives. It draws on and is intended to complement a very rich, developing body of research on how biases operate within organizations and on what organizations can do and what they are actually doing to reduce discrimination. Close analysis of the law is lagging behind advances in the social sciences. Although there has been some recent study of plaintiff and defendant success rates in employment discrimination litigation,[12] particularly on the heels of several significant procedural decisions of the Supreme Court, and also some recent work on litigant perceptions of fairness in employment discrimination litigation,[13] there has been relatively little attention paid to how the substantive law of employment discrimination as a whole has been shifting or to the consequences of that shift.

The book tells the story of discrimination laundering primarily through legal cases, many but not all decided by the Supreme Court of the United States. It situates these legal cases in the context of broader movements in law, legal scholarship, social science, organizations and the personnel profession, and society, seeking not to establish precise causal connections but to expose a general movement in understandings of and discourse around discrimination. Research shows that discrimination discourse – what we say about what discrimination is and who is at fault or responsible – has broad reach, from boardrooms to courtrooms. The future of equal opportunity in employment law will depend on shifting this discourse as much as on revising the legal doctrine.

Although principally about the law, the book is also about the relationship between the law and social science. Social science has driven critique of employment discrimination law for many years now. Understanding how biases operate in the workplace helps us to see better how and where the law is inadequate, and to see when it relies on stories that are incomplete. A less frequent (but potentially more productive) approach to the relationship between law and social science works the other way around. What should the law look like in light of the social science on discrimination within work organizations, including its limitations? How should the law incorporate knowledge from the social sciences, now and over time? There are better and worse ways for the law to structure its relationship with the social sciences on questions of how discrimination operates and how organizations can best avoid or reduce discrimination within their walls, and we should be careful to select the better ones over the worse.

TERMINOLOGY AND CLARIFICATIONS

On Talking About Discrimination

Discrimination today can refer to many things. It can mean simply treating one person differently than another on any basis, or even simply noticing difference. For example, I can discriminate between two people, one wearing red shoelaces, the other blue, or I can have a discriminating eye. More often, however, the colloquial, everyday meaning of discrimination overlaps with its legal meaning. Treating a person differently than another because of their protected group status in making an employment decision or creating an environment that is hostile to members of a protected group is discrimination legally (it violates Title VII of the Civil Rights Act and sometimes the U.S. Constitution). But the law also defines as discrimination some employer actions that are not typically included in more colloquial use: disparate impact is a common example. The Supreme Court and Congress have determined that an employer can violate Title VII when it uses an employment practice that has a disparate impact on members of a protected group if the employer's use of the practice is not justified by business necessity. The employer is sometimes said to "discriminate" in this scenario, even though neither it nor its agents have made distinctions on the basis of a person's protected characteristics.[14]

When I use the term "discrimination" I usually mean the more colloquial, human process of bias influencing decisions or interactions in ways that result in different treatment of people belonging to different groups, whites and blacks, whites and Asians, men and women, etc. This book is most concerned with discrimination as different treatment operating within institutions, specifically work organizations. When I do not intend the term to have that meaning, I will explain how and why I use the term.

Why Race and Sex (and What About Other Protected Groups?)

This book focuses principally on race- and sex-based discrimination. It does this for several reasons, both purposeful and practical. The Civil Rights Act was passed in 1964 after years of intense political battle, and many failures. It passed on a wave of tumult and social unrest, including when peaceful marchers, many of them schoolchildren, were met with fire hoses by Eugene "Bull" Connor, the police commissioner of Birmingham, Alabama. The images that flooded the media at the time were images of a racial caste system, white power, and black disempowerment, and they generated new momentum for a civil rights movement that envisioned minimal protections against longstanding racial inequality and discrimination.[15]

Neither the Civil Rights Act, though, nor Title VII is limited to race. Each also includes religion and national origin – and sex. Popular accounts once held that sex was added to the bill as a "joke," or a means of tanking the bill, though history tells us otherwise.[16] It was the result of an ongoing and hard-fought battle for women, who had long been kept in certain jobs and mostly out of the workplace. They entered the factories in droves during World War II, only to be sent back home when the men returned from war.

Race and sex have been and continue to be the most common forms of discrimination alleged by individuals in the United States.[17] National origin discrimination claims are also common, particularly involving discrimination against Latino and Latina workers, but also against Asians and Native Americans, and I include these claims under the broader terminology of race.[18] These categories – race and sex – also dominate in the social science research, and in the media.

It is also difficult to think about the big picture, a law of nondiscrimination obligation that involves multiple legal theories, without narrowing down the realm of inquiry in some way. Indeed, even with my focus on race and sex, readers will see places where I do not fully flesh out differences between the two, both in their legal histories and their lived experiences, yesterday and today.

The law of employment discrimination is nonetheless generally considered trans-substantive in that its major theories and doctrines carry across protected categories, even across statutory enactments, to inform the law, for example, of disability-based and age-based discrimination, which are covered by different statutes. The Age Discrimination in Employment Act (ADEA), passed in 1972, prohibits age-based discrimination;[19] the Americans with Disabilities Act (ADA), passed in 1990 and substantially amended in 2008, prohibits disability-based discrimination.[20] These Acts differ in some important respects from Title VII, but they share core principles and the law of Title VII is, for the most part, applied to cases brought under these statutes, and vice versa. Indeed, in several places I draw on cases that involve allegations of discrimination on the basis of age and even veteran status when the legal theories applied in the cases can be expected also to apply to cases involving race and sex filed under Title VII. At the same time, I hope that telling the story of discrimination laundering as it is occurring in Title VII law, focusing on race and sex, will advance our capacity to address discrimination beyond these categories.

On Talking About the Law

I resist using legal theories to organize the conceptual frame for how we think about employment discrimination. Some legal scholars in particular may find this awkward, even off-putting. We are so accustomed to juxtaposing disparate impact theory against disparate treatment theory around proof of intent, for example, that we find it almost impossible to talk about the law in this area without doing so. But this habit of allowing legal theories to frame our conceptions of how discrimination operates is a mistake. To start from legal theories cabins us from seeing clearly what the law is missing and it constrains us from thinking practically about where the law should go. I will explain and address legal theories in this book, and I will propose amendments to the law that build on existing theories. However, I will try to start one step back, at the point of how discrimination is (and might be) identified in workplaces. I frame the law roughly around two principal categories: claims seeking redress and change focused on individual instances of discrimination and claims seeking redress and change focused on systemic discrimination, discrimination that is pervasive and often cannot be identified at the level of individual instance, with hostile work environments sometimes falling in the former category and sometimes in the latter.

MAP

Part I tells the story of discrimination laundering. Chapter 1 sets important theoretical and empirical groundwork, including an initial tracing of the conceptual steps of organizational innocence. Chapters 2, 3, and 4 illustrate three different ways that discrimination is being laundered through law.

Two are doctrinal shifts: first, narrowing employer responsibility for individual instances of discrimination by introducing a duty of care (employers are expected to establish processes for complaint and to process complaints within that system); and second, hampering the law's ability to identify those organizations in which discrimination is widespread through aggregate statistics. The third is more subtle in the judicial perception of events and of Title VII purview: casting racial and gendered interactions as interpersonal conflict and resisting Title VII as a statute intended to disrupt gendered and racialized work cultures.

Part II shows what is wrong with discrimination laundering. Chapter 5 takes a close look at the laundered workplace, examining measures being taken by organizations to avoid or reduce discrimination. In the laundered workplace, organizations focus their attention on providing written nondiscrimination policies and systems for complaint, and on responding to individual complaints with investigation and appropriate discipline of individuals. The additional measures that organizations take to reduce discrimination are usually narrowly focused on training and trying to insulate key decisions from bias. Research suggests, however, that these measures are unlikely to reduce discrimination, and may actually hinder progress.

The diversity rhetoric that pervades organizations also translates narrowly into efforts to increase the numbers of women and racial minorities in higher status positions within organizations. Not only are these efforts minimal (and often ineffectual), even at this level, but no efforts at all are made at the lower levels of many organizations. Moreover, individuals are policed while organizational influences on biases and stereotypes remain in place.

Chapter 6 shows that organizations are not innocent bystanders to discrimination. It challenges organizational innocence by presenting a fuller picture of how employment discrimination operates – and how organizations discriminate. Research shows that organizations play a significant role in creating and sustaining discrimination and inequalities. Organizations actively construct and capitalize on race and gender, from enhancing their diversity banners to leveraging race and gender for market share to devising low-cost, disempowered labor classes. And they devise and shape the policies and structures, the practices and cultures that form the conditions for interaction and decisions by their employees and ultimately that shape their employees' opportunities for work success.

Part III proposes a way forward and identifies several key questions for debate. We need to tell new stories about how discrimination operates. The full story of how discrimination operates includes organizational sources as much as individual ones, and our law should reflect that reality. The law should incentivize organizational choices that will result in work environments that reduce or minimize discrimination, not incite it.

GETTING STARTED: THINKING ABOUT INDIVIDUALS, ORGANIZATIONS, AND DISCRIMINATION

Discrimination is a human problem. We have a long history in the United States of categorizing along racial and gender lines and of subordinating out-groups in a multitude of ways. Whether we think about it in terms of stereotypes or animus, cognitive biases or emotions and discomfort and avoidance, people can and do continue to discriminate. We have made progress, no doubt. More Americans today are moving toward openly subscribing to an egalitarian ideal. But this progress does not mean that we are free of our discriminatory biases, no matter how much we may want to be. This is the human side of discrimination.

Discrimination is also an organizational problem. Organizations are actively involved in producing discrimination, even today, long after they have taken down their signs indicating that "No Negroes Need Apply." Some executives today continue to make consciously race- and sex-based decisions. But organizations also incite discrimination by creating the context for human decision making and day-to-day interaction at work. I will turn in later chapters to draw out more comprehensively the research indicating that organizations are active participants in discrimination.

For now, two brief introductory stories, one situated in the legal department of a large organization in the late-1980s, the other in a small venture capital firm in Silicon Valley in the 2010s. These stories are not intended to resolve controversial legal questions about when employers should be held responsible for discrimination; those questions will be addressed (if not entirely resolved) much later in the book. Rather, these stories are thought-provoking starters. They are intended to give readers some initial grounding, a taste of how discrimination can operate, raising questions and I hope also at least a vague awareness of why we should be troubled, even alarmed, by the discrimination laundering that is occurring on our watch.

INTRODUCTORY STORY NUMBER ONE

Large Company X, a successful product manufacturing and sales organization, was ordered by a federal court in the 1970s to create and implement an affirmative action program upon a judicial finding that the company had engaged in a pattern of "egregious discrimination" against women and blacks.[21] By the

1980s, the company had improved substantially the representation of women and minorities in the lower echelons of the company, jobs like sales, clerical work, and factory work. However, the representation of minorities and women in higher level jobs remained quite small. In 1989 there were three black attorneys (two men and one woman) in the forty-three-person legal department at the company.

That year, sociologist Jennifer Pierce took a job as a paralegal in the company's legal department. Over the next ten years, she would observe behavior within the organization (for the nine months that she worked there) and conduct numerous informal and formal interviews with attorneys who worked at the firm, including interviews with attorneys who had worked at the firm during her time there.[22] Her goal was to better understand how professionals in one workplace understood affirmative action and its effects.[23] I draw on Pierce's work in telling this story about discrimination and bias. In doing so, I focus more closely on the experience of one African American male attorney, Randall Kingsley,[24] his colleagues, and the organization in which they worked.

Most of the white male attorneys whom Pierce interviewed described their work at Large Company X in positive terms, but they described the affirmative action mandate imposed upon the company as having a mostly negative impact on their working experience. They told of being afraid to share jokes or to use certain words, of "walking around on eggshells."[25] They also expressed a view that affirmative action meant that positions sometimes went to people who were unqualified and specifically that the policy at the firm had "outlived its usefulness."[26]

Kingsley and the other two black lawyers at Company X had all left the company by the late 1990s. Kingsley started working in the legal department of the firm in 1985 and left four years later, in 1989. His reasons for leaving the firm were, as he puts it, a "long story": "It started with a lot of small stuff, and the small stuff just added up."[27]

But before I get to Randall Kingsley's impressions of his experience at Large Company X, a bit more about the white male attorneys and their impressions of Kingsley, his departure, and his career trajectory after he left the firm. According to the head of the legal department, Kingsley had "done very well for himself" since leaving the firm.[28] Another lawyer in the department said that Kingsley had landed a much higher-paying job at another firm, after he "cashed in on all the opportunities available for minorities" at Large Company X.[29] This lawyer also confided that he found Kingsley "demanding" and "abrasive" and said that he had doubted Kingsley's "qualifications from the beginning," adding that "this assessment has nothing to do with the fact that Randall Kingsley is an African American."[30] Other white attorneys also said that Kingsley took a much better job elsewhere. Many mentioned that he was "too flashy" and "too demanding" in his requests for help while he was at the company.[31] The white men described any difficulty that Kingsley had at the firm as isolated incidents with individual attorneys and as a matter of style and personality. As one attorney put it, Kingsley just did not "fit in."[32]

Kingsley described his experience differently. But first, the facts. Kingsley did not leave Large Company X for a higher-paying job. The first job he took was a lateral job at another big company, earning the same amount that he was earning at Large Company X, $45,000 a year. He left that company in 1993 to open up a firm with a friend from law school, and in 1998, ten years after he left Large Company X, he was earning $47,000 per year.[33]

The "small stuff" as Kingsley calls it started with his first assignment.[34] Kingsley's interest and expertise were in employment law, but the head of the department gave him a first assignment in the field of patent law. Kingsley expressed his concern about taking on work outside his area of expertise, but the head assured him that there were plenty of people in the department to help him if he had any questions. When Kingsley later approached senior lawyers for help, however, they reacted negatively or indifferently, telling him they were "too busy." He heard from some of the paralegals that the senior attorneys joked among themselves about his style of dress and personal manner. There were other incidents, too: one attorney "forgot" a lunch date he had made with him; another made jokes whenever Kingsley came into his office; another ignored his contributions in meetings. It was clear to Kingsley that the other new associate, a white man, was not being treated in the same way. Kingsley began to feel alienated from his colleagues, isolated, and angry. Finally, he decided to "call them on it." When he did, their responses varied from excuses to assuring him that their behavior had nothing to do with his race, to the head of the department yelling, "Are you calling me a racist?"[35]

How can this story help us in our thinking about discrimination and how it really operates? It is possible that Kingsley was treated the same as his white counterparts, perhaps not well but no differently than others. But assuming that he was treated differently from his fellow associates at the firm, who were white, this story of Randall Kingsley's and his colleagues' experience shows how seemingly minor, individualized actions and interactions can operate over time to exclude and undermine success. It also shows how employment discrimination can be more relational than static, involving perceptions that coalesce through intragroup interaction (and often in less public settings) – interactions between the white men in their offices or in the halls when Kingsley was not around – as well as through intergroup encounters. And it shows the difficulty that whites can have in seeing or at least acknowledging racial issues and the ease with which they can create dominant stories that revolve around personality and individual choice. Kingsley in their version chose to take other opportunities, and his choice was entirely independent from their treatment of him.

The story of Kingsley and his time at Large Company X can also widen the lens so that we can more easily see the active role of the organization in the discrimination that Kingsley may have experienced. The company's affirmative action policy, after all, jumps out as an obvious backdrop for the racial disadvantage that Kingsley may have faced. The policy arguably worked to skew white male attorneys' perceptions of the competency of black attorneys like Kingsley. It led them to believe that all black attorneys were less qualified than their white peers. The policy need not have resulted in this thinking, but as implemented from leaders down through the rank and file at the firm, the plan was perceived by the white attorneys as having "outlived its usefulness" and as having generated the context that created their feelings of discomfort in telling racial jokes and using certain words, their sense of "walking on eggshells."

The mere existence of the affirmative action policy, moreover, may have lulled leaders into thinking that any problem of discrimination had been fully resolved. By instituting a policy of affirmative action – albeit under order from a court – they could insulate themselves from any charges that they were consciously working to keep racial minorities down, even as they may have continued to shape a work environment that made it nearly impossible for African Americans to succeed.

In this way, the story of Kingsley, his colleagues, and Large Company X can open our eyes to the other ways in which organizational action can incite biases and result in discrimination. The three-out-of-forty-three demographics in the legal department (a result in part of Large Company X's recruiting and hiring practices)[36] provided additional context for the interactions between Kingsley and his colleagues. Large Company X's system for allocating work and for providing help may also have played a role. The lead attorney was given full discretion to allocate work among the attorneys, and the company relied on an informal, seek-help system that left Kingsley asking for help and being penalized for doing so. The culture of the legal department and perhaps even more broadly of the firm as a whole may also have played a role in the experience of both Randall Kingsley and his colleagues. Male attorneys (or at least male black attorneys) were expected to act and dress in a certain way (not too "flashy" and not to "demanding"), a way that Kingsley did not adhere to, or at least was perceived as not adhering to.

Today, few organizations are either legally compelled to implement or voluntarily implement affirmative action plans like the one imposed on Large

Company X in the 1970s and 80s, but organizations are still actively involved in creating organizational practices, cultures, and structures that produce discrimination. Indeed, organizations whose leaders do not consider the ways in which their practices can incite biases are easily setting up their employees to engage in discrimination, when many of them would prefer not to. The lead attorney in Large Company X, for example, may have been genuinely shocked when Kingsley raised the issue of race-based unequal treatment, even if his reaction may have been exaggerated by racial indignation and anger. Similarly, Randall Kingsley's colleagues who found him "too demanding" may have been influenced by the context in which they received his requests. Did he appear too demanding because he was one of just a few black attorneys assigned to work in a field of law with which he had no experience or expertise? Did he appear too demanding because he was a black attorney looking for help, while his white counterpart received help without asking?

The story of Randall Kingsley, his colleagues, and Large Company X also illustrates the difficulty of law in addressing all individual moments of discrimination. As I will soon show, Randall Kingsley is unlikely to have a viable individualized legal claim (proving individual discrimination is difficult on the evidence that he is likely to have, and the law's increasing focus on complaint and response would likely doom his claim anyway). But his experience may also not have been unique. Not every black man or woman working in the legal department at Large Company X will necessarily experience the same relational moments (some black attorneys, for example, may perform in a way that eases the discomfort of their white colleagues), but the structures, systems, and cultures at Large Company X may have been operating to exclude black lawyers, which may over time result in significant disparities between white and black attorneys in success outcomes such as retention, pay, and promotion.

The story of Randall Kingsley should get us thinking, too, about the disconnect between what firms want and what they are getting. Organizations like Large Company X are often lamenting that they cannot keep their minority and women workers, particularly in professional jobs such as law or accounting. We hear the same story from firms in technology, medicine, science, and finance. Yet these same organizations may be simultaneously structuring their workplaces to incite bias and discrimination, whether they know it or not.

INTRODUCTORY STORY NUMBER TWO

Story number two aired much more recently in a courthouse in Silicon Valley. Venture capital is an industry almost exclusively run by men. One recent study suggests that women make up just 6 percent of partners at venture capital firms.[37] In 2012, Kleiner Perkins Caufield & Byers, one of the most prominent venture capital firms in the technology industry, was sued for sex-based discrimination and the case went to trial in the spring of 2015.[38]

Ellen Pao, a Harvard-educated, Asian female former junior partner of the firm, alleged in the case that she was denied senior partnership because of her sex. Pao said that the firm's male leaders ignored her complaints that a male colleague, Ajit Nazre, had pressured her "relentlessly" for sex and then retaliated against her when she broke off the relationship. She also presented evidence that male partners excluded women from a firm ski trip, that female partners were excluded from all-male dinners with entrepreneurs because, according to one male partner, they would "kill the buzz," and that talk among the men turned on a business trip to female porn stars, "hot" female executives, a Victoria's Secret fashion show, and the Playboy mansion. Pao was seated around the edge of the room at meetings rather than at the table, and at one meeting she and another female junior partner were asked to take notes, when male junior partners were not asked to do the same.

Kleiner Perkins, meanwhile, maintained throughout the trial that it was supportive of women in the tech industry and at the firm, and that it had not discriminated against Pao. A juror asked John Doerr, Pao's former boss and one of the most successful venture capitalists in the world, whether women were simply not interested in becoming venture capitalists or "did the venture capital world fight them off?" Doerr responded that the dearth of women was not the company's fault: few entrepreneurs are women, and venture capital firms draw their partners from leaders of successful new companies.

The Kleiner Perkins case was lauded in the press as a "wake-up call," a case that would necessarily lead to great change in the industry, regardless of whether Pao won or lost. "Thanks Ellen," proclaimed a crowdfunded ad put together by female tech workers in Palo Alto. Pao was deemed a "disrupter" by one national columnist, and others echoed the sentiment, declaring that "the high-profile case will force more Silicon Valley companies to pay attention to their gender dynamics."[39]

But the case itself quickly became less about women working at a male-dominated firm and more about Pao's performance reviews and the firm's reactions to her complaints about Nazre. Kleiner Perkins said that Pao was not promoted (and was ultimately fired) because she received bad performance reviews and that she lacked the attributes for succeeding in venture capital – in John Doerr's words, "the ability to lead others, build consensus and be a team player." Lawyers for Kleiner Perkins focused closely at trial on drawing out that Pao did not complain about any objectionable conduct early on, and that she was an unpleasant person to work for and with.

The jury found in favor of Kleiner Perkins.[40] One juror who was interviewed after the verdict explained that the jury narrowed in on Ellen Pao's performance evaluations, affixing them along the walls of the deliberation room next to those of her male colleagues and walking through each one in comparison to the others.[41] As this juror remembers it, the jury spent almost no time deliberating over the evidence of a male-dominated, boorish, sexist firm culture, and almost all of their time scrutinizing the performance reviews of Pao and her colleagues. Was Pao really just a prickly, pushy person whose personality did not fit into the firm? Or was she made out to be that person by Kleiner Perkins at trial when she was really no different from the men who were given the senior partnership nod? This same juror who found for Kleiner Perkins said he saw similar critiques of Pao and of some of her male colleagues, but he thought that the male colleagues improved in response to the feedback, while Pao did not. Another interviewed juror, this one who found for Pao, said she thought the critiques of Pao and of her male colleagues who made senior partner were similar enough throughout to suggest that Pao was denied the partnership position because she was a woman.

The jurors in the case narrowed in on Pao's performance evaluations in part because that is what the law told them to do. The jury instructions issued by the judge in the case explained that to find for Pao the jurors would have to find that her gender was a "substantial motivating reason for Kleiner Perkins' not promoting her to senior partner, not promoting her to general partner, and/or terminating her employment."[42] Instructions like these get jurors thinking narrowly about discrete decisions and the state of mind of specific decision makers.

But what of the rest of the story of women in venture capital firms like Kleiner Perkins? Kleiner Perkins is a firm that actively builds its work culture and grooms its partners for strong leadership ability, including hiring speech coaches so that Pao and others could "own the room." Yet high-level partners at the firm could not find their employment policies when asked, and they presented no evidence that they were thinking institutionally or systematically about equality in the firm. If the firm's structures, systems, and its work cultures work against women, reinforcing exclusion and keeping them out of the top echelons – or even the bottom echelons – of the business, why is that not part of the legal story?

It is a lot easier to focus on comparing what was stated in Pao's and others' performance evaluations than it is to decide whether a gendered culture may have affected Pao's interactions with her colleagues, her colleagues' interactions with other male employees, even her own un-team-like behavior, all of which may have influenced the content of the evaluations in the first place.

But if the male-dominated dynamics at Kleiner Perkins played a role in how Pao and other women were evaluated and how they experienced and negotiated their relationships within the firm, should we expect Kleiner Perkins to change those dynamics?

As with Randall Kingsley, it is certainly possible that Ellen Pao was not the victim of discrimination. She may in fact have been pricklier and pushier than her male colleagues and this may have been why she was not chosen for senior partnership. But, contrary to the suggestion of many commentators in the media during the trial, the law, as I will show, is pushing us away from rather than toward the bigger, harder questions about how discrimination and disadvantage operates at firms like Kleiner Perkins and Large Company X. And this means that the organizations are not going to feel any legal pressure to consider themselves as sources of discrimination. Even when Pao or women generally are victims of discrimination, in other words, the law is developing in ways that make it harder and harder for us to see the possibility of that discrimination, and in so doing it is releasing organizations from responsibility for discrimination that is occurring within their walls.

I expect readers to have differing reactions to these two introductory stories, and to my explanations of them. The stories and my explanations raise many questions about what the law should require of employers to satisfy their non-discrimination obligation and about what it should require of litigants seeking to prove discrimination. These are the questions at which this book is aimed.

ON THE RELEVANCE OF CLASS: HIGH-END AND LOW-END JOBS

Both of the introductory stories that I have told involve professional, high-paying jobs in what are largely service sector industries, law and venture capital financing, where soft skills like collegiality, intuition, and ability to navigate people and social situations tend to outweigh those skills that are more objectively quantified. Randall Kingsley and Ellen Pao were both critiqued for their failure to fit in to the culture of the firm in which they worked.

Low-end jobs and industries, too, are affected by discrimination laundering. Indeed, as I will show in Chapter 4, some judges are straining to protect segregation and the gendered and racialized work cultures that can emerge in the segregated environments of industries such as construction and oil drilling. Many of the recent legal cases that I will discuss also involve working-class plaintiffs seeking equality in pay or in promotions or complaining about the racial and gender harassment that they endured in their jobs. In her book, *Grace and Grit*, one of these plaintiffs, Lilly Ledbetter, describes her desire to get paid work and her improved sense of freedom and self-value when she did, but she also explains that she felt she needed to work to earn money to sustain her family: "What I hadn't told [her doctor, who had asked about stress in the family] was that Charles's job was only part-time, and the income, even with his supplement from the National Guard and selling encyclopedias, just wasn't enough."[43] Another plaintiff, Betty Dukes, the lead plaintiff in the prominent *Wal-Mart* case, started working at Wal-Mart as a part-time cashier earning 5 dollars an hour.[44] Yet another, Maetta Vance, worked in the Dining Services division of a state university dining hall.[45]

Regardless of whether these individuals lost or won their legal cases, and on what grounds, as working people representing a vast range of employment, they – like Randall Kingsley and Ellen Pao – give a face to discrimination in the United States. They remind us that discrimination is a problem across pay sectors, and that we need to keep our radar on the full range of industries and workplaces in which it operates.[46]

1

The Threads of Organizational Innocence

Organizational innocence represents a change in the way that Americans view discrimination, its individual, human components, its structural, organizational components, and the interplay between the two. Although my focus in this book is on developments in the law, the rise in the frame of organizational innocence on which discrimination laundering rests is a societal shift as much as a legal one. I start this chapter by showing that organizational innocence was not always the dominant frame in employment discrimination cases. The story of discrimination once included organizations as much as individuals, and we can see this in a number of judicial opinions issued in the early years following the enactment of Title VII. I then develop three key extra-legal threads that will re-surface throughout the book: the influence of the cognitive bias revolution in the social sciences on our understanding of discrimination, the increase in attention to diversity management in the personnel profession and in organizations, and the turn to complaint processes as the principal solution to discrimination.[1] These threads intertwine, overlap, and sometimes pull against each other, but together they provide the social background for the rise of organizational innocence and the discrimination laundering in law that is occurring today.

EARLIER TIMES: ORGANIZATIONS AS DISCRIMINATORS

There was a time when in cases of discrimination courts were suspicious of organizations and their high-level decision makers. This should not be surprising. After all, judges like everyone else of this time had witnessed widespread resistance to civil rights laws across all sectors of American society. And organizations, whether schools, realtor associations, private clubs, unions, or employers, were part of that resistance.[2]

In 1964, Congress passed the Civil Rights Act, which included Title VII, the employment Title. Title VII makes it unlawful for employers to discriminate on the basis of certain protected characteristics or status. Specifically, the Act states that it "shall be an unlawful employment practice" for an employer:

> to fail or refuse to hire or to discharge any individual, or otherwise to discriminate against any individual with respect to his compensation, terms, conditions, or privileges of employment, because of such individual's race, color, religion, sex, or national origin.[3]

The term "employer" is defined in the Act to include any "person engaged in an industry affecting commerce" who employs fifteen or more employees and "any agent of such person."

After Title VII came into effect, some employers continued to overtly discriminate, often relying on express discriminatory policies. They maintained dual seniority lines for black and white employees and excluded black employees from certain employee facilities like bathrooms and locker rooms.[4] Companies also excluded women from certain jobs and maintained separate seniority rosters for men and women.[5]

The law could have stopped there, focusing only on these companies, and saying that if a company has stopped expressly discriminating, that is enough. But it did not. The law that emerged out of Title VII recognized that employers might abandon their express policies of discrimination but nonetheless continue to treat members of groups differently or adopt "neutral" policies that locked in segregation without sufficient business reason. These practices, too, were declared unlawful by the Supreme Court.

In the famous case of *Griggs* v. *Duke Power*, the Supreme Court saw how even neutral policies that treat members of all groups the same can in practice lock in segregation and disadvantage members of some groups over others.[6] Prior to the passage of Title VII, black employees at Duke Power were relegated to a handful of physically demanding jobs, and until the early 1960s, locker rooms, showers, drinking fountains, and other facilities were segregated. The case involved fourteen black employees from Duke Power's "labor" department. None had ever been promoted even though several had been working there for close to twenty years. The company disavowed its express policies of discrimination on July 2, 1965, the day that Title VII went into effect, but it continued to segregate its facilities, and its managers continued to provide blacks and whites with different privileges. Blacks, for example, were not generally given overtime work, while whites were. Pay differences also remained. At the time the plaintiffs filed suit, no black employee earned more than $1.65 per hour, while the lowest-paid white employee earned $1.81 per hour.[7] Black workers naturally wanted the higher-paying jobs, but when black workers in the labor department requested transfers to higher-paying departments, they were referred to a company policy (adopted by Duke Power on the effective date of the Act) requiring either a high school diploma or a satisfactory score on an aptitude test to be eligible for transfer.

A unanimous Supreme Court famously held in the *Griggs* case that an employer's use of neutral practices – a high school diploma requirement or a score on an aptitude test – can be an unlawful employment practice in violation of Title VII if the employer's use of the practice has a disparate impact on members of a protected group and if the employer cannot justify its use of the practice as a business necessity, or if it refuses to adopt an alternative practice that has a lesser impact. This, the Court said, was true even with no showing of motive on the part of high-level policy makers to use the practices to keep members of a protected group out or down.

Although *Griggs* is known for its embrace of the idea of discrimination as disparate impact, ushering into Title VII enforcement a legal theory with that name, it most surely was also a case that would have raised judges' suspicion of employer motive. Given the timing of the adoption of the testing and diploma requirement and the organization's past practices, the Court surely would have suspected that high-level policy makers at Duke Power wanted to retain a system of segregation and advantage for whites and adopted practices that had a disparate impact on blacks in an effort to do so. But the Court did not rest its holding on that reality. Instead, the Court in *Griggs* saw organizations and particularly their use of policies and practices as a substantial barrier to equality in employment.[8]

The Court during this time also faced cases in which employers had abandoned their expressly discriminatory policies, but continued to treat members of different groups disparately. Here, too, the Court accepted that the law would have to go beyond outlawing formal, expressly discriminatory policies in order for Title VII to be effective. In several early cases, it held that plaintiffs seeking to prove a "pattern or practice" of discrimination needed only to prove that different treatment of members of different groups was widespread, the "regular rather than the unusual practice" within an organization, in order to establish employer liability. And the Court permitted plaintiffs to prove this pattern or practice through use of statistics comparing the actual makeup of an employer's job category with what one would expect the makeup of that job category to look like, assuming nondiscrimination, given a relevant labor pool.

In the first case of this kind, *International Brotherhood of Teamsters v. United States*, the government alleged that the T.I.M.E. trucking company had engaged in a pattern or practice of discrimination in violation of Title VII by failing to place black and Latino truck drivers into the more lucrative long haul, "line driver" positions.⁹ T.I.M.E. had purged all of its openly discriminatory policies after the enactment of Title VII, and its high-level executives had made no public comments suggesting that the company was continuing an informal policy of exclusion or discrimination. The government sought to prove its case instead by pointing to the stark disparity between the small percentage of blacks and Latino line drivers in the company and the larger percentage of blacks and Latinos in the populations surrounding the company's terminals. It also submitted testimony of individuals who recounted over forty specific instances of discrimination, instances in which, for example, a manager told a black applicant that he did not think the company was "ready" for a black line driver. The Court held that this evidence could establish employer liability for a system-wide pattern or practice of discrimination on the part of the company in violation of Title VII, and that such proof, in addition to warranting equitable remedies aimed at eliminating the practice of discrimination, would create a legal presumption that individual black and Latino workers who had sought such positions had suffered discrimination. The company could avoid paying back pay to any specific individuals only if it could prove that it had not excluded that individual from a line-driver position because of his race.

This focus on organizations and institutions over individuals carried over to judicial decisions beyond system-wide cases like *Griggs* and *Teamsters*. Judges who were trying to figure out whether a particular plaintiff had suffered discrimination in a specific employment decision – a decision by a manager not to hire or promote, for example – tended also during this time to conflate questions of employer and manager motivation. One of the earliest Title VII cases decided by the Supreme Court, *McDonnell Douglas* v. *Green,* involved a claim of discrimination by Percy Green, a black man who worked as a mechanic and laboratory technician for the giant aerospace and aircraft manufacturer McDonnell Douglas.¹⁰ Green worked for McDonnell Douglas at its headquarters in St. Louis for eight years before he was laid off during a reduction in the workforce. Percy Green had a strong streak of racial rights activism in him, and he believed that his layoff and the general hiring practices at McDonnell Douglas were racially discriminatory. Taking to the streets, he picketed and participated in a "stall-in" during which he and others stopped their cars on the road to tie up traffic going to McDonnell Douglas during the morning rush hour. Green also may have participated in a "lock-in" during which a chain and padlock were placed on the front doors of a McDonnell Douglas building to prevent workers from leaving.¹¹ Several weeks after the lock-in, McDonnell Douglas publicly advertised for qualified mechanics, and Green applied. He was not hired, and he was told that he was not hired because of his involvement in the stall-in and lock-in against the company.

He filed suit against McDonnell Douglas, alleging that the real reason he was not rehired was his race. In its opinion in the case, the Supreme Court explained that the ultimate question in the case was whether Green had been denied reemployment because he was black. Instead of focusing exclusively on the state of mind of a particular decision maker, the person who rejected Green's application, however, the Court asked more broadly whether the "employer" had discriminated. It went to on to explain that "[e]specially relevant to such a showing would be evidence that white employees involved in acts against [McDonnell Douglas] of comparable seriousness ... were nevertheless retained or rehired."[12] This could have been a decision by another employee, not just the one who decided not to rehire Green. The Court also said that evidence of "McDonnell Douglas's" treatment of Green while he was working there and its reaction to his "legitimate civil rights activities"[13] could be evidence of discrimination in the rehire decision.

Finally, the Court mentioned that "even statistics as to McDonnell Douglas's 'general policy and practice with respect to minority employment'" would be relevant to the determination of whether Green was discriminated against when he was rejected for rehire.[14] In a footnote, the Court did caution that statistics, "while helpful, may not be in and of themselves controlling as to an individualized hiring decision, particularly in the presence of an otherwise justifiable reason for refusing to rehire."[15] Indeed, Justice Blackmun, expecting that Green on remand would be unlikely to find evidence that whites who had engaged in similar practices were rehired or evidence that McDonnell Douglas had taken discriminatory action against Green in his past employment, specifically requested that this footnote be added to the opinion.[16]

This point – that statistics do not establish individualized discrimination – is an especially good one, and one that I will revisit later, in Chapter 3. For now, it is important merely to see that the Supreme Court in *McDonnell Douglas* did not insist that all of Green's evidence involve the specific person who denied him reemployment. Instead, the Court assumed that evidence of general race-based treatment toward Green and even toward others would be useful in proving that Green was denied reemployment because of his race.

There were other cases like this during this time. A group of black bricklayers sued Furnco Construction in *Furnco Construction* v. *Waters*.[17] The bricklayers alleged that the superintendent in charge of hiring at the defendant company (a company that specialized in the relining of blast furnaces for steel mills) had refused them work because they were black. Instead of considering applicants who showed up at the jobsite looking for work, this superintendent hired exclusively from a compiled list of people whom he claimed had come recommended to him or whom he claimed to know personally to be competent at bricklaying work.

The justices of the Supreme Court all agreed with the lower court judges in the case that the black bricklayers' claims were properly analyzed using individual disparate treatment theory, the theory that the Court had laid out for individual claims of discrimination several years earlier in *McDonnell Douglas*.[18] They also agreed that under that theory the bricklayers had established a prima facie case of discrimination by proving that "they were members of racial minority; … they did everything within their power to apply for employment; … they were qualified in every respect for the jobs which were about to be open; they were not offered employment; … and the employer continued to seek persons of similar qualifications."[19]

From there, the Court might have asked next whether the superintendent acted with discriminatory bias when he refused the plaintiffs work.[20] But this is not how the Court framed the question. Instead, the Court asked whether the *employer's* hiring practices – its "refusal to engage in on-the-job training or to hire at the gate" – were a pretext for discrimination. And it explained that "[p]roof that [the employer's] work force was racially balanced or that it contained a disproportionately high percentage of minority employees" would be relevant to that question. Nowhere did the Court consider the state of mind of the allegedly discriminating superintendent who had made the decision not to hire at the gate and who had created a list that included no black bricklayers.

Employers did try to separate themselves from their employees as a way of avoiding liability in many of these early cases, but largely to no avail. In *Slack v. Havens*, for example, a case that I will discuss in greater detail in Chapter 2, the employer argued that the racially biased action of a supervisor could not be attributed to the company, but the court rejected the argument.[21] Even as recently as the early 1990s, the Court seemed to reject similar arguments. *Price Waterhouse* v. *Hopkins*, for example, was a sex-based discrimination case in which Ann Hopkins, an accountant and senior manager at the accounting conglomerate Price Waterhouse, was denied partnership.[22] Partnership decisions were made at the firm according to a two-step process: first, partners were invited to provide comments and to vote; second, members of the policy board reviewed recommendations and made a final decision. The Supreme Court in its opinion in *Price Waterhouse*, however, did not delineate between the partners who submitted the initial review forms and the board members who made the final decision. Nor did it draw a sharp distinction between evidence that tended to suggest that high-level decision makers within "the firm," as the Court put it, were tolerating gender-based bias and stereotyping and evidence that the partners or board members in Hopkins's case were biased when they evaluated her and decided to put her partnership on hold.[23]

My point here is a purely descriptive one. In an earlier era, the Supreme Court drew little distinction between the individuals who discriminated and the organizations for which they worked. This has changed dramatically in an era of organizational innocence. But organizational innocence goes one step further than merely acknowledging the reality that individual employees can be distinct actors from their employers. The story of organizational innocence draws causal and normative conclusions: the individual employees are understood to be the wrongdoers, acting in isolation and against the interest of the organizations in which they work, and the organizations are understood to be mere bystanders that can do little more as a practical matter to curb discrimination than to police their employees.

THE RISE OF ORGANIZATIONAL INNOCENCE

It should not surprise us that when it comes to discrimination today courts are less likely than they were in the past to be suspicious of organizations and their high-level decision makers. We have come a long way from the blatant discrimination and purposeful resistance to civil rights of the late 1960s and 70s. In fact, it would be hard to find an employer in America today that does not declare a strong commitment to nondiscrimination and equality, and many of those employers have adopted measures of some kind that are commonly expected to combat discrimination.

For instance, Wal-Mart's nondiscrimination policy states:

> We are committed to maintaining a diverse workforce and an inclusive work environment. Walmart prohibits discrimination in employment, employment-related decisions or in business dealings on the basis of an individual's race, color, ancestry, age, sex, sexual orientation, religion, disability, ethnicity, national origin, veteran status, marital status, pregnancy, or any other status protected by law or local policy. We should provide an environment free of discrimination to our associates, customers, members and suppliers.[24]

That sounds pretty good, and Wal-Mart goes further than just stating a policy. It has a formal complaint system for harassment and other forms of discrimination, and it includes diversity training as a requirement for all new employees. In 2005 Wal-Mart began to measure the "institutional diversity performance" of the top 100 outside law firms that it uses and threatened to end or limit its relationship with firms that did not comply with its requirements.[25]

Without evidence to suggest otherwise, it may make sense for courts to assume that organizations such as Wal-Mart are not purposefully excluding members of any particular group. But courts today have not just become less suspicious of organizations. They have bought in to a story of organizational innocence that stages employers as the victims of their employees' biases and of the civil rights laws that hold employers responsible. Take, for instance, the Court's reasoning in a more recent case, decided in 2007, *Ledbetter v. Goodyear Tire*.

First, some background: Lilly Ledbetter grew up in Possom Trot, Alabama, and she knew from an early age that the Goodyear plant brought with it good wages. Her best friend Sandra's father worked there, and every few years they would get a brand-new Mercury to drive around in. In her book, *Grace and Grit*, Ledbetter describes her early childhood picking cotton, her love of math and numbers, and her marriage before she had turned eighteen.[26] She started working at General Electric on the assembly line, doing piece work with radios and televisions. She dropped out of the workplace for a few years after her children were born, but when her two children were still small, she went back to work. Her husband had only part-time work at the time, and she wanted to make money to pay for speech therapy for their son and school trips for their daughter. And she wanted to start savings to send them to college, where she had never gone. She took a job at H&R Block filling out tax returns for four years, then a job at Jacksonville State University for three, and back at H&R Block as a district manager for four. In 1979, she saw an article in a magazine about women becoming part of a new management team at Goodyear Tire. She applied, and was hired. And so began her chapter at Goodyear.

Ledbetter worked at Goodyear for almost twenty years. She says that she had long suspected that she was getting paid less than her male counterparts, but she did not know for sure until she found an anonymous note in her cubicle one morning listing her name and pay (to the exact amount) and names of the other tire room managers, all men, and their pay. The paper listed three men who had started in 1979, the same year as Ledbetter. Ledbetter was earning $44,724 a year by 1998, while those men were earning over $58,000. The next morning, she drove to the federal Equal Employment Opportunity Commission (EEOC) building in Birmingham and filed a charge of discrimination.[27]

Ledbetter's legal case would last the next nine years. Her Title VII claim went to trial, and she won, but Goodyear appealed, ultimately petitioning to the Supreme Court. The issue before the Supreme Court involved the timing of Ledbetter's complaint with the EEOC. Victims of discrimination are required to file a charge of discrimination with the EEOC within a certain number of days, in Ledbetter's case 180 days, of the unlawful employment practice.[28] Ledbetter filed her charge in March of 1998, which would reach back until late 1997. But she had evidence of biased interactions and decisions that went back much further. In particular, as evidence of discrimination, she pointed to biased statements and harassment by Mike Maudsley, her supervisor in the 1980s and her performance auditor in the early to mid-1990s, and to later statements made by a plant manager expressing bias against women at the plant. She also presented statistical evidence showing the stark disparity between her pay and that of other managers and of women's pay as compared to men's generally within the company, as well as evidence of her work experience and skills as compared to the men who were paid more, and testimony by other women of sex-based incidents at the plant.[29]

Now to the Court's opinion, and especially its reasoning. Despite the breadth of Ledbetter's evidence, the Court focused narrowly on her allegations about Mike Maudsley: that he retaliated against her in the 1980s by recommending low pay increases after she rejected his sexual advances, and that he did so again in the 1990s by submitting false audit reports.[30] Once the Court focused in on Ledbetter's experience with Maudsley, organizational innocence came to the fore. The Court isolated Maudsley's actions from the employer. Indeed, the Court insisted that it would be *unfair* to require Goodyear to defend what the Court saw as several specific incidents that occurred many years in the past. According to the Court:

> Ledbetter's claims turned principally on the misconduct of a single Goodyear supervisor who, Ledbetter testified, retaliated against her when she rejected his sexual advances during the early 1980's, and did so again in the mid-1990's, when he falsified deficiency reports about her work … Yet by the time of trial, this supervisor had died and therefore could not testify. A timely charge might have permitted his evidence to be weighed contemporaneously.[31]

The Court's holding in *Ledbetter* – that Lilly Ledbetter's claims could not be pursued in court because she had not filed a charge within 180 days of the discrete incidents of discrimination experienced in the 1980s and 90s – was highly problematic for victims of pay discrimination. As Justice Ginsburg pointed out in her dissent (appealing to Congress for action), workers in the United States often do not know the pay of their co-workers and even when they do, pay raise differences can be so small that they only add up to a claim worth pursuing over time. Congress responded to the Court's *Ledbetter* decision in 2008, creating a new statutory rule that each paycheck amounts to a discriminatory incident from which the filing period begins to run.[32] The Ledbetter Fair Pay Act, as it is called, however, did nothing to disturb the underlying organizational innocence that drove the Court's view of her case.

The Court may have homed in on Maudsley and his pay decisions in part because of the facts suggesting that he sexually harassed Ledbetter. As I will show in Chapter 2, sexual harassment cases have presented a first foothold for discrimination laundering. But as I will show in later chapters, the Court today sees most employment discrimination in much the same way that it saw Lilly Ledbetter's experience at Goodyear. Organizational innocence, in other words, carries well beyond sexual harassment. And the rise of organizational innocence can only be explained through a broader lens, a lens that sees shifts in organizations and in frames, and ultimately in beliefs about what discrimination is and how it operates.

THREADS OF ORGANIZATIONAL INNOCENCE

Our views about how discrimination operates derive from a host of influences, from our own personal and professional experiences to those of our families, our friends, even the subjects we learned in school. I cannot make a precise causal case for any specific judge's views about how discrimination operates and the role that organizations play, but I do develop here what I argue are three of the principal threads that may have contributed to the rise of organizational innocence and discrimination laundering. These are some of the changes outside the law that seem to be influencing the ways that judges understand employment discrimination and its solutions. The first of these threads is the rise in the predominance of cognitive bias research in mainstream understanding of how discrimination operates. The second is the shift within the management literature and organizations toward emphasizing a business case for diversity and diversity management. The third is the rise in complaint processes as the principal measure taken by organizations to reduce discrimination. Together, these threads operate to generate a paradigmatic view of employment discrimination as something that is carried out by rogue, lower-level, often managerial individuals within a work organization acting in isolation from and against the interest of the organization. As I will show in greater detail in later chapters, these threads – and particularly the organizational innocence that they fuel – are inextricably intertwined with the discrimination laundering that is occurring in the law.

THE COGNITIVE BIAS REVOLUTION

He's a racist. So are you. So am I.[33]

We are in the midst of something of a cognitive bias revolution in the United States. Over the past several decades, social science research on cognitive bias has exploded, and it has revealed that we all hold biases and stereotypes deep inside our brains that come out as we process information and make judgments.[34] These stereotypes and cognitive biases can involve neutral things such as the tendency to value something that we have over something that we do not. More important for understanding discrimination, however, is the fact that cognitive biases tend to develop around socially salient categories like race and sex, and they lurk behind our mundane decisions as much as our life-changing ones.[35]

Research on unconscious, cognitive bias and its role in discrimination in the modern world, including the workplace, has been underway for some time.[36] In the early 1990s, for example, social scientists developed the concept of "aversive racism" to describe what they called "a subtle, often unintentional, form of bias that characterizes many white Americans who possess strong egalitarian values and who believe they are nonprejudiced."[37] This research suggested that whites and others who do not wish to discriminate often nonetheless still do, even if unconsciously, and that they are particularly likely to do so when they are able to justify their actions in nonracial terms. Justifying their decisions in nonracial terms allows people to insulate themselves from having to believe that their behavior was racially motivated.

Beneath this idea of aversive racism, and much of the cognitive bias revolution, lies a better scientific understanding of how our brains work and particularly of how our brains use categories and prototypes, or schemas, to make sense of the world. Categorization helps us sort the vast array of information that we come across in the world. We all categorize, and given the social salience of race and sex in our society, we also all (or almost all) categorize along racial and gender lines. And once we categorize, put someone in the box of black or woman (or both), for example, we then process information according to that category and its associated stereotypes. From there, there are all sorts of ways that our categorical biases affect our perceptions and judgments of both people and situations. And all of this can and often does operate entirely outside our mental awareness.

Research shows, for example, that the image of an ideal hire is often infused with beliefs about gender that influence decisions about whom to hire. In one study, managers were asked to describe the required characteristics for the job of manager, and also to describe the typical characteristics of men and women. Both male and female managers' descriptions of the good manager substantially overlapped with their descriptions of typical men but were less similar to their descriptions of typical women.[38] In another study, sociologist Elizabeth Gorman coded the hiring criteria that large U.S. law firms listed for their jobs by marking the extent to which they included stereotypically gendered traits.[39] Stereotypically masculine traits (e.g., ambitious, assertive) were more common, but feminine traits (cooperative, friendly) were listed as well. Controlling for other factors that might affect the percentage of men and women applying for and qualified for the jobs, Gorman found that the more masculine characteristics listed in the hiring criteria, the less likely it was that a woman was hired for the job.[40] The more feminine characteristics in the hiring criteria, the more likely it was that a woman was hired.[41]

What really blew cognitive bias onto the main stage, though, was the development of a test called the Implicit Associations Test, or IAT.[42] The basic idea behind the IAT is that our minds work faster when we make stereotype-consistent associations and more slowly when we fight against the associations that we hold. By measuring differences in the speed of cognitive processing, researchers therefore can identify biases not found in our responses to explicit questioning. For example, I may say, honestly and with conviction, that I think women can be as good as men in math, but when I see math on a screen, I am likely to associate it more quickly with a man than with a woman. This is because I am likely to hold implicit stereotypes about women and men and math, even if I find these stereotypes objectionable and would prefer not to hold them. The same is true for most people's associations between older age and quick-witted thinking. We find it more difficult to associate older age with positive attributes, and this goes even for the "we" that includes older people.

When it comes to race, the results are consistent, and striking. For example, one IAT tests response rate when associating white faces and black faces with weapons and harmless items. The automatic "Black equals weapons" stereotype was stronger than "White equals weapons" for all groups who took the test. It was larger in whites and Asians, but even African Americans showed a modest "Black equals weapons" stereotype. Moreover, while level of education did affect explicit endorsement of this stereotype (the higher the education level, the lower the endorsement of the stereotype), the degree of automatic stereotyping did not vary according to level of education.[43]

The IAT and the larger cognitive bias revolution of the 1990s changed the way people think about discrimination and opened many people's eyes to their own biases and the biases of others. It arguably tipped us as a society toward a better understanding of discrimination and how it operates to the detriment of women and racial minorities. Malcolm Gladwell devoted a substantial part of his bestselling book, *Blink*, to the science of cognitive bias, and in 2010 Oprah Winfrey brought Gladwell and Anthony Greenwald, one of the designers of the IAT, onto her show.[44] The IAT had hit the big time. By the mid-1990s and early-2000s, the concept of implicit or unconscious bias had become part of our social world, even if we were still uncertain about what we should do about it.

The Effects of the Cognitive Bias Revolution on the Law

Despite the importance of cognitive bias research to our understanding of how discrimination operates, the effect of the cognitive bias revolution on the law of employment discrimination has tended to be more perverse than positive. Indeed, the direct effect of the cognitive bias research – its ability to tip individual claims toward a finding of discrimination rather than not – has actually been relatively weak. The cognitive bias literature was introduced into the legal lexicon in the 1980s by legal scholars arguing against a narrow definition of actor intent in antidiscrimination law. Mining the wealth of social science research on implicit bias, these scholars showed that it makes little sense for the law to focus on motive (asking whether a person was consciously aware of their biases or consciously motivated to discriminate on the basis of race or sex) when race- and sex-based biases are so likely to creep into our decisions without our knowledge, giving rise to the same differential treatment of members of protected groups.[45] They argued in favor of a focus on causation rather than on conscious motivation. A Title VII plaintiff under this approach would be able to succeed in proving discrimination, for example, by showing that bias "played a role in" her supervisor's decision not to promote her, even if the supervisor did not act with a purpose to harm or even awareness that harm would result.

These scholars were right. Given the harm to victims of discrimination and the injustice of group-based subordination, it hardly makes sense to give employers an out simply because the supervisor making the decision "didn't mean to discriminate." Indeed, although there remains some scholarly debate around the edges, it seems safe to say that the cognitive bias case for causation has been a success, at least when thinking about identifiable individuals making key employment decisions such as whom to hire or to fire. Causation over conscious motive seems in this area to have secured a substantial foothold both among commentators and in the courts.[46]

As a practical matter, though, this success has made little difference in the way that most cases of discrimination are proved. It remains very difficult for an individual plaintiff to prove that discriminatory bias played a role in any particular decision unless the decision maker was aware of and bold enough to express his or her bias out loud (or in writing) and in such a way as to leave no doubt about the nature of the bias and its seriousness.[47] And, even then, most courts think the biased statement has to be uttered close in time to the decision.[48] My supervisor not only has to declare aloud that "Women aren't cut out for this work" or something along those lines; for many courts he has to declare it within a few months, sometimes even weeks, of the decision to pay me less than my male counterpart.

Because most plaintiffs lack biased statements by the key decision makers involved in their claims (for example, the manager who denied them the promotion), many plaintiffs end up trying to prove that a decision was based on protected group membership through comparative evidence. A Latino man, for example, might submit evidence of his qualifications and compare those qualifications to the white man or woman who was selected for the promotion. This was at least partly how Ellen Pao tried to prove her case against Kleiner Perkins: she argued that she had better evaluations (and that sometimes men were critiqued in the same way) but nonetheless she was denied the promotion while her male counterparts were promoted. This was the evidence the jurors took very seriously, affixing the reviews to the walls of the deliberation room for comparison.

Other plaintiffs seek to prove that a decision was because of a protected characteristic by proving that the reason that the employer put forward for the decision – that the applicant for the promotion was regularly late to meetings, for example – is false.[49] These plaintiffs hope that a judge or jury will infer from the fact that the employer provided a false reason that the real reason is the plaintiff's protected characteristic, their race or sex. These methods of proving that a manager acted with bias have long been the only realistic ways for a plaintiff to prove discrimination in a specific employment decision, and these methods have not changed at all with the advent of the cognitive bias revolution.

The Cognitive Bias Revolution and Organizational Innocence

Instead of making individual cases easier to prove, the singlemost impact of the cognitive revolution in the law to date lies in its message about the nature of discrimination. As Michael Shermer for the *Los Angeles Times* put it in defense of Seinfeld actor and comedian Michael Richards: "He's a racist. So are you. So am I."[50] The reality that biases are neither static nor isolated from others or from context, as the research also shows, has been overshadowed by the splash of the idea of implicit or unconscious bias and its pervasiveness through all segments of society. I will talk more about the expanded realm of research and the realities of how discrimination operates in Chapter 6. For now, it is enough to see that by emphasizing biases of individual actors as the principal, if not sole, source of discrimination and by opening awareness of the ubiquity of those biases (that they are in all of us), the cognitive bias revolution may have unwittingly fueled the rise of organizational innocence and discrimination laundering in the law. Individual employees acting in their capacity as managers, supervisors, or even as co-workers or subordinates, tend to take center stage in a cognitive bias account, to the exclusion of the broader policies, systems, and cultures that can influence those biases.

The tone around discussion of biases has also shifted from one of disparagement to something of neutral acquiescence. Early literature on some of the subtle ways in which our stereotypes can influence behavior and decisions, for example, spoke of "aversive racism." Mahzarin Banaji and Anthony Greenwald, in contrast, titled their 2013 book on the subject of cognitive biases and the IAT *"Blindspot: Hidden Biases of Good People."* A *Business Week* magazine article in 2006 titled an article about unconscious biases that might be operating at Wal-Mart "White Men Can't Help It." This shift in tone may be warranted in some respects.[51] However, turning from an animus-based understanding of discrimination (the stigma-laden form) to a cognitive-based one replaces one individual mindset frame for another. "White men can't help it" makes bias seem like a private state of being that is pervasive across our lives, despite our best intentions, and regardless of the context in which we think and act. And this frame leaves organizations and the contexts in which those individuals interact entirely out of the picture.

Moreover, removing much of the stigma associated with bias and discrimination means that the relational act of discriminating is more likely to be seen as personal and localized to the individuals involved. Here, the cognitive bias revolution dovetails with post-racialism as racial or gendered encounters are viewed as inevitable and not necessarily problematic or indicative of broader patterns of segregation and subordination. We can admit to seeing race and sex, we may even acknowledge that all of us are biased, but in a sense our frank honesty about that fact absolves us from facing the socially destructive reality of our actions.

There is also something of an organizational control-to-blame element lurking behind the cognitive bias revolution. When overt racists are running amok within a firm, we might think that that says something about the firm's dedication to nondiscrimination, at least in part because we tend to think that the firm can do something about it: It can threaten the racists with punishment, or fire them. With the cognitive bias revolution though comes the idea of organizational helplessness: What do we expect organizations to do when everyone is potentially a discriminator? Indeed, the ubiquity of cognitive biases – and, again, a narrow focus on individual mindsets over context – may lead to the pervasive concern about organizations "over-policing" individuals who hold or act on implicit biases. The more that bias is framed as a personal characteristic shaped by society wholly outside work and uninfluenced by work context, the less likely we are to hold organizations responsible.

THE RHETORIC OF DIVERSITY MANAGEMENT AND
ORGANIZATIONAL INNOCENCE

We are committed to maintaining a diverse workforce and an inclusive work environment.[52]

Organizations today declare that they care about diversity and about managing diversity, not just (or even) because the law requires it, but because it makes good business sense. According to the case for "diversity management," a diverse workforce is a resource – a way of getting ahead – and a business imperative. Diversity allows organizations to better reach and serve an increasingly diverse and globalized market and to benefit from an increasingly diverse and globalized workforce. As one firm puts it, "A culturally sensitive diverse workforce is better able to … generate the wealth of ideas that are key to innovation."[53] The CEO of the firm also emphasizes reaching consumer markets: "[D]iversity is good for business. Importantly, we're a consumer goods company. So we need to reflect the consumers we sell to."[54]

This business case for diversity is actually relatively new. Sociologists trace the diversity management rhetoric to the mid-1980s and 1990s, when personnel managers and equal opportunity officers turned to managing diversity over developing affirmative action plans. The term "managing diversity," for example, was coined in the 1980s when consultant and former Harvard Business Professor R. Roosevelt Thomas founded the American Institute for Managing Diversity.[55] In several pieces published in the early and mid-1990s, he and others argued that diversity management was a business imperative for organizations in an increasingly globalized business environment.[56]

The diversity management push also drew steam from the Supreme Court's affirmative action decision in *Regents of the University of California* v. *Bakke*, where Justice Powell's opinion characterized race as one of many "pertinent elements of diversity."[57] Justice Powell went on to identify "diversity" as an acceptable goal for college admissions, authorizing race as a legally permissible factor to consider, among other factors, in achieving that goal. Businesses submitted briefs to the Court in later cases emphasizing the importance of diversity in their workforces in serving an increasingly international market and in reaching specific racial and cultural communities.[58]

As the managing diversity rhetoric caught on, organizations began to act according to that rhetoric. They hired diversity consultants, implemented diversity training programs, and disseminated diversity narratives. There remains a substantial question whether any of these and other "diversity" efforts have been effective in keeping women and racial minority employees or increasing demographic diversity across levels of organizations generally.[59] There is little doubt, however, that diversity management has become a dominant refrain in the business community.

Managing Diversity and Organizational Innocence

An organizational response to equal opportunity law framed in terms of business sense is nothing new. Indeed, organizations responded to equal opportunity pressures in the early days of Title VII by favoring various internal labor market practices.[60] The EEOC's 1974 guidelines for employers suggested that employers could avoid Title VII liability by formalizing their hiring and promotion procedures and expanding personnel record keeping.[61] Personnel professionals, too, pushed organizations to create formal evaluation and promotion systems as a way of avoiding Title VII liability and also as good business sense.[62]

What is different about the rise of diversity management is the signal that it sends of organizational innocence. The diversity management movement sends an express signal that organizations care about diversity itself, that they celebrate difference as a business advantage. Managing diversity is not just an organizational effort to avoid discrimination (and gain efficiency), but a proactive organizational drive to value employees of diverse backgrounds. And this means that organizations who espouse diversity management rhetoric and take measures consistent with that rhetoric are more likely than ever to be seen as innocent, even when biased decisions take place within their walls. Biased employment decisions are easily seen as contrary to the organization's genuine interest, not just legally but also financially. Diversity management, after all, tells us that organizations *want* to manage diversity successfully; their very business success depends on it.

Research shows that judges deciding employment discrimination lawsuits tend to defer to organizational structures without questioning the efficacy of those structures. This is part of the process of legal endogeneity studied by sociologist Lauren Edelman and her colleagues.[63] Their research shows that particularly in individual discrimination cases where judges are often asked to decide whether a specific person or group of people acted on the basis of a protected characteristic in a key decision, such as promotion, judges will defer to organizational structures like formalized promotion procedures as a signal of employer rationality and fair treatment.[64]

The work of Edelman and her colleagues also shows that diversity man-agement as implemented tends to push concerns about discrimination that are raised by employees out of the legal realm and into the realm of business prerogative.[65] Indeed, in many organizations there is a stark structural division between departments engaged in diversity management and those overseeing equal opportunity. One researcher explained her observation of American companies this way:

> There are "compliance" or "EEO/AA people," who put together socio-demographic "numbers," fill out "EEO-1 form" and other reporting require-ments, write "affirmative action plans," make sure employees and managers are aware of the antidiscrimination legislation, and sometimes handle internal complaints. On the other hand, there are "diversity and inclusion people," whose work is about "intercultural training," "employee resource groups," "di-versity events," multicultural marketing strategies, "talent management," etc.[66]

Even those diversity officers who also handled compliance roles in these com-panies tended to separate the two functions. One study participant described the two roles as making her feel "like two different people."[67]

These structural divisions between diversity management and equal oppor-tunity carry over to the human side, with diversity officers distancing them-selves from equal opportunity. The equal opportunity side is often associated with "paperwork" and "numbers," nothing as "exciting" as diversity and inclu-sion. Compliance people are seen by diversity personnel as the "bad cops" of the organization. Diversity work, in contrast, is considered "strategic" with diversity officers seeing themselves as "change agents" "from within."[68] A diversity officer of a large New York banking company explained:

> In the U.S., diversity and discrimination are completely different subjects. So, discrimination and harassment … this is absolutely legal. It's about compli-ance. It's about risk. There's mandatory training for everyone in the company … Diversity and inclusion is more about having an employment culture where diverse talent is empowered to succeed, a management culture which cre-ates an inclusive environment for the clients … the shareholders … for the employees, to add business value. So it's a very separate proposition.[69]

Within the diversity management realm, moreover, individuals are seen as the problem, if there is one. In one company, a diversity officer explained: "[The] Leadership Team gets it. Maybe one or two layers down get it," but "[m]an-agers don't get it."[70] Diversity trainings similarly often frame the problem of racial and gender inequality in terms of insults and other individual behav-iors that might denigrate a member of a minority group or make them feel uncomfortable.[71] These trainings present the "culturally sensitive employee" as the solution to racial and gender inequality.[72]

My point here is not that the turn toward diversity management is entirely problematic, or necessarily subversive of meaningful social change, although there is some reason to believe that it may be.[73] Instead, it is that, as currently conceived and implemented, the turn contributes to a sense of organizational innocence by framing organizational action in terms of proactive, business-driven efforts to manage diversity and by sweeping individual bias into the business realm of the personal and relational for managers and workers.

THE EMPHASIS ON COMPLAINT AND GRIEVANCE PROCEDURES

The management's position is if the misconduct or the bad performance is established, whatever disciplinary action is appropriate will be taken.[74]

In the Kleiner Perkins litigation one of the most surprising things to many people, including one of the jurors who found against Ellen Pao, was the audacity of the high-level partners: that they could not even find their employment policies on discrimination and harassment. The question of following proper procedures also came up *against* Ellen Pao. Kleiner Perkins's lawyers spent some time at trial making the case that Pao should have complained earlier and more forcefully about the harassment and retaliation that she experienced.

Formal complaint or grievance systems have become the principal discrimination-reducing measure adopted by organizations. The systems emerged in the American workforce in the 1950s and 60s as part of a broader due-process revolution, beginning with unions and rolling over into non-union workplaces soon after.[75] Complaint procedures appeared in some of the first union contracts covering race discrimination in the early 1960s, and the Department of Justice had a nonunion equal opportunity grievance procedure by 1969. Personnel experts advised as early as the 1970s, when the EEOC was gearing up to file some of its first law suits, that a "freestanding civil rights grievance procedure could intercept employees en route to complain to the EEOC and at the same time signal the employer's good faith in trying to quash discrimination."[76] That advice spread like wildfire. A national survey taken in 1989 found that 31 percent of employers had created a grievance procedure specifically to handle discrimination complaints. Over time, judges began to defer to the procedures, at least in harassment cases, and by 1991, the Supreme Court had endorsed them as a way for employers to avoid liability for discriminatory harassment that takes place (more on this in Chapter 2). The

Supreme Court's decisions drove the popularity of complaint processes even higher. According to a broad national sample of 389 employers, nearly half had a sexual harassment grievance procedure in 1990; by 1997, 96 percent had one.[77]

Complaint Procedures and Organizational Innocence

The focus on complaint processes as the principal measure for reducing discrimination tends to individualize the problem, and also turns it into a management problem rather than one of discrimination. Research shows that internal investigators tend to recast complaints of discrimination as typical managerial problems like poor management or interpersonal difficulties and to remedy the problems with managerial solutions such as training programs, separating employees, and counseling.[78] The complaints within these systems are also likely to be individualized as employees feel pressure to describe specific relational incidents or comments or behaviors.[79]

Focusing on complaint procedures as the principal organizational measure situates organizations as mere policing bodies of the individual actions about which individual employees complain. Individuals and their interactions take center stage; organizations are rendered secondary actors responsible only for responding to complaints within their established systems. This emphasis on complaint systems also heightens concerns about over-policing as organizational influence is cabined around tamping down on expressions and actions of individual employees.

Putting the Contextual Threads Together: The Power of the Personal

How can we understand these contextual threads as they operate together to fuel organizational innocence? On the whole, these contextual threads present discrimination as an individualized, personal problem that is not likely to be incited or even affected by the organizations in which people work. Indeed, the individualized problem of discrimination is considered contrary to organizational interests. The cognitive bias revolution softens the stigma associated with discriminatory decisions, and it reinforces organizational innocence by making discrimination seem to stem from biases that are localized in individuals. The cognitive bias revolution works together with post-racialism to make intergroup biases and conflict seem personal, or at least not problematically racial (particularly to whites) or gendered. Meanwhile, diversity management sends the message that organizations are actively working on managing diversity. Finally, implementation of complaint systems as the principal means of reducing discrimination reinforces this story as organizations are positioned as the police of the individuals who may act on their biases in the workplace.

The threads work together to suggest that there should be both less discrimination (nonracial or gendered interpersonal conflict is considered equally likely), and also that when discrimination does take place, it is personal to the discriminators, resulting from biases socially constructed entirely outside work and uninfluenced by work context. Personalizing is doing two kinds of work here: it is turning incidents of racial and gender bias into interpersonal conflict, which actually means that discrimination tends more often today to fall out of view of antidiscrimination law entirely. In other words, the swath of action that is recognized as legally actionable, what we would call "discrimination" that violates Title VII, is becoming smaller. I will return to this effect of personalizing in Chapter 4. Personalizing, though, is also occurring within the discrimination frame. An act of discrimination, whether conscious or unconscious, may be recognized as discriminatory, as taken because of a person's race or sex, but it is considered a discrimination that is personal to the individual who discriminates and in contravention of the nondiscrimination goals and efforts of the organization in which the individual works. This latter personalizing is the core of organizational innocence that is pushing change in the law, narrowing the law to focus closely on individual instances of discrimination (thereby making it impossible to identify discrimination in the aggregate) and also reshaping the law to provide a new layer of protection to employers from liability for the discriminatory actions carried out by their employees.

ORGANIZATIONAL INNOCENCE – THE CONCEPTUAL PARADIGM

What is it, then, that judges may be thinking when they redraw employment discrimination law to protect employers? As the threads described here suggest, organizational innocence involves three conceptual components.

First, courts have come to believe that high-level decision makers within organizations, the policy makers of organizations, are unlikely to be personally discriminating. These people are assumed not to be acting with a purpose to keep women or minorities down. And, interestingly, they are also assumed not to be influenced by less conscious biases in making policy decisions. This latter point at first glance may seem in tension with the cognitive bias revolution. But it is one thing to acknowledge that cognitive biases are common, and another to believe that executives are likely to be affected by those biases when they are setting policies and general practices for an organization. Indeed, the prominent cognitive bias story tends to emphasize biases as they influence perceptions and decisions of lower-level managers involving assessment of individual merit (whether I am likely to hire a female applicant or to pay her more than a male counterpart, for example), not biases as they can influence decisions about what structures and practices are adopted in an organization. What's more, judges themselves are likely to be influenced by their own cognitive biases in thinking that high-level executives can control their biases when important decisions are at stake.

We might take a somewhat extreme recent case as illustration: *Ashcroft v. Iqbal*.[80] This case was not a run-of-the-mill Title VII case, but rather a constitutional one involving the seizure and detention of a man named Javaid Iqbal after the September 11 attacks in New York. Iqbal alleged that he had been subjected to unusually harsh conditions in detention because he was Arab and Muslim. He brought what is called a *Bivens* claim, which allows individual citizens to sue federal officials for violation of citizens' constitutional rights.[81] Iqbal alleged that John Ashcroft, the Attorney General of the United States at the time, and Robert Mueller, the Director of the FBI, had violated his constitutional right to equal protection by adopting the policy that resulted in his harsh detention. In order to win on his claim, however, he had to show that Ashcroft and Mueller had adopted the policy "not for a neutral, investigative reason but for the purpose of discriminating on account of race, religion, or national origin."[82] And this, the Court held, he could not do. In fact, the Court held that Iqbal's claim should be thrown out before any discovery (the process used to uncover evidence from the organization) because Iqbal's allegations were "implausible." Although the Court was willing to find plausible Iqbal's allegations that low-level officers on the street or in the detention center had acted on bias when seizing him or in their treatment of him while they had him in custody, the Court could not see how Ashcroft or Mueller could have been acting with bias in adopting the policy when they obviously had more important national interests in mind.[83]

The federal government may be a unique organization, and national security a uniquely important interest, but this same idea – high-level decision makers have more important things in mind when making policy decisions (and are unlikely to allow biases to infect their minds when making important decisions) – carries over easily and regularly to private organizations. Without evidence to suggest otherwise, there is no reason to suspect that high-level policy makers at Wal-Mart, for example, set their pay and promotion policies with an express purpose to keep women down. Moreover, although the research shows that executives can be biased in their decisions about which structures or policies to adopt, the reality is that it is difficult to show that high-level actors acted with bias in making policy decisions. Policy decisions do not lend themselves well to comparative evidence. And most people can come up with a reason that is nondiscriminatory for a policy, which means that proving the stated reason for a decision false is not a promising way of proving bias. This leaves plaintiffs grasping for statements made by high-level actors that reflect bias, and these statements are naturally hard to come by when CEOs and other policy makers usually know better than to express their racial or gender stereotypes or biases.

Turning to the second component of organizational innocence, with most high-level decision makers out of the picture, discrimination, when it does occur, is seen as a problem of low-level decision makers, the managers and supervisors who make the decisions about who receives what kind of pay raise and who is transferred or promoted (or even the lower-level managers and co-workers who make decisions about who does what job tasks or conducts evaluations or writes up disciplinary reports). Sometimes these managers and supervisors may be acting on conscious biases and animus. Other times, they may be acting on implicit biases and stereotypes, even if they do not act with a purpose to discriminate, and courts seem to accept this as a possibility.

As for the third component, courts see the low-level decision makers who do make biased employment decisions, whether consciously or unconsciously, as rogues, as individuals acting in isolation and against the interest of their employers. Biases carried out in the workplace are thought to be personal to the individuals that hold them, to vary according to outside-of-work socialization, media, and upbringing, and to have little or nothing to do with the organizations in which the individuals act.

Once the individual rogue discriminator is isolated from the organization, it is easy to worry about fairness to the organization that defends the lawsuits and pays the price of any judgments in plaintiffs' favor. The organization becomes innocent, disconnected from the act of discrimination that is committed by a low-level actor, indeed harmed by the action that is contrary to the organization's proclaimed and, as demonstrated by diversity management efforts, actual interests.

PART I

Discrimination Laundering

2

Individual Discrimination: The Emerging
Law of Complaint and Response

Critics of individual discrimination law have long maintained that the law as it has evolved focuses too closely on identified moments of decision and specific states of mind.[1] Scholars have also shown that courts are increasingly less inclined than they once were to find discrimination when there are other possible reasons for decisions.[2] The shift in law that I document in this chapter, however, is different. It is a shift in the legal doctrine not around the evidence required to prove discrimination, but around whether employers are liable for discrimination once it is proved.

Employers have been pushing since the beginning of Title VII to get courts to separate individual discriminators from their employers in determining employer liability. The early 1970s case of *Slack* v. *Havens*, which I mentioned earlier, serves as a textbook example.[3] Three black women working at Havens Industries, a manufacturing plant in San Diego, were fired for refusing to do heavy cleaning that was outside of their job description. Ray Pohasky, the women's immediate supervisor, instructed them to do the work, and when the women objected, he told them that they would do the work "or else," adding that "Colored people should stay in their place" and "colored folks were hired to clean because they clean better." At trial, Havens Industries argued that it should not be liable for the discriminatory action of Pohasky because "no top level management officials of [Havens] Industries intended to discriminate against plaintiffs." The court flatly rejected this argument. It was enough, said the court, that Havens Industries required the women to do the work, and later fired them for refusing to do the work, regardless of top-level management officials' knowledge of the discriminatory nature of Pohasky's action.

Twenty years later, the major accounting firm Price Waterhouse pushed the same argument, this time with an emphasis on cognitive bias – and to some success in the courts. Ann Hopkins sued Price Waterhouse, the accounting giant, for discrimination in its decision to deny her admission to partnership.[4] As described earlier, decisions on partnership at Price Waterhouse were made by a board based in part on evaluations submitted by the existing partners of the firm, and those evaluations in Hopkins's case included statements reflecting sex stereotypes (e.g., that Hopkins would be more successful at the firm if she were to dress and act more femininely). Price Waterhouse argued to the trial court that it should not be held liable for the unconscious biases of partners in their evaluations when those partners did not make the ultimate decision on Hopkins's partnership.[5] That court agreed, holding that the firm could not be liable for unconsciously biased evaluations by the partners. However, the court said the firm could be liable for its own system that made evaluations based on "outmoded attitudes" determinative. According to the court, the evidence in the case suggested that "Price Waterhouse should have been aware of the danger that women being evaluated by male partners might well be victims of discriminatory stereotypes. Yet ... the firm made no efforts to make partners sensitive to the dangers, to discourage comments tainted by sexism, or to investigate comments to determine whether they were influenced by stereotypes."[6]

The court of appeals saw the issue differently. In response to the same argument on appeal, the appellate court stated that it was enough that Hopkins was "treated less favorably than male candidates because of her sex."[7] She did not also have to show that the firm should have been aware of any danger of stereotyping or that it otherwise knew that stereotyping was taking place in the partner evaluations.

The Supreme Court did not expressly acknowledge the argument in its opinion in the case, but as I explained in Chapter 1, it also did not separate the employer or the board decision from the partner evaluations.[8] This might be read as a signal that the Court was steadfast, resisting the organization's attempt to disavow itself of discrimination merely by pointing to lack of knowledge or of purpose on the part of high-level decision makers. The Court instead focused on the question of when, if ever, the employer must prove that a decision was the result of legitimate factors, even if discriminatory bias may also have played a role. A plurality (four justices) held that it must do so when the plaintiff has proven that her race or sex was a "motivating factor" for a decision.

Justice O'Connor in her concurrence, however, did draw a distinction between the employer organization, which has control over practices and policies, and the individual decision makers who evaluated Ann Hopkins. She framed her discussion in terms of causation, just as the plurality did, but she expressed concern in her opinion about what the employer would do in response to a law that shifted the burden of proof on causation (requiring the employer to prove that it would have made the same decision anyway, absent any consideration of race or sex) upon presentation of evidence by a plaintiff of general attitudes or biased statements in the workplace.[9] In an earlier decision, Justice O'Connor had expressed similar concern, although that time based on her sense that making it too easy for plaintiffs to establish that an employer's use of a neutral practice has a disparate impact on members of a protected group (or too difficult for employers to justify their practices in response) would lead employers to rely on quotas, or what Justice O'Connor calls "inappropriate prophylactic measures."[10] Requiring a plaintiff like Ann Hopkins to present evidence of biased statements in the formal decision-making process before shifting the burden of causation was wise, according to Justice O'Connor, because then all the employer needed to do to avoid having to justify its decisions on nondiscriminatory grounds was to "avoid substantial reliance on forbidden criteria in making its employment decisions."[11] All it needed to do, in other words, was purge its evaluations of biased statements. It need not go further to consider whether bias was operating more pervasively within the workplace. As it turns out, Justice O'Connor was articulating some of the early glimmers of organizational innocence.

Today, resistance to a new layer of employer protection like that pushed by the defendants in *Slack* v. *Havens* and *Price Waterhouse* is at breaking point. Courts and commentators alike increasingly declare distinct limits as to what employers should be expected to do when it comes to discrimination at work. These limits rest on empirical assumptions about how discrimination operates and about what organizations can (and should) do to avoid or reduce discrimination. What often goes unstated – and always goes unexamined – is the pervasive belief that institutions can do little more to reduce discrimination than police their discriminating employees and purge their formal decisions from expressions of bias.

With this belief also comes concern about over-policing. The idea is that employers should be liable only for discrimination that they can prevent "without overly draconian policing of the expressions of their employees."[12] If employers establish complaint procedures and respond adequately to specific, reported incidents of harassment and discrimination, this idea goes, they should not be responsible for discriminatory harassment or even ultimately for discrimination like that experienced by the black women in a case such as *Slack* v. *Havens*.

This dramatic shift in employer liability – a move toward a law of complaint and response – is taking place behind the scenes, buried beneath seemingly technical doctrinal questions of agency, causation, statutes of limitations, and civility codes. In this chapter, I show how the law of individual discrimination is changing and is likely to continue to change, pushed by the frame of organizational innocence, to protect employers from liability for discrimination carried out by employees so long as the employer implements a complaint system and responds adequately to complaints. This new version of Title VII law puts pressure on victims of discrimination to complain, often very early on, and it asks employers to address those discrete complaints. Employers are under no obligation under this law to monitor for structural and other organizational causes of discrimination, or to reduce discrimination otherwise.

INDIVIDUAL DISCRIMINATION LAW

Most employment discrimination claims are filed by individuals who allege that they were discriminated against in a key employment decision, like a hiring, pay, promotion, discipline, or discharge decision. These claims isolate specific decisions as having been made because of the plaintiff's membership in a protected group. Hostile work environment claims, known colloquially as harassment, are also most often litigated as individual claims of discrimination, even if sometimes the acts of harassment only amount to a work environment hostile enough to violate Title VII when they amass over time. An identified individual or small group of individuals is alleged in these cases to have treated the plaintiff in a hostile or abusive way because of that plaintiff's race, color, religion, sex, or national origin.

Recall that in all cases the employer, and not any individual employee, is held liable for discrimination in violation of Title VII. Title VII was a major inroad into the private realm of business, cutting into managerial prerogative to otherwise hire and fire employees for any reason, and courts from the start accordingly read the term "agent" in the statute to signal Congress's intent for a broad definition of "employer," a definition that includes the informal decisions of lower-level employees as well as the more formal policy decisions of high-level executives.[13] Indeed, this indirect, often called "vicarious" employer liability for the actions of employees is central to Title VII. Without it, most acts of individual discrimination would go entirely unaddressed.[14]

We can see this indirect, vicarious liability at work in a case like *Slack v. Havens*, where the employer was liable for the blatantly discriminatory action of its low-level manager, Ray Pohasky. Similarly, when a human resources officer discriminates against an applicant in a hiring decision based on the applicant's race, the employer, not the human resources officer, is liable under Title VII. The employer's liability depends on the plaintiff's establishing discriminatory bias in the decision taken by the human resources officer, not in their proving discriminatory bias or purpose at higher levels of the company.

The organization may have influenced the human resources officer in various ways, but in these claims the employer's liability typically does not hinge on that influence. High-level executives need not have adopted a policy of discrimination against members of a particular race or even have encouraged the human resources officer more indirectly to discriminate. Moreover, the employer is liable regardless of the precautions that may have been taken to prevent discrimination and regardless of whether high-level executives knew that the discrimination was occurring.

This said, an employer could be both directly and indirectly liable for the actions of its agent. If the human resources officer acts pursuant to company policy to discriminate, for example, the employer would be both directly liable and indirectly (vicariously) liable for discrimination. Or if high-level executives knew of prior discriminatory decisions by this officer and did nothing about it, the employer might be directly liable for its own negligence – its carelessness in the face of knowledge of discrimination – as well as indirectly (vicariously) liable for the lower-level officer's discriminatory decision. In both these cases we would expect to see remedies that focus on making whole the individual who suffered the discrimination and also on eliminating the organization's role in perpetuating or in some cases commanding discrimination by its employees.[15] Most cases of individual discrimination, however, involve only the first type of employer liability: indirect, vicarious liability for the discriminatory acts of the employer's agents.

Cases of individual discrimination are often difficult for plaintiffs to win. After all, evidence that a particular decision was made because of the plaintiff's protected characteristic can be hard to come by in a modern age when managers are less likely to make their racial and gender biases known. The personalizing of racialized and gendered interactions, which I will talk more about in Chapter 4, also makes proving individual discrimination difficult. But discrimination laundering is protecting employers from liability in another important way, by cutting back on vicarious liability. Even when a court finds that a specific decision was discriminatory, for example, when a manager expressly states his bias in the context of the decision, the employer is increasingly likely to find protection from liability. This second layer of protection emerged in the area of sexual harassment law in the 1990s, and it is quickly gaining momentum beyond harassment to include all individual claims of discrimination. The precise doctrinal issues in the cases differ, but through each weaves the subtext of organizational innocence: that discrimination is a problem of individuals acting in isolation and against the interests of the organizations for which they work, and that the principal, if not only, way to reduce discrimination and harassment at work is by policing individual behavior. This assumption leads to concerns that imposing vicarious liability on organizations will lead to "draconian" measures and over-policing of individual behavior and expression.

THE BEGINNING OF A NEW ERA: ORGANIZATIONAL INNOCENCE AND HARASSMENT

The law of employment discrimination shifted dramatically in 1998, when the Supreme Court first drew limits around employer liability for individual acts of discrimination by employees. In its 1997–98 term, the Court heard two cases in which plaintiffs had suffered discriminatory harassment at work. The trial courts in both cases found discrimination. In one case, Kimberly Ellerth, a saleswoman for Burlington Industries, was sexually harassed over a period of fifteen months by a mid-level manager, Ted Slowik.[16] In the other case, Beth Ann Faragher, a part-time summer lifeguard for the City of Boca Raton, was sexually harassed during two summers by her immediate supervisors, Bill Terry and David Silverman.[17] The courts said that the harassment experienced by Ellerth and Faragher was severe and pervasive enough to violate Title VII. Discrimination, in other words, had occurred.

The doctrinal question for the Court in the cases, therefore, was not about whether the harassment amounted to discrimination (it did), but rather about whether the employer should be vicariously liable for the discrimination carried out by the men. Is there a limit to the liability of an employer for the discriminatory acts taken by its employees, and, if so, what is that limit?

The question arose out of concerns about discriminatory harassment as a recognizable form of discrimination. In its earlier cases, the Supreme Court had held that discriminatory harassment could be discrimination in violation of Title VII so long as it was severe or pervasive enough so as to alter the terms and conditions of the plaintiffs' employment.[18] But concerns about employer liability for harassment continued to percolate.

For example, the court of appeals in the *Faragher* case had held that because the harassing acts by Terry and Silverman were in that court's view a "frolic" and were motivated solely to further their own personal ends (rather than to serve the ends of the employer), the city employer would be liable only if the plaintiff could show that the city was negligent in allowing the harassment to take place.[19] A majority of the Supreme Court ultimately rejected this broadreaching negligence standard (which would have jettisoned entirely vicarious liability for harassment cases), but the Court did not entirely reject the underlying idea: that there should be limits on vicarious employer liability for discriminatory harassment. Rather, in *Faragher* v. *Boca Raton* and *Burlington*

Industries v. *Ellerth* the Court agreed with the defendants that there should be limits on employer liability because, in the Court's view, harassment is generally motivated by personal ends, and is therefore carried out against the interests of the employer.[20]

Specifically, the Court held that an employer will be vicariously liable for harassment only when the harassing employee was the victim's supervisor with immediate (or successive) authority over him or her and when the harasser took tangible employment action, "such as discharge, demotion, or undesirable reassignment," against the victim. If the harassing employee was a supervisor of the victim but did not take tangible employment action, then the employer will be vicariously liable only if it cannot meet the elements of an affirmative defense, by showing: "(a) that the employer exercised reasonable care to prevent and correct promptly any sexually harassing behavior; and (b) that the plaintiff employee unreasonably failed to take advantage of any preventive or corrective opportunities provided by the employer or to avoid harm otherwise."[21] In practical effect, this holding shifted employer liability for a class of individual employment discrimination cases (those involving harassment by co-workers and by supervisors who do not take tangible employment action) from vicarious liability to direct liability grounded in concepts of notice and reasonable response to known harassment. An employer will be liable for harassment by a supervisor when the supervisor does not take tangible employment action only if the employer fails to show that it acted reasonably under the circumstances.

Why did the Court limit employer liability in this way? The answer lies at least in part in organizational innocence. The Court sees harassers like Slowik, Terry, and Silverman as acting on their own, for personal reasons. In this view, the organizations, Burlington Industries and the City of Boca Raton, have no influence on the discriminatory actors apart from providing the venue for the harassment to occur. And their role in preventing the harassment is thereby narrowly construed as one of policing – adequate response to victim complaints.

One legal commentator describes the rationale behind the Court's holding in this way:

> Employers must make an effort to prevent harassment and the corresponding damage to women's career opportunities, but no employer can prevent every ill-considered comment, unwelcome pass, or off-color joke. As entities, most employers can't harass or refrain from harassment – but they can establish procedures to ensure that unwelcome comments and overtures can be reported and dealt with.[22]

The Court's opinions in *Faragher* and *Burlington Industries* map precisely this line of thinking – and share its underlying assumptions. The Court expressed concern that without a tangible employment action requirement for vicarious liability, employers would be held automatically liable for actions by supervisors that could just as well be carried out by co-workers, who are merely brought together with their victims through the employment relationship, nothing more.[23] Simply providing access to victims for rogue harassers who act for their own personal motives rather than for the interests of the employer, in the Court's view, is insufficient organizational involvement to warrant automatic employer liability. Similarly, the Court couched its reasoning for the specific contours of the affirmative defense in terms of pragmatism and effectuating Title VII's prophylactic goals. The Court stated that "Title VII is designed to encourage the creation of antiharassment policies and effective grievance mechanisms" and "limiting employer liability could encourage employees to report harassing conduct before it becomes severe or pervasive."[24]

THE DRIVING CONCERN ABOUT OVER-POLICING

The concern that Title VII law, if not adequately cabined, will drive employers to "over-police" private behavior was also doing more work in *Faragher* and *Burlington Industries* than the Court let on. Harassment law in the United States has long been controversial and contested by those who think that its enforcement risks substantial infringement on personal liberties, like free speech. This frame consistently presents harassment as an interpersonal problem that merely takes place at work (instead of on the sidewalk, in a bar, or in a private home) and as a problem that is deterred exclusively, if at all, by policing individual behavior. The frame is behind the early development of sexual harassment law, including the Court's decisions in *Faragher* and *Burlington Industries*, and it is likely to drive the development of employment discrimination law beyond harassment in various ways in the years to come.

The movement to include sexual harassment as discrimination in violation of Title VII gained momentum in the early to mid-1970s in the United States, and by the early 1980s, the appellate courts and then the EEOC had declared sexual harassment a violation of Title VII.[25] Prior to this, many lower court judges had held that sexual harassment was personal in nature, motivated by personal sexual urges, and could not be the basis for a sex-based discrimination under Title VII.[26] Controversy continued to brew, however, over whether to extend the concept of legally actionable harassment to include hostile work environments and not just explicit demands for sexual favors (often called quid pro quo harassment). Historian Leigh Ann Wheeler describes, for example, the debate at the time within the prominent and influential civil liberties organization, the American Civil Liberties Union (ACLU).[27] Board members of the ACLU demanded that "pure speech" be excluded from the ACLU's sexual harassment policy. They insisted that the "office prude" should not be permitted to set the standards for sexual behavior in the workplace.[28] "Calendar pinups" in particular dominated the discussion within the ACLU on devising a policy on harassment. In one discussion, committee member Carolyn Simpson argued that pinups were as threatening to women as photos of lynchings were to black men. Another committee member responded by asking Simpson if she thought car mechanics should be forced to take down their pinups, and when Simpson said yes, she was accused of class bias for assuming that blue-collar men used pinups to intimidate women. Pinups alone, in the absence of "other harassing behavior," these members maintained, should not be considered a form of sexual harassment.[29]

When the ACLU finally came out with its policy in 1984, the policy defined sexual harassment as "intentional unwanted physical contact of a sexual nature which is clearly offensive."[30] The policy included "sexual expression" only when "directed at a specific employee" and only when the behavior "demonstrably hinders or completely prevents" the victim from functioning at work. It excluded altogether generalized harassment "that has no other effect on its recipient than to create an unpleasant working environment."[31]

In 1986, the United States Supreme Court granted certiorari in its first sexual harassment case, *Meritor Savings Bank* v. *Vinson*.[32] Mechelle Vinson had worked at Meritor Savings Bank as a teller-trainee under the supervision of Sidney Taylor, a vice president and branch manager at the bank. Vinson alleged that while she was working at the bank, Taylor asked her to have sex with him, and she did for fear of losing her job. After that, Taylor made repeated demands for sexual favors, usually at the bank, and over the course of the next several years Vinson had intercourse with him many times. In addition, Taylor fondled Vinson in front of other employees, exposed himself to her, and forcibly raped her on several occasions.

The EEOC's 1980 guidance stated that employers were strictly liable for harassment by supervisors, but when *Meritor* came up to the Supreme Court, the Department of Justice (DOJ) and the EEOC, headed at the time by now-Justice Clarence Thomas, filed an amicus brief on behalf of the bank arguing that the bank should not be liable for the harassment by Taylor unless it had failed to implement a procedure designed to resolve sexual harassment claims or had actual knowledge of the harassment and failed to do anything about it.[33] The DOJ/EEOC brief insisted that to impose vicarious liability upon an employer for a hostile work environment created by any employee would be

"practically unfair to the employer and perhaps even productive of unneces-
sary harmful side effects."[34] As the brief explained: "Given the naturalness, the
pervasiveness, and what might be called the legal neutrality of sexual attraction ..., we find much wisdom in Judge Bork's observation that a rule of strict
liability would create an incentive for employers to 'monitor ... or police ...
employees' voluntary sexual relationships.'"[35]

The district court in the case had dismissed Vinson's claim on three distinct grounds: first, that she could show no tangible or economic harm (it was
undisputed that her advancement within the bank was based on merit alone);
second, that Vinson had engaged in a sexual relationship with Taylor that
was "voluntary" and therefore not sufficient basis for a finding of discrimination; and third, that the bank should not be liable even if the circumstances
amounted to discrimination because the bank lacked "notice" of the harassment.[36] The Supreme Court quickly rejected the first two grounds. It held
that Vinson did not need to prove a tangible economic harm in order to prove
a violation of Title VII, that, in other words, a hostile work environment that
alters the "terms and conditions of employment" is sufficient. Nor would
Vinson lose her case simply because she "voluntarily" engaged in sexual conduct with Taylor, so long as his behavior toward her was "unwelcome."[37]

But when it came to the third ground, the issue on which the EEOC had
submitted its brief, the Court provided only a partial answer. The Court's
opinion in *Meritor* is often described as not deciding the issue at all, but that
is not quite right. The Court stated in *Meritor* that courts should look to tort
law agency principles for guidance in placing limits on vicarious employer
liability for harassment (as the EEOC had recommended in its brief),[38] and
this opened the door to the narrowing of employer liability.[39]

These same ideas – that harassment is an individualized, interpersonal
problem and that imposing liability on employers will lead to over-policing of
employee behavior – were put forward again to the Court six years later in a case
called *Harris* v. *Forklift Systems, Inc.*[40] The plaintiff in the case, Teresa Harris,
had worked as a manager at the equipment rental company Forklift Systems
for almost two years. During her time there, the company's president, Charles
Hardy, regularly insulted Harris, saying things like, "You're a woman, what do
you know?" and calling her a "dumb ass woman." Hardy also asked Harris and
other female employees to get coins from his front pants pocket, and made sexual innuendos about Harris's and other women's clothing. The legal issues in
the case involved the standard for proving harassment. The magistrate judge
(affirmed by the district court) had held that although some of Hardy's comments
offended Harris, they would not offend a reasonable woman and were not "so
severe as to be expected to seriously affect [Harris's] psychological well-being."[41]

Harris came to the Supreme Court not long after the Thomas–Hill hearings at which Anita Hill, an employee at the EEOC under Clarence Thomas, recounted Thomas's relentless requests for dates, comments on her appearance, and persistent and graphic talk about pornographic videos and his own sexual prowess. Some of the public debate around the hearings included concern that declaring behavior such as that described by Hill as harassment would infringe on individual liberties, including freedom of expression.[42]

For the most part, however, the Thomas–Hill hearings drew attention to the problem of sexual harassment for working women, and made it more likely that the law would turn in favor of plaintiffs, even if only in the shorter term. Indeed, although briefs were filed in *Harris* arguing that a high standard for harassment is necessary to avoid overzealous policing by employers, the Supreme Court made no mention of these concerns in its *Harris* opinion, where it unanimously held that plaintiffs need not show "tangible effects" or "psychological injury" from harassment in order for the harassment to violate Title VII.[43] The standard, said the Court, is simply whether the environment "would reasonably be perceived, and is perceived, as hostile or abusive."[44]

But the concerns about harassment law and employer policing did not die with *Harris*. They resurfaced, this time in *Faragher* and *Burlington Industries*. In the Seventh Circuit Court of Appeals decision in one of the cases leading up to the Supreme Court, Judge Richard Posner explained his view of why the law should impose vicarious liability for some supervisor actions but not for others and not for co-worker actions. According to Posner, the limitation on employer liability turns on the feasibility of deterrence and the risk of over-policing. "Why," he asks, "is the standard negligence rather than strict [vicarious] liability?" "The reason," he answers, "is the infeasibility of an employer's stamping out this sort of harassment without going to extreme expense and greatly curtailing the privacy of its employees, by putting them under continuous video surveillance." According to Posner, "courts know, more or less, what is reasonable for the employer to do about hostile-environment harassment – institute a tough policy, disseminate it, establish a procedure by which a worker can complain without fear of retaliation …, [and] respond promptly and effectively to any report of possible harassment."[45]

This kind of thinking is exactly the kind that the Supreme Court relied on in formulating its holding in *Faragher* and *Burlington Industries*. The details may have differed. Posner, after all, argued for a negligence standard (on which plaintiffs bear the burden of proof) for all hostile work environment harassment claims, while the Court shifted the burden to the defendant in some cases by devising an affirmative defense for hostile work environments created by supervisors. But the basic idea is there. It fuels the Court's

understanding of how harassment operates – that it is an individualized undertaking motivated, as the Court puts it, by "gender-based animus or a desire
to fulfill sexual urges" that is not within the scope of employment.[46] And the
idea underlies the Court's decision to limit employer liability by imposing
vicarious liability only in cases of supervisor harassment that result in tangible
employment action, such as decisions to fire or discipline or deny a pay raise.
Indeed, Justices Thomas and Scalia nearly shout out their concern in dissent in *Burlington Industries*, insisting that "Sexual harassment is simply not
something that employers can wholly prevent without taking extraordinary
measures – constant video and audio surveillance, for example – that would
revolutionize the workplace in a manner incompatible with a free society."[47]

One way to limit the reach of harassment law is by constructing a high
standard for proving harassment that amounts to discrimination. That the
Court in *Harris* was unwilling to do. Another way is by limiting employer
vicarious liability for proven discrimination. This is what the Court did in
Faragher and *Burlington Industries*.[48]

With *Faragher* and *Burlington Industries*, the Supreme Court set up a new
legal regime under which employers are protected from vicarious liability for
acts of discrimination by their employees. While the early Supreme Court
cases involved sexual harassment, the law has not been confined to that area. It
has been applied to cases where the harassment is not sexual at all, but nonetheless sex based,[49] and to cases of race-based harassment as well. Moreover,
the Court recently expanded employer protection by defining the category of
"supervisor" narrowly and thereby pushing more cases into the co-worker category, where the plaintiff must prove negligence on the part of the employer.
Given the organizational innocence frame that underlies these decisions,
we should expect the Court to expand the realm of protection even further,
beyond harassment. As this realm expands, the employer obligation shifts.
Where employers were once under an obligation not to discriminate, not to
treat employees and applicants differently based on race or other protected
characteristics, employers are increasingly under an obligation today merely
to provide a system of complaint and to respond adequately to any complaints
that arise.

ONE STEP FURTHER: A LOOK AT RACIAL HARASSMENT, WHO IS A "SUPERVISOR," AND THE DRIVE TOWARD A LAW OF COMPLAINT-AND-RESPONSE

Maetta Vance started work in 1989 at the University Banquet and Catering
(UBC) division of Dining Services at Ball State University in Muncie, Indiana.

She was the only black employee in her division. Her legal case involved her overall experience working in UBC and particularly her experiences with at least four fellow Ball State employees, all of whom were white, and who Vance alleged together created a racially hostile and intimidating work environment.[50] Vance presented evidence of the following specific experiences. She was subjected to harsh treatment (berating and yelling) by her immediate supervisor, Kimes, who was known to "pick favorites" and treat others terribly, but who nonetheless treated Vance worse than any of the nonminority employees. She was called "monkey" by a fellow employee, McVicker, who was also overheard calling African Americans, including Vance and students at Ball State, "nigger" and bragging about having Klan members in her family. She was "blocked" in the elevator by another fellow worker, Davis, who asked Vance "Are you scared?" "like she had a southern accent." And she was "mean-mugged" by another supervisor, Adkins, who also stared intently at Vance when they were alone in the kitchen.

Vance complained. She used the grievance procedure in place at Ball State. Each time she complained, someone at Ball State would investigate. A decision would be made whether to discipline any of the employees involved, and the incident would be closed. The conduct continued, and Vance eventually filed a charge with the EEOC and later a lawsuit in federal court alleging violation of Title VII.

The trial court granted summary judgment for the defendant, meaning that the case did not go to trial. Kimes and Adkins were both identified in the Ball State hierarchy as Vance's superiors, and the lower courts in the case considered Vance's allegations involving those two separately from the incidents between Vance and Davis and McVicker. Kimes, said the courts, had expressed no racial reason for treating Vance more harshly than non minority employees and therefore Kimes's treatment of Vance could not be a basis for Title VII liability – it was not "because of race." Adkins's mean face and staring, said the courts, "while not the most mature things to do, fall short of the kind of conduct that might support a hostile work environment claim," meaning that Vance's experience with Adkins too was not considered as part of her Title VII claim.[51] As to McVicker and Davis, whom both the district court and circuit court considered co-workers of Vance, Ball State was not liable because Vance failed to put forward sufficient evidence to establish that Ball State was "negligent in failing to 'take reasonable steps to discover and remedy the harassment.'" As the circuit court put it, "While it is unfortunate that Ball State's remedial measures did not persuade Davis or McVicker to treat Vance with respect, and we have nothing but condemnation for the type of conduct Vance has alleged, we find that Ball State satisfied its obligation under Title VII by promptly investigating each of Vance's complaints and taking disciplinary action where appropriate."[52]

Even if we believe that none of Maetta Vance's experiences rose to the level of harassment that is severe enough to violate Title VII, the court's isolating of each incident from the others for analysis is problematic. It masks the reality that sometimes multiple, seemingly "minor" incidents when considered in isolation can nonetheless add up when viewed together to be sufficiently pervasive to violate Title VII.[53]

The case went to the Supreme Court, though, solely on the issue of whether Davis, considered a co-worker by the lower courts, was in fact a supervisor. Recall that whether a harassing employee is a supervisor or co-worker matters in a case like this one because if the employee is a supervisor, then under *Faragher* and *Burlington Industries* the employer is vicariously liable, unless it can establish the stated affirmative defense. If the employee is a co-worker, in contrast, the plaintiff has to prove that the employer was negligent. In *Vance*, the Court held that an employee is a supervisor only if he or she is formally empowered by the organization to take tangible employment actions such as hiring, firing, or promoting. Having control over other employees' daily work tasks, as Davis was alleged to have, is not enough.[54]

The holding of *Vance* restricts the circumstances in which employers will be liable by pushing more cases into the negligence category rather than the supervisor-who-takes-no-tangible-action affirmative defense category. And under a negligence standard, an employer will be liable for a hostile work environment only if high-level management knew or should have known about the environment and failed to act reasonably to address it. This means that a victim has to not only complain (which she also has to do under the *Faragher/Burlington Industries* defense when harassed by a supervisor); she has to make sure that her complaint goes high enough within the organization to count as notice, and the response to the complaint needs to be considered inadequate.[55]

In one recent case involving a question of notice, Samantha Stabenchek, a seventeen-year-old cashier at Safeway, experienced sexual harassment, including a sexual assault, by her "front-end manager."[56] The court held that the manager was not Stabenchek's supervisor under *Vance* and therefore the employer would be liable only for negligence in its treatment of the harassment. Stabenchek complained about the manager's behavior (he had made hundreds of sexual comments and sent thousands of sexual text messages) only after the physical assault. The court held that the employer was not liable for the harassing discrimination, the assault, because the employer did not know about the harassment until after that incident. Evidence that the harasser had slapped other women on the buttocks and that he and other employees had engaged in sexual "joking" was insufficient to support an inference that the employer should have known of the harassment.

Vance also shows that the law limiting employer liability extends beyond sexual harassment to racial harassment. Indeed, the extension is not likely to stop there. As organizational innocence takes hold, courts, including the Supreme Court, have begun to apply similar thinking to cases involving discrimination other than harassment – to discrete employment decisions.

BEYOND HARASSMENT

The more the courts view discriminatory decisions by individuals as rogue acts, driven by socially constructed biases carried out against the interests of the employer, the more likely courts are to develop the law so that it focuses inquiry on notice (victim complaint) and employer response. These are the hallmarks of a liability standard that protects organizations from perceived unfairness at being held vicariously liable for individuals' acts and eases concerns about the risks of over policing.

Organizational innocence is leading the Court to alter individual discrimination law beyond harassment through two avenues. The first is quite subtle, building around ideas of organizational fairness in a seemingly procedural context: the timing of the filing of a victim's complaint with the EEOC. The second is the more radical, whole-scale shift. Ultimately, if organizational innocence continues to dominate, the Court may simply hold that organizations should not be vicariously liable for any of the discriminatory actions of their employees, or at least of those employees who are not high enough in the hierarchy to be acting on behalf of the organization as a whole.

THE INDIRECT ROUTE TO NARROWING EMPLOYER LIABILITY: STATUTES OF LIMITATION AND DELAYED ACTION

The first route to narrow employer liability has been in the works in the Supreme Court for some time. It traces back to 2007, when the "cat's paw" issue, as it is sometimes called, first came before the Supreme Court. Stephen Peters, an African American man, had sued BCI Coca-Cola Bottling Co. for discriminatory discharge.[57] Peters had worked as a merchandiser for BCI in its Albuquerque, New Mexico facility for six years. During that time, he reported to Cesar Grado, a District Sales Manager, who was responsible for monitoring and evaluating employees but who was not authorized to discipline or terminate anyone's employment. Grado was expected to bring disciplinary matters to the attention of the Human Resources Department, which was responsible for taking any disciplinary action.

On Friday, September 28, 2001, Grado reported Peters for insubordination to Pat Edgar, a Human Resources official based in the Phoenix, Arizona office, after Peters refused to come into work on a Sunday as directed. Three days later, on October 1, 2001, Edgar decided to terminate Peters's employment for insubordination. She explained that she based her decision "first and foremost" on "the conduct of Mr. Peters toward Mr. Grado on Friday." Edgars did not know that Peters was black. Grado, however, not only knew that Peters was black; he had a history of treating black employees less favorably than other employees and of making disparaging remarks about blacks at work.

The district court ruled in favor of BCI. It held that the discrimination inquiry must focus exclusively on whether Edgar, the ultimate decision maker, "honestly believed that Mr. Peters was guilty of insubordination on Friday, September 28."[58] Grado's bias, according to the court, was immaterial. The circuit court reversed, holding that BCI could be liable for discrimination if "the biased subordinate's discriminatory reports, recommendation, or other actions caused the adverse employment action."[59] The Supreme Court granted certiorari. Was it enough that the termination decision was the result of biased action by Grado? Or did Edgars herself need to act with discriminatory bias?

The *BCI* case settled before the Supreme Court could hear argument or issue an opinion, but the Court faced the issue again several years later in *Staub* v. *Proctor Hospital*.[60] The plaintiff in *Staub* brought his claim under the Uniformed Services Employment and Reemployment Rights Act (USERRA), alleging that his employment was terminated because he was a veteran. Although the statutory language of USERRA is slightly different than that of Title VII, the issue presented in *Staub* was identical to that presented in *BCI*: Is an employer liable for discrimination when a low-level supervisor (with the responsibility to monitor and report on work behavior but not the authority to take final disciplinary actions) acts with discriminatory bias against an employee and that act later results in discipline or termination of the employee's employment? The Court's answer: Yes, so long as the initial act was taken with requisite intent and so long as that act was a proximate cause of the ultimate disciplinary action.[61]

We might look at this issue as a reframing of the longstanding push by employers to limit employer liability by arguing that the high-level, final decision makers did not act with bias. This was roughly the argument made by the employer in *Price Waterhouse*, and two decades earlier in *Slack* v. *Havens*. But the defendants in *Staub* and *BCI* tweaked the argument just enough to give it a fresh look. This time, they presented facts that the person making the ultimate decision was not aware of the bias, or, in the case of *BCI*, even of the race of the victim. This lured the Court into thinking about individual states of mind. The Court still resisted the full extent of the employers' argument: that an employer should not be liable unless the final decision maker was motivated by discriminatory animus or bias. But once we put *Staub* together with cases such as *Ledbetter* (discussed in Chapter 1) and *Vance*, and the organizational innocence that underlies them, it becomes easy to see that the Court is likely to move even further toward a complaint-and-response law than most people have realized.

Indeed, the importance of *Staub* lies in something much deeper that the Court barely acknowledges. Cases like *Staub* and *BCI* are commonplace. Many cases of discrimination involve multiple judgments and seemingly minor decisions made by several people that culminate later in an adverse decision such as a denial of promotion or discharge. Employment discrimination law has long focused its attention closely on those later decisions, the decisions to deny promotion or discharge, rather than on the earlier ones, even if the earlier ones are part of the overall package of evidence. *Staub* changes that. It focuses the lens directly onto the earlier decisions.

With the lens focused on these earlier decisions, the Court is likely to begin to question whether the plaintiffs challenging those decisions ought to be required to complain to their employers about any discriminatory behavior. The Court's response, if organizational innocence holds, will bring the bulk of individual discrimination claims largely in line with those of harassment after *Vance* and *Faragher* and *Burlington Industries*.

As described earlier, employment discrimination law has long required victims of discrimination to file a charge with the EEOC before filing a claim in court. This charge requirement operates as a de facto statute of limitations, requiring individuals to complain about suspected discrimination within a specified time, usually 300 days, of a discriminatory event. The law has also long required individuals who suspect discrimination, though, to wait to file a charge with the EEOC until at least a "materially adverse action" has occurred. Claims challenging poor evaluations, changes in job title, failure to train, and intra-department transfers have all been held to be legally insufficient to support a Title VII claim, even if the plaintiff has strong evidence that the specific decision was based on protected group status. The rationale here has always been that these actions may never result in the tangible economic employment detriment that Title VII cares about.

Putting these two aspects of long-standing law together with the Court's holding in *Staub* raises this question: In a case involving a discriminatory action that is a proximate cause of a later materially adverse action, which act, the initial discriminatory action or the later materially adverse action triggers the running of the filing period? Or, putting it to facts, which decision in a case like *BCI* triggers the filing period, the ultimate decision to terminate Peters's employment or the initial decision to write him up for insubordination? The facts of *BCI* render the issue relatively unimportant there because the termination followed just four days after the insubordination report, but the timing will not always be so close. *Staub* involved actions (e.g., a written warning accusing him of shirking his duties) that were motivated by discriminatory bias that went three months back from the date of his firing. And although the law governing filing within statutes of limitation does not typically require actual knowledge on the part of the victim, Staub actually was aware of the discriminatory biases of his supervisors and of their actions based on that bias more than four years earlier, beginning in 2000 when his supervisor started scheduling him for extra shifts without notice. She explained then that she thought Staub's military duties were "bullshit" and that the extra shifts were his "way of paying back the department and everyone else having to bend over backwards to cover [his] schedule for the Reserves."[62]

The issue also goes beyond disciplinary reports and discharge. Take the case of *Thomas v. Eastman Kodak Co.*[63] Myrtle Thomas was the only black customer service representative in Eastman Kodak's Wellsley, Massachusetts office when she was laid off in 1993. She filed a charge with the EEOC within the statutory period as measured from the layoff decision. Her claim, though, alleged that the 1993 decision was discriminatory because it resulted from a ranking process that relied on racially biased performance appraisals in 1990, 1991, and 1992. The court of appeals in the case held that the layoff decision rather than the performance appraisals triggered the limitations period because the appraisals did not have "crystallized implications or apparent tangible effects" at the time that they were conducted. Kodak sought certiorari in the Supreme Court at the time, but the Court denied the request.

What would the Court likely hold if it were to grant certiorari in *Thomas* today? One option would be for it to hold, as the court of appeals in *Thomas* did, that the ultimate layoff decision triggers the running of the limitations period. This would be consistent with the line of cases requiring a materially adverse action before a plaintiff can sue. But it would be inconsistent with the rise of organizational innocence, the Court's growing concern about organizational responsibility for what it views as isolated acts by rogue employees. It would mean that evidence relating to intent or bias by those rogue employees in some cases could be years in the past, something about which the Court has expressed concern, again out of fairness to organizations in litigating claims involving low-level, rogue discriminators.

A second option would be for the Court to hold that the decision involving discriminatory bias (in Myrtle Thomas's case, the performance evaluations), even if not yet resulting in an ultimate or materially adverse employment action, triggers the statutory filing period. The Court is unlikely to adopt this option, though, because it would undoubtedly lead to a surge in EEOC charges and lawsuits, and it would result in litigation over actions that may never have resulted in tangible harm.

The third option is for the Court to hold that the ultimate adverse decision triggers the statutory filing period, but that the employer will be liable for that discrimination only if it was negligent or failed to satisfy an affirmative defense like the one in *Faragher* and *Burlington Industries*. Taking this option would further narrow employer liability by expanding the law of *Faragher* and *Burlington Industries* beyond the realm of harassment to claims involving discrete acts of discrimination, including acts by supervisors or other agents of the employer.[64] It would put an obligation on victims of discrimination to complain internally early on, and would put pressure on employers to respond to those complaints.

And this change is likely to reach much further than we might even initially imagine. We tend to think of discriminatory actions – including the tangible employment actions envisioned in the harassment context – as discrete decisions, such as decisions to discharge or to deny a promotion or a pay raise. We imagine that the question is whether the person who made this particular decision was acting with bias when he or she made it. But when employers can avoid liability for discrimination by showing that a seemingly discrete decision, the decision to discharge, for example, was really based on earlier discriminatory actions about which the plaintiff failed to complain, those defendant employers are likely to push courts to see that discrimination often operates over time, only resulting in a materially adverse action after years of smaller discriminatory actions coalesce and build. This highlights the similarity between "soft" decisions affecting terms and conditions of employment and harassment. Performance reviews, job assignments, decisions about whom to invite into a work team, whom to invite to an important client dinner, even criticisms or complaints by co-workers about performance, are all decisions that are unlikely to have an immediate material effect but can easily translate into a materially adverse decision down the road. Each action itself may not now be actionable, even if discriminatory, but it nonetheless can become actionable if it adds up over time with others or even on its own later results in an ultimate employment decision (or a hostile work environment).

As a practical matter, moreover, a requirement that victims complain early on, when "softer" forms of discrimination are experienced, will reach quite broadly. This is because plaintiffs' evidence of bias in a particular, actionable decision often consists of anecdotal testimony of earlier interactions with that decision maker. My supervisor denies me a promotion today, but he told me three months earlier that he did not think women should be put in management positions. If courts think that my supervisor's action is a matter of personal biases, and that he is acting against the interests of the organization, then courts are likely to rely on the same rationale as expressed in *Faragher* and *Burlington Industries*. The law under this view might require that I notify my employer of my supervisor's statement so that the employer can do something – can alter my supervisor's bias or otherwise insulate the decision-making process from his bias – before the promotion decision is made.

THE DIRECT ROUTE AND END RESULT

Some cases, of course, will still involve discriminatory bias in a materially adverse decision made at a discrete point in time, with no hint that the plaintiff should have complained earlier. Imagine a supervisor who denies a black man a promotion because he thinks black men are lazy troublemakers. He has made no mention of his views prior to the decision, but at the moment of the decision he states that this is the reason for his decision. The Court insists that it has established a line over which the complaint-and-response law of *Faragher* and *Burlington Industries* will not creep, that of supervisors who take tangible employment action. But if the Court believes that discrimination truly is a problem of rogue actors, of supervisors and others acting on their own socially constructed biases and against the interests of the employer (the employer, after all, tells its employees not to discriminate), then even in these cases of tangible action, hiring or firing, the Court will be tempted to shift the law from vicarious employer liability for the discriminatory acts of employees to a direct liability standard, a duty of care, like negligence. Conceptually, in other words, there simply is no logical stopping point for organizational innocence in these cases. Once discriminating employees are viewed as rogues, it is too easy to shift to thinking about whether the employer failed in some duty to control that rogue actor.

Indeed, without always acknowledging the dramatic shift from indirect, vicarious liability to direct liability, several prominent legal commentators situated across the political spectrum seem to have already bought in to organizational innocence, arguing that this shift is (and should be) the future direction of the law. These and other commentators talk about discrimination in much the same way that the EEOC brief talked about sexual harassment in *Meritor*. They talk of constraining individual behavior,[65] of notice and cost to the employer,[66] and of how hard it is "for employers to control bias in the air."[67]

Once individual disparate treatment law evolves in this way, employers will be focused even more closely on responding to complaints as the principal method of reducing discrimination. The shift in law affects employers' obligation under Title VII for individual acts of discrimination. Employers under this new law are no longer consistently required to avoid or reduce discrimination by their employees. Rather, they are merely expected to provide a system for complaint and to investigate complaints or other known discriminatory acts, and to take disciplinary action where "appropriate." Employers have long been protected by the difficulty that plaintiffs alleging individual discrimination encounter in proving discrimination. Now they are increasingly protected by an additional layer of inquiry into employer responsibility for that discrimination, once proved.

My point in this chapter is not that the doctrinal move is necessarily bad because it will mean fewer successful employment discrimination claims, although it surely will. Rather, it is that individual disparate treatment law, driven by organizational innocence, is evolving into a law of victim complaint and employer response. As I will show in Chapter 5, the narrowing of employer obligation is problematic because it misses the many other ways that organizations contribute to workplace discrimination, and it unduly cabins organizational incentives toward measures such as policing that put responsibility for discrimination solely on individuals and that are unlikely to be effective in achieving Title VII equality goals.

3

Systemic Discrimination: Erasing the Aggregate and Entrenching a Law of Complaint and Response

At the same time that organizational innocence is driving the law of individual discrimination toward narrow emphasis on complaint and response, it is also driving the law of systemic discrimination in new and narrowing directions. Indeed, the narrowing in the law of systemic discrimination is arguably both more dramatic and further underway than in the individual realm – and more devastating for the future of equal opportunity in employment. What is happening in this area? Two things: First, the Supreme Court is erasing the aggregate, dispersing what were once systemic discrimination claims into many individual claims, both as a matter of procedure (for private plaintiffs seeking class certification) and substance (for all plaintiffs seeking to establish employer liability). Second, some of the justices seem to be considering adopting a standard of deliberate indifference for entity liability, a move that would only further entrench the complaint-and-response law that is emerging in the individual discrimination area.

The Supreme Court's recent decision in *Wal-Mart* v. *Dukes*[1] takes center stage in this chapter. The case against Wal-Mart was brought by private plaintiffs seeking to proceed as a class, and this fact is important to the historical build-up to the case and to its outcome in the Supreme Court. To see *Wal-Mart* as just a class action decision, however, is a serious mistake. The chapter digs deeper into the story of *Wal-Mart*, and the many cases like it, to show the shifts in the law that are already underway, and the organizational innocence that underlies them.

Like the story of discrimination laundering in individual discrimination law, the story here, too, involves the contextual/causal threads of organizational innocence, intertwined and overlapping: the cognitive bias revolution, the rise of diversity management, and increased reliance on complaint processes. Add to this the at times fever-pitched controversy around class actions, particularly large class actions seeking monetary payments, and the stage is set for discrimination laundering in systemic discrimination law.

As I described in Chapter 1, in addition to prohibiting individual instances of discrimination, Title VII also made unlawful more systemic forms of discrimination. Express policies of discrimination, for example, are unlawful under Title VII. Formally endorsed segregation as well as hiring or promotion bans fall into this category, and for the most part these went by the wayside soon after Title VII went into effect. An employer can no longer place help-wanted ads seeking only men or members of specific racial groups;[2] nor can it maintain formal policies that pay men and women differently for the same work. The *Griggs* v. *Duke Power* case, and later Congress by statutory enactment, also made unlawful employers' use of employment practices, such as a high school diploma requirement or testing requirement, that have a disparate impact on members of a protected group and that are not justified by business necessity.

Beyond formal discriminatory policies and use of practices that have a disparate impact, Title VII also prohibits employers from engaging in "patterns or practices of discrimination."[3] This pattern-or-practice theory became known over time as systemic disparate treatment theory. Under systemic disparate treatment theory, plaintiffs have established employer liability by using statistics and other evidence to show that discrimination within their work organization was or is widespread, that discrimination, in the Court's words, is "the regular rather than the unusual practice."[4]

All three of these systemic theories traditionally have been understood to impose direct liability on employers, liability that, unlike in the individual claims context, is not derivative of any specific agent's action. In other words, when it comes to systemic discrimination, the employer is held responsible for something it has done (e.g., relying on an express policy of discrimination or using a practice that has a disparate impact or engaging in a pattern or practice of discrimination) rather than for something that one of its lower-level agents has done (e.g., a supervisor making a discriminatory promotion decision or supervisors or co-workers engaging in harassment). While courts have consistently maintained this understanding of systemic discrimination as a form of employer liability that is independent of individual agents when it comes to organizations with facially discriminatory policies and organizations using practices that have a disparate impact, they have recently backed away from this understanding in the area of systemic disparate treatment law.

SYSTEMIC DISPARATE TREATMENT THEORY:
FROM THE BEGINNING

Two early and significant cases set the contours of what is now known as systemic disparate treatment theory. In the first (discussed briefly in Chapter 1), *International Brotherhood of Teamsters* v. *United States*, the government alleged that the trucking company T.I.M.E.-D.C. Inc. had engaged in a "pattern and practice of employment discrimination against Negroes and Spanish-surnamed Americans" throughout its transportation system by failing to place minorities equally with whites in long-distance, line-driver positions. T.I.M.E. had purged all of its obvious discriminatory policies after the enactment of Title VII, so the government sought to prove its case by pointing to the stark disparity between the small percentage of blacks and Hispanics employed as line drivers within the company and the larger percentage of blacks and Hispanics in the general population surrounding the company's terminals. The government "bolstered" its statistical evidence, in the words of the Supreme Court, with "testimony of individuals who recounted over 40 specific instances of discrimination." These individual accounts described managers who blatantly refused to place black or Hispanic workers in line-driving positions.

The *Teamsters* Court explained that to establish liability for systemic disparate treatment plaintiffs must prove "more than the mere occurrence of isolated or 'accidental' or sporadic discriminatory acts."[5] They must prove "that racial discrimination was the company's standard operating procedure – the regular rather than the unusual practice."[6] This was what distinguished systemic disparate treatment cases from claims of individual discrimination, even claims brought by several plaintiffs who wanted to join together in a single lawsuit. Pointing to the government's statistical and anecdotal evidence, the Court said that the government had met its burden. In doing so, the Court flatly rejected the defendant's argument that statistics could not be used to prove employer liability.

What statistics are we talking about here? Statistics come in many forms. The term statistics is really just a term that refers to the collection, analysis, and presentation of data. We can have statistics showing the number of days with temperatures over 100 degrees Fahrenheit in a single year, or statistics showing how many people have immigrated to the United States. These are raw data statistics, but statistical analyses can also tell us things about raw data. Among the statistics that the parties were arguing about in *Teamsters* were statistical analyses of disparities between the demographic makeup of the job pool involved in the lawsuit, the line drivers, and the demographic makeup of the labor pool in the area around the trucking terminals, the labor pool from which the employer might be expected to hire. For example, in Atlanta at the time, the population in the metropolitan area surrounding the terminal was 22.35 percent black, but all of the fifty-seven line drivers employed at the Atlanta terminal were white. Similar disparities were presented of other major metropolitan areas around the country, including Los Angeles, Denver, San Francisco, and Dallas.[7]

The Supreme Court in *Teamsters* held that statistics like these can tell us something about an employer's practices, even though employers are not required by law to maintain certain numbers of minority employees or to engage in quota hiring (indeed, using quotas may itself be unlawful discrimination[8]). The statistical analysis, the comparison between what we see – the observed outcome – and what we would expect to see, given the relevant labor pool – the expected outcome – can serve as evidence that discrimination is operating within an organization. How? If the disparity between the two is greater than we would expect to occur by chance (for example, almost no women in the job that we are looking at but lots of qualified, interested women in the labor pool from which the employer is drawing), then that statistical disparity can support a legal inference that the observed outcome is due to discrimination, unless otherwise explained by the defendant employer. The statistics do not mean, of course, that discrimination necessarily caused the disparity. The idea instead is that one possible explanation for the disparity is discrimination, and the law is willing to credit that explanation if the defendant cannot attribute the disparity to a legitimate reason.[9] The Court went on to caution that statistics "are not irrefutable; they come in an infinite variety, and, like any other kind of evidence, they may be rebutted."[10] But, as a legal matter, they can be evidence of systemic disparate treatment, evidence that discrimination was widespread within the company even if the company has done away with its formal policies that favored white workers over black ones, or men over women.

Proving systemic disparate treatment in a case like *Teamsters*, rather than merely proving a single or multiple individualized cases of discrimination, meant that the government could obtain broader, generalized injunctive relief. For example, an organization might be required to make changes to its promotion or transfer policies and practices or to hire a consultant to develop a plan for reducing discrimination or increasing racial minorities and women into certain positions. As the Court constructed the law, a finding of systemic discrimination also meant that employers would redress many claims of individualized discrimination.[11] This is not because proof of systemic discrimination necessarily proves discrimination in any individual instance.[12] Most often it does not. Finding that sex-based discrimination explains an overall observed pay disparity, for example, does not mean that each woman working at the firm has proven that she was discriminated against in her pay. Instead, the Court in *Teamsters* created a legal rule. It held that once systemic disparate treatment is established by proving that discrimination is the regular rather than the unusual practice, then a legal presumption of individual discrimination arises for each member of the group on whose behalf the claim was brought. In other words, each individual plaintiff does not have to prove that his or her promotion decision or pay decision was based on his or her race or sex. Instead, the organization has to prove the opposite: that the decision was not based on the individual's race or sex.

The statistics involved in the *Teamsters* case are sometimes referred to as the "inexorable zero," meaning that the defendant organization had hired almost no black or Hispanic line drivers. In that case, given the percentage of minority workers in the relevant labor pool, the "inexorable zero" meant that the difference between what we would expect the line driver force at T.I.M.E. to look like and the actual makeup of the line driver force at T.I.M.E. was quite stark.[13] The starkness of the disparity raises immediate suspicion that discrimination might be taking place.[14] Other early cases, though, involved less stark disparities. *Hazelwood School District* v. *United States*, decided just one month after *Teamsters*, involved allegations of discrimination in hiring teachers in the Hazelwood School District, located in a predominantly white suburb of St. Louis. In its opinion in this case, the Court again endorsed plaintiffs' use of statistical analyses, specifically the binomial distribution analysis, which calculates the likelihood that a particular outcome, when there is a random choice between two outcomes, is due to chance.[15]

Since *Hazelwood*, even more sophisticated statistical techniques have emerged that can better account for nondiscriminatory factors that might distinguish members of different groups, such as level of education, interest, or years of experience. Statistical analyses using these techniques might show disparities between men and women in pay, for example, that is not explained by identified nondiscriminatory factors. Again, statistics of any kind cannot tell us whether we would see a particular observed disparity in the absence of discrimination. In other words, they cannot establish with certainty that discrimination is the reason for a disparity. They can, however, indicate the likelihood that an observed group disparity (after accounting for legitimate variables) is due to chance. If it is unlikely to be due to chance, then, according to the Supreme Court in *Teamsters* and in *Hazelwood*, an inference of systemic disparate treatment can be drawn.

Most plaintiffs, though, do not typically rely exclusively on statistics to prove systemic disparate treatment. They present additional evidence that supports an inference that discrimination, rather than some other factor, explains the observed disparity. This evidence often includes anecdotal testimony of individual instances of discrimination or expression of discriminatory bias or stereotyping, and expert testimony, particularly testimony by a social science expert to the effect that the particular structures, systems, and cultures in place at the defendant organization are likely to result in regular, widespread disparate treatment. Like the anecdotal testimony in *Teamsters*, the expert social science testimony in these cases contributes to an inference that discrimination within the organization more likely explains the observed disparity than other possible explanations, such as poor work performance, lack of interest due to caregiving responsibilities, discrimination in education, poverty, or other possible explanations.

WHO SUES: THE GOVERNMENT (INCLUDING THE EEOC) AND PRIVATE INDIVIDUALS

Title VII is a civil rights statute that relies heavily on private enforcement, meaning that it expects individual plaintiffs to sue, putting pressure on organizations to change their ways. Private litigants have always been able to sue under the Act. Moreover, they can recover attorneys' fees in most cases when they are the "prevailing party."[16] A prevailing defendant, in contrast, will be awarded fees only in cases in which the action brought is found to be unreasonable, frivolous, meritless, or vexatious.[17] Individuals are therefore encouraged to bring suit under this scheme, to act as "private attorney generals" for the fight against discrimination.

Despite this private-attorney-general aspect of Title VII, the government, too, can bring cases. *Teamsters* and *Hazelwood* both involved systemic disparate treatment claims brought by the Attorney General, in the Department of Justice. The lawsuits were filed under section 707 of Title VII, which authorized the Attorney General to bring a civil action whenever there was "reasonable cause" to believe that any person or group of persons is engaged in a "pattern or practice" of discrimination. Today, the EEOC has this authority, and also the authority to sue to enforce private rights and to vindicate the public interest under section 706 of Title VII, which allows suits by private individuals.[18]

Employers argued in several cases in the 1970s that the EEOC lacked authority to sue under section 706 without certification as a class representative under Rule 23, the class certification rule of the Federal Rules of Civil

Procedure. The Supreme Court rejected those arguments, holding that the EEOC need not comply with Rule 23 to pursue a claim under section 706 and obtain relief for a group of individuals.[19] Since then the EEOC has regularly brought systemic disparate treatment claims under section 706 and section 707 without obtaining class certification.

Private individuals can also still bring claims of systemic disparate treatment against their employers. But while in theory a private plaintiff can allege systemic discrimination theories as well as individualized ones, in practice they are often limited to their individualized claims unless they obtain class certification.[20] These plaintiffs, as any private plaintiff without express statutory authorization of class treatment, must satisfy the requirements of Rule 23 to proceed on behalf of a class. And, after a decade in which courts readily certified "across-the-board" class actions in employment discrimination cases without much attention to the requirements of Rule 23,[21] the Court signaled in 1982 that trial courts should more closely examine whether proposed employment discrimination classes meet each of the specific requirements of the Rule.[22]

THE "SUBJECTIVE DECISION-MAKING" CASES

All of this is history, and for the most part it is uncontested.[23] Things began to change in the late 1980s and early to mid-1990s, when plaintiffs began to bring more of what are sometimes known as "subjective decision-making" cases. These cases alleged widespread discrimination at major corporations through largely decentralized, highly subjective decision-making systems that lacked specific or objective criteria or oversight. The general idea behind the cases was that white men who predominated in positions of power in the defendant organizations were left to exercise their discretion in biased ways, leading to disparities in hiring, work assignments, training, discipline, promotion, and/ or pay.

These kinds of cases were actually not new. A number of earlier cases also involved employer reliance on subjective, highly discretionary decisions of managers and observed disparities in hiring, pay, and promotion for women and racial minorities. *Teamsters* and *Hazelwood*, for example, can both be read in this way. The anecdotal testimony in *Teamsters* revealed individual managers making discriminatory decisions based on their own views about the perceived difficulty of having nonwhite line drivers. One manager responded to a black applicant for a line driver job that in his view there would be "a lot of problems on the road … with different people, Caucasians, etc."[24] The Hazelwood school district also followed "relatively unstructured procedures in hiring its teachers" and it was "undisputed that each school principal possessed virtually unlimited discretion in hiring teachers for his school."[25] As the Court described, "The only general guidance given to the principals was to hire the 'most competent' person available, and such intangibles as 'personality, disposition, appearance, poise, voice, articulation, and ability to deal with people' counted heavily."[26] *Leisner* v. *New York Telephone Company* was another early case, brought in 1971, in which a class of women managers working at the New York Telephone Company sued for discrimination in placement, pay, and promotion.[27] They pointed to stark pay grade and position disparities between men and women managers and to the organization's reliance on supervisors to "look to the individual as a total individual" to decide: "Is this person going to be successful in our business?"[28]

Even though the cases were not new, there was a substantial rise in the number of private employment discrimination class action cases filed in the 1990s,[29] and many of these cases fit the same basic mold. Plaintiffs' evidence included statistical analyses showing significant disparities, sometimes quite stark, in pay and promotion or other measure of job success and a system of highly subjective, discretionary decision making carried out mostly by white, male managers.[30] Defendants in the cases included a number of well-known, large organizations, including Home Depot, Coca-Cola, and American Express. The cases more often than not ended in settlement, and they made big news.[31] The cases involved substantial monetary payouts – from $65 million by Home Depot in 1998 (sex-based discrimination)[32] to $113 million by Coca-Cola in 2001 (race-based discrimination)[33] and $31 million by American Express (sex-based discrimination) in 2002.[34] They were seen, as one *New York Times* reporter put it, as "part of a new stage in the civil rights movement, transforming many companies' rules for hiring, pay scales and promotions."[35]

THE CONTROVERSY OVER CLASS ACTIONS

Commentators (and judges) during this time began to worry about the fairness of holding organizations liable for the discriminatory decisions of their low-level managers. This concern tended to make its way to the surface early on in the process of litigation, when courts were asked to decide whether named private plaintiffs could be certified to represent a broader class. Under Rule 23, a court can certify a group of plaintiffs to proceed as a class in federal court if several requirements are met. One of those requirements is commonality, which requires that the judge find that all of the plaintiffs' claims share at least one common question of law or fact.[36]

Commonality may seem a simple enough inquiry, and for years courts did readily certify plaintiff classes in employment discrimination lawsuits. Employment discrimination class actions had been long considered structural reform cases, lumped together with prison reform, desegregation of schools, and other "public law" reform,[37] but over time they came to be mentioned increasingly in debates over mass tort and other consumer litigation.[38] By the 1990s, class actions, particularly those with large numbers of plaintiffs who together seek a substantial monetary award, had come under attack in the United States. This attack extended across areas of law, from securities fraud to antitrust to consumer fraud. Roughly put, folks far on one side of the issue see large money award class actions as an important, in some cases the only, way for many plaintiffs to obtain relief and/or for the public interest behind laws to be enforced, while folks far on the other side see these class actions as legal "blackmail" and as inappropriately twisting the substantive law in a variety of legal areas to hold organizations liable.[39]

THE BUILD UP TO *WAL-MART V. DUKES* AND THE FRAME OF ORGANIZATIONAL INNOCENCE

Into this broader debate entered Betty Dukes and several fellow female plaintiffs seeking to represent a nationwide class of over 1.5 million women in an employment discrimination action against the country's largest employer, Wal-Mart Stores, Inc. Filed in 2001, the lawsuit alleged that Wal-Mart had engaged in (and continued to engage in) systemic discrimination against women resulting in disparities in pay and promotion between men and women in its U.S. stores in violation of Title VII. Among other things, the plaintiffs claimed that Wal-Mart's personnel system, which provided a mostly white, male managerial force with highly subjective and relatively unguided authority to make pay and promotion decisions, resulted in discrimination against women across Wal-Mart stores. Plaintiffs presented statistical evidence showing significant disparities in amount of pay and promotion rates between men and women (and analyses indicating the disparities were not due to chance, accounting for legitimate variables such as experience and interest),[40] testimony of social scientists to the effect that Wal-Mart had a policy of decentralized decision making regarding pay and promotion, testimony of managers and other employees reflecting a work culture permeated with gender stereotypes and bias, and individual testimony by women who alleged that they had been denied promotions and were paid less than men at Wal-Mart because of their sex. In 2004, the trial court certified a class estimated at 1.5 million women.[41] A panel of the Ninth Circuit Court of Appeals affirmed the trial court's decision in 2007,[42] and in April 2010, a majority of the Ninth Circuit Court of Appeals sitting en banc (meaning an eleven-judge panel) affirmed, with five judges dissenting.[43] The Supreme Court granted certiorari.

ORGANIZATIONS AS MERE "CONDUIT" FOR
SOCIETAL BIASES OF EMPLOYEES

Between the time that the *Wal-Mart* case was first filed in 2001 and 2010 when the case came before the Supreme Court, commentators began to crystallize their concerns about large class actions, and in particular about large employment discrimination class actions. This is where the cognitive, unconscious bias turn and the appeal of organizational innocence began to bubble up. An article in *Fortune* magazine described the *Wal-Mart* case as "The War Over Unconscious Bias,"[44] while an article in *Business Week* used the title, "White Men Can't Help It."[45] These articles described *Wal-Mart* as just one among many cases involving showings of statistical analyses of observed disparities between men and women, or whites and racial minorities, and claims by plaintiffs that organizations were not doing enough to keep unconscious biases from seeping into employment decisions.

Some of this perception may have come from the judicial decisions (in addition to commentators and even plaintiffs' framing) in the *Wal-Mart* case, which was working its way through the courts at the time. District Judge Martin Jenkins who initially certified the class did describe some of the plaintiffs' evidence of commonality as evidence "that Wal-Mart's policies governing compensation and promotion are similar across all stores, and build in a common feature of excessive subjectivity, which provides a conduit for gender bias that affects all class members in a similar fashion."[46] The word "conduit" suggests a mere channel or physical architecture for individual biases.

Lost in translation was Judge Jenkins's further explanation that the plaintiffs in *Wal-Mart* had also presented evidence to provide "a nexus between the subjective decision making and discrimination" – evidence of "gender stereotyping and a corporate culture of uniformity" that would add further support to an inference that discrimination rather than some other factor explained the disparities in pay and promotion at Wal-Mart.[47] This additional evidence included, for example, declarations from women describing senior managers referring to female store employees regularly during executive meetings as "Janie Q's" and "girls" and a Wal-Mart company newsletter that featured a photograph from a company event showing Wal-Mart's Executive Vice President of Operations and Chief Operating Officer at the time posing at

a company event on a leopard-skin stiletto high-heel-shoe chair while surrounded by women singing and dancing.[48]

Regardless of Judge Jenkins's intent, though, the idea that the class action
against Wal-Mart was an effort to hold an employer liable as a mere "conduit" for broader societal biases took hold. The idea gained even more trac-
tion from an influential law review article published in the *New York Law
Review* in 2009, not long before the Ninth Circuit's en banc decision and
the Supreme Court's decision to hear the case.[49] In that article, law professor
Richard Nagareda skillfully cast the plaintiffs' case in *Wal-Mart* as trying to
hold private employers responsible for broader societal forces. According to
Nagareda, "[T]he inference of a common wrong [required for class certifica-
tion] depends crucially on whether prohibited discrimination under Title VII
encompasses the 'conduit' or 'nexus' notions advanced in [*Wal-Mart*]" which
he characterized as a "bold, new conception of prohibited discrimination"
advanced by scholars relying on cognitive bias research.[50]

Nagareda's view holds great appeal. It envisions Wal-Mart's role in any
discrimination that women experienced as limited to the firm's mere existence. Indeed, people across the political spectrum adopted descriptions of the
debate about Wal-Mart that tracked this idea: that the *Wal-Mart* case is controversial largely because it involves allegations that an organization should be
liable for discrimination when it has simply allowed people to act upon the
fully formed and unwavering biases that they bring into the workplace from
their outside lives. Professor Samuel Bagenstos, for example, despite declaring
his own normative commitment to combatting discrimination through law,
has been widely cited for his claim that employment discrimination law is at
its "limits" because courts are "unlikely to conclude that particular employers
are at fault for failing to police conduct that has been programmed into our
brains by overarching societal influences."[51]

EMPLOYMENT DISCRIMINATION CLASS ACTIONS AS MASS TORTS

With organization-as-mere-"conduit" firmly rooted in mind, the idea that
employment discrimination cases such as *Wal-Mart* v. *Dukes* were really just
a mass of individual claims brought together in a single lawsuit also gained
strength during this time. Systemic employment discrimination claims had
increasingly appeared in discussion of mass torts, rather than the public law
litigation of the earlier era, and *Wal-Mart* was no exception.[52]

Some of this shift in perception may have been driven by a change in procedural and remedial aspects of litigation under Title VII during this time.
In 1991, Congress amended the Civil Rights Act to provide plaintiffs with

the possibility of obtaining compensatory and punitive damages for discrimination suffered.[53] Prior to the amendment, plaintiffs could and did obtain monetary relief, but the relief was considered equitable and was calculated as back pay from the time between the discriminatory decision and the legal judgment. This disadvantaged harassment plaintiffs who often do not suffer a discrete, tangible economic injury on which to base a back pay award, and so Congress added the compensatory damage provision, including a punitive damage provision as well.

For most plaintiffs, the amendment providing for compensatory and punitive damages should have had little impact on their cases. Successful plaintiffs who had suffered economic harm – denial of a promotion or a raise, for instance – could still obtain back pay, as they always had. But the amendment turned out to have several very practical effects that may have contributed to the growing sense that systemic discrimination claims were just another mass tort. First, it opened employment discrimination cases to adjudication by juries, whereas, before the amendment, judges had made all findings.[54] Juries decide factual issues in tort claims, so this may have signaled a similarity in the types of cases. Second, the amendment brought money to the forefront and, with the addition of punitive damages, may have contributed to the increased involvement of the private bar. The number of employment discrimination class actions filed not only rose during this time, but many more of these cases were brought by law firms that had historically specialized in representing plaintiffs in mass tort class actions.[55]

Nagareda was again one of the scholars who pushed the idea that employment discrimination (systemic cases) are an amassing of individual claims, a mass tort, like asbestos, gun, and tobacco litigation.[56] So that ultimately when Nagareda argued that the *Wal-Mart* plaintiffs were seeking endorsement of a "bold new theory" of discrimination, he was starting from the premise that what the plaintiffs presented were merely simultaneous individualized claims. Aggregation in his view skewed the case in favor of the plaintiffs by allowing them to prove something other than individualized discrimination, to prove instead that discrimination was widespread (the regular rather than the unusual practice) within the organization.

WAL-MART V. *DUKES*: ORGANIZATIONAL INNOCENCE AND PROVING SYSTEMIC DISCRIMINATION

In 2011, the Supreme Court issued its decision in *Wal-Mart* v. *Dukes*.[57] As explained earlier, in order to certify a class under Rule 23, a court must find that each of four initial requirements for class treatment are met, including commonality; the court must also situate the class within one of three categories.[58] The district court found the four initial requirements met and certified a class under the category 23(b)(2), which has historically been used for employment discrimination claims seeking predominantly injunctive relief (including back pay for individuals, long considered equitable in nature), and the Ninth Circuit Court of Appeals affirmed the district court's certification of the class. The Supreme Court, however, held that the plaintiffs had not established the commonality required for class certification, and (this part unanimously) that even if commonality had been met, the class should not have been certified under Rule 23(b)(2), but rather should have been certified only if it met the requirements of the Rule 23(b)(3) category, the category historically used for mass torts and other cases primarily seeking damages.

The *Wal-Mart* decision and its effects on private class actions have been analyzed and debated extensively now for several years. The common take is that the *Wal-Mart* decision makes it more difficult for private plaintiffs to sue as a class. But the piece of *Wal-Mart* that is likely to have the biggest long-term impact on equal opportunity at work in the United States has less to do with class action certification (the EEOC, after all, can sue on behalf of a group without obtaining certification) and more to do with the substantive law of systemic discrimination. Organizational innocence takes strong hold in the majority opinion in *Wal-Mart*, and this leads the Court to fashion an ever narrower realm of employer liability.

Recall the three conceptual threads of organizational innocence from Chapter 1: (1) high-level decision makers within organizations are generally understood not to be acting with bias in setting organizational policy; (2) discrimination is understood to be largely a problem of low-level actors, specifically managers and supervisors; (3) those managers and supervisors who do discriminate are rogues, acting on personal biases in isolation from and against the interest of the organizations for which they work. Each of these steps is evident in the Court's *Wal-Mart* opinion.

Wal-Mart had adopted and disseminated a nondiscrimination policy, to which the Court gave full and unwavering credit. "Wal-Mart's announced policy forbids sex discrimination," said the Court, and, even more, "the company imposes penalties for denials of equal opportunity."[59] The company is against discrimination and it is policing its employees, penalizing its individual discriminators. Enough said, thought the Court.

Second, the Court viewed the plaintiffs' case and their request for class certification as an effort to bring together each of their 1.5 million individual claims of discrimination in specific employment decisions made by their respective managers.[60] Regional and district managers made the decisions about pay increases and admission into the Wal-Mart management training program, the pipeline program to management at Wal-Mart. The case under this frame was simple: Managers across Wal-Mart are discriminating against women in their pay and promotion decisions. With these individual managers placed at the center of the lawsuit (and the case looking to the Court exactly like a mass tort, an amassing of claims alleging discrimination against individual employees in pay and promotion decisions by individual managers), the Court naturally wanted evidence that a substantial portion of the managers were discriminating.

This is why the Court thought the plaintiffs' anecdotal evidence inadequate. In the eyes of the majority, the anecdotal evidence needed not to merely buttress plaintiffs' argument that discrimination rather than some other reason explained the observed disparities in pay and promotion between men and women at Wal-Mart, as most people understood the anecdotes in *Teamsters* to do. The anecdotes needed on their own to support an inference that "all the individual, discretionary personnel decisions [at Wal-Mart] are discriminatory."[61] It is no wonder then that the majority insisted that the ratio of anecdotes to class members was too small. As the Court pointed out, the ratio of anecdotes to class members in *Teamsters* was 1 to 8, while in *Wal-Mart* it was 1 to 12,500.[62]

This is also why the Court thought it could "safely disregard" what the plaintiffs' expert, sociology professor William Bielby, had to say.[63] Bielby testified that the particular features of Wal-Mart, including its heavy reliance on subjective decisions, its culture imbued with gender stereotypes, and its minimal measures taken to ensure equality, were likely to result in biased employment decisions and disparities between men and women in pay and promotion.[64] But Bielby could not answer, in the Court's words, "[w]hether 0.5 percent or 95 percent of the employment decisions [meaning the managerial pay and management decisions] at Wal-Mart might be determined by stereotyped thinking."[65] Bielby's testimony, particularly together with the evidence of a work culture in which bias and stereotypes were common, could support an inference that bias was operating pervasively within Wal-Mart and resulting in the observed disparities in pay and promotion, but Bielby could not tell the Court how many of Wal-Mart's managers were discriminating in a similar way. No one could.

Third, any discrimination going on at Wal-Mart was understood as a problem of managers acting exclusively on their own personal biases, biases that these managers brought into the workplace from broader society. The Court explained that the plaintiffs needed to show that managers at Wal-Mart "exercise[d] their discretion in a common way" (and for class certification the plaintiffs needed to submit significant proof of this).[66] Statistical analyses cannot make this kind of showing. Indeed, the Supreme Court was particularly suspicious of the statistics presented by the plaintiffs. It was skeptical that nationwide or even regional breakdowns can tell with certainty whether disparities occur across Wal-Mart stores.[67]

Moreover, even if the statistics could show store-by-store disparities, explained the Court, the Court expected that individual managers within each store would surely provide different reasons for their decisions and therefore would not be acting on similar biases or on biases in similar ways.[68] Some managers may discriminate on their own without direction from on high, but they are going to be rogues acting on their varied personal biases. According to the Court, "In a company of Wal-Mart's size and geographical scope, it is quite unbelievable that all managers would exercise their discretion in a common way without some common direction."[69]

Nowhere in its opinion did the Court hold that systemic disparate treatment theory requires plaintiffs to prove that the employer (or its high-level decision makers) acted with bias or a purpose to keep women down, at least as a matter of principle or theory (as Nagareda and others have suggested *Teamsters* required). But the Court did buy in to organizational innocence, and in practice, if not in theory, this led to much the same place: it left plaintiffs with only one way to bring their individualized claims together. In the Court's words, they needed to prove (and at the class certification phase needed to submit significant proof) that the entire company "operates under a general policy of discrimination."[70] And to do this they needed to submit evidence sufficient to support an inference that the managers at Wal-Mart were being instructed to discriminate. Evidence, for example, of statements reflecting bias of high-level executives and communication with the rank-and-file managers, or evidence that Wal-Mart's record – the disparity between men and women in pay and promotion – was substantially worse than the industry or the labor market as a whole.[71] This kind of evidence may be one way of proving systemic discrimination, but it has never been the only way. The Court required this evidence because it saw the plaintiffs' case as an amassing of many individualized claims against each of their managers, the rogue discriminators.[72]

What all of this misses is that discrimination in violation of Title VII is rarely litigated like a mass tort, where individuals come together to sue en masse for their individual injuries. Individual plaintiffs can come together under Title VII, just like plaintiffs suffering injury due to a mass tort can come together, but the law of Title VII provides its plaintiffs with another option. Indeed, plaintiffs in a systemic discrimination case are situated differently under the law of Title VII than are individual plaintiffs coming together under tort law, regardless of whether the cause of tort injury was gun-related violence, environmental toxins, or a refinery fire.[73] They are situated differently because Title VII law – through systemic disparate treatment theory – has long provided plaintiffs in employment discrimination cases with a way of establishing employer liability without proving individualized discrimination, by proving instead that discrimination was widespread within the defendant organization, the regular rather than the unusual practice.

THE MOVE TO DELIBERATE INDIFFERENCE: ENTRENCHING COMPLAINT-AND-RESPONSE

Something else happened at the Supreme Court during the *Wal-Mart* case that is worth considering. Several justices at oral argument asked in various ways whether the Court should not be thinking about applying a deliberate indifference standard to determine employer liability (and class action commonality) for systemic disparate treatment claims. One reading of the holding of *Wal-Mart* is that the law requires plaintiffs to prove individual discrimination (which as a practical matter is hard to prove without evidence from which to infer that managers were being instructed to discriminate), but that it does not require plaintiffs to prove wrongdoing by the employer. In this view, the apparent wrongdoing of high-level executives instructing managers to discriminate is merely evidence – the "glue" as the Court puts it – that ties each of the individual claims together. At the end of the day, the employer is being held vicariously liable for the discrimination of its managers.

Justice Kennedy's (and Chief Justice Robert's, and even Justice Alito's) questions at oral argument, however, suggest that they might be thinking in a slightly different way about organizational responsibility.[74] They still see the claims as individualized, requiring proof that managers were discriminating in a similar way in pay and promotion decisions, but a deliberate indifference standard for employer responsibility asks whether the high-level executives knew or should have known that a pattern of manager discrimination was occurring and whether they deliberately failed to act to stop those managers from discriminating in the face of that knowledge.

It might be tempting to think of a deliberate indifference standard as softening the blow of *Wal-Mart*. It may be easier to show deliberate indifference on the part of high-level executives than to show that the executives instructed managers to discriminate. It is important to see, though, that the justices' reach for deliberate indifference is equally grounded in organizational innocence – and that it would likely just further entrench the complaint-and-response law that is developing in the individual discrimination realm.[75]

The deliberate indifference standard is used in several areas of law, including most prominently in claims alleging constitutional violations that seek to hold entities responsible under section 1983 of the Civil Rights Act of 1866, and also claims of harassment and discrimination in educational settings where plaintiffs seek to hold schools liable for discrimination under Title IX of the Civil Rights Act. The laws under each of these statutes vary slightly, but in each of these areas the Court has firmly held that entities are not to be held vicariously liable.[76] Instead, the entities will be liable only if the plaintiff proves a violation, such as an incident of police brutality that rises to the level of excessive force or an incident or series of incidents of harassment in school, and also if they prove that the entity acted with deliberate indifference to the constitutional or statutory rights of the victim. In the context of section 1983 violations, courts often talk of the agent of the entity acting pursuant to a "policy," though that policy can be an informal custom to which the entity is deliberately indifferent, including a pattern of violence and victim complaint that is inadequately investigated and addressed.[77]

Early in oral argument in the *Wal-Mart* case, Justice Kennedy asked the lawyer for Wal-Mart whether the law of section 1983 governing city liability for constitutional violations is not a good analogue for the law of employer liability for employment discrimination under Title VII.[78] Organizational innocence underlies this reach for deliberate indifference. Indeed, what Justice Kennedy really seemed to want to know was whether organizations should be held liable for discrimination that arises out of socially constructed biases. Toward the end of the oral argument, Justice Kennedy asked again about applying a deliberate indifference standard, this time of the plaintiffs' lawyer. He presented the following hypothetical:

> Let's suppose that experts' testimony, sociologists and so forth, establish that in industry generally and in retail industry generally, women still are discriminated against by a mathematical factor of X. You have a company that has a very specific policy against discrimination, and you look at the way their employees are treated, and you find a disparity by that same mathematical factor X, does that give you a cause of action ... even if you could not show deliberate indifference?[79]

Drawing on the law of section 1983 (or Title IX) would further entrench the complaint-and-response law that is developing in the individual discrimination area. The best way to see this is to take a look how "pattern or practice" cases are proved in that context. Take police brutality. Plaintiffs seeking to prove deliberate indifference on the part of a police department often present statistics, but the statistics that they rely on are quite different from those historically relied upon in the employment discrimination context.[80] For police brutality, plaintiffs rely on incident statistics. Sometimes the statistics give the number of complaints filed against a particular officer or in a particular police force. In other cases, the statistics present the percentage of relevant complaints sustained within the department or against a particular officer. Even the more sophisticated statistical presentations in section 1983 cases focus closely on complaints about officer abuse and the department's investigations of and decisions with respect to those complaints.[81] In one case, for example, the plaintiff's experts used a data set from the Chicago Police Department to calculate the discipline rates for complaints involving abuse of civilians and also the "sustained rates," the percentage of cases where the Chicago Police Department found that sufficient evidence existed to believe that the charged abuse occurred.[82] The experts then compared Chicago's rates to other major metropolitan police departments in the United States, showing that Chicago had sustained rates that were much lower than the average rate for excessive force complaints in major metropolitan police departments nationwide, and to those departments that the DOJ had found to have engaged in a pattern or practice of excessive force. All of these statistical presentations are about complaints and department response to complaints.

In employment discrimination cases, in contrast, the statistical analysis has historically focused not on complaints and employer response to complaints, but on employment outcomes, such as pay and promotion. This make sense because section 1983 is aimed at curbing moments of police brutality and compensating victims for harm caused in those precise moments, moments of brutality. Title VII is also aimed at reducing discriminatory moments (and compensating victims), but it is most concerned about the effect of biased decisions on employment outcomes, the success of employees in work. This means that Title VII law includes various limitations, like the adverse employment action requirement for individual disparate treatment claims and in hostile work environment law the requirement that the harassment be severe or pervasive so as to alter the terms or conditions of employment. It also means that the legal wrong of employment discrimination includes widespread discrimination within a work organization that results in disparities in pay and promotions or other adverse employment actions, even if each incident of discrimination would not be independently actionable.

To draw from the law that governs police brutality would shift the legal inquiry dramatically toward evaluating entity response to complaints rather than identifying whether discrimination was widespread within the organization. Indeed, Justice Roberts asked a question at oral argument in *Wal-Mart* in just this way, framing employer liability around complaint and response. He asked of the defendant's lawyer: "[S]o they've got thousands of stores, and ... every week they get a report from another store saying that ... there's an allegation of gender discrimination. At some point, can't they conclude that it is their policy of decentralized decisionmaking that is causing or permitting that discrimination to take place?"[83]

Maybe. But the entity's knowledge of complaints is not what the law of systemic employment discrimination has historically emphasized. Instead, the question has always been whether discrimination is the regular rather than the unusual occurrence. Under *Teamsters* and *Hazelwood*, the law asks whether discrimination explains the observed disparities in success between men and women at Wal-Mart. That is all.

As with individual discrimination law, where the law is shifting from vicarious to direct liability grounded in complaint and response, here, too, commentators across the political spectrum seem to be leaning toward a negligence or deliberate indifference standard for employer liability for systemic discrimination without recognizing that this would be a drastic – and devastating – shift in existing law. This new systemic discrimination law puts a different kind of pressure on organizations, a pressure that focuses narrowly on knowledge about individual complaints of discrimination and response to that knowledge.

4

Class, Culture, and Limiting the Purview of Title VII

Organizational innocence is also pushing courts to narrowly construe what is considered discrimination in the first place. Racialized interactions are deemed personal, and thereby not discriminatory, and considered too minimal to count as harassment except in the most extreme cases. "Vulgar" work environments involving sexually charged conduct, particularly in all-male workplaces, are deemed environments of "mere horseplay," and thereby not discriminatory. And hostile work environment claims and disparate treatment claims are being driven by judges into disparate impact theory, which changes substantially the legal and remedial inquiry.

This chapter examines the current judicial inclination to place discrimination outside Title VII concern. Instead of tracing and predicting doctrinal shifts, as Chapters 2 and 3 did, this chapter takes a snapshot of several cases that have been decided by trial and appellate courts over the past several decades. It excavates beneath the surface and exposes the often overlooked pressure of organizational innocence. Discrimination is being laundered in the most basic sense in these cases: judges are cleansing the workplace of discrimination by labeling race- and sex-based conduct "personal" and placing it outside Title VII purview altogether.

There is arguably a class and even a geographic element to what is going on in these cases. Many of the racialized interaction cases involve workplaces located in the southern states. And almost all of the jobs in these cases are relatively low-wage, nonprofessional jobs. The judges deciding the cases seem to think that racialized and gendered cultures in these jobs and geographic areas are part of life, something to be tolerated, not disrupted by law. These judges also seem to think that workers in these jobs, often white men, should be protected from legal disruption of their gendered and racial work cultures, almost as if such legal disruption would be an invasion into these workers' private space.

PERSONALIZING RACIALIZED INTERACTION

Despite progress in the law of sexual harassment toward understanding how sexualized harassment can amount to discrimination on the basis of sex, when judges come across situations involving heated racialized encounters at work, they tend to "personalize" those encounters, labeling them nonracial. The Supreme Court arguably set the foundation for this judicial willingness to categorize racial emotion as personal (and not racial) in *St. Mary's Honor Center v. Hicks*, decided in 1993.[1] The case involved a claim by Melvin Hicks, a black man, who alleged that he had been demoted and later fired because of his race in violation of Title VII. Hicks had been hired in 1978 as a correctional officer at the St. Mary's Honor Center, a minimal-security correctional facility, and he was promoted to a supervisory position in 1980. In 1984, though, the facility made several personnel changes, including hiring John Powell, a white man, as Hicks's immediate supervisor and Steve Long, another white man, as the new superintendent. After Powell and Long came on board, Hicks's disciplinary record took a downward turn. He was cited for several violations and demoted. When Hicks was notified of the demotion, in the words of the trial court, he "was shaken by the news and requested the day off." His request was granted, but as he was leaving, Powell and Hicks got into a heated exchange that ended with Hicks asking if Powell wanted to "step outside." Hicks was fired for his involvement in that incident.

The trial judge, sitting as a fact finder in the case, found that Powell and Long had fabricated the disciplinary incidents that led to Hicks's demotion and also that Powell had provoked the threat that formed the basis of the discharge.[2] Nonetheless, the court found in favor of St. Mary's. According to the court, Hicks had "proven the existence of a crusade to terminate him," but he had not "proven that the crusade was racially rather than personally motivated."[3] The court cited to no evidence suggesting a nonracial source of the acrimonious relationship between Hicks and Powell and Long. Powell, in fact, had testified that he harbored no personal animus toward Hicks.

The Supreme Court affirmed, holding that the plaintiff in an individual discrimination case must prove not just that the reasons put forward for an employment decision, like the disciplinary violations, were false (for example, that they were fabricated by Powell and Long), but also that the real reason for the decision was the plaintiff's race or sex.[4] This holding itself is not particularly controversial today, but in practice it gives courts leeway to find that heated relational encounters, even those involving racialized and gendered language, are personal and not evidence of discrimination. Indeed, when courts see negative emotion – animosity, acrimony, resentment – in a work relationship, they tend to label the emotion as "personally" motivated and thereby not motivated by race or gender, even though we could certainly imagine that the two might be (and often will be) intertwined.[5]

Take a more recent example: Judith Sweezer, a black woman, worked as a supervising corrections officer at the Michigan Department of Corrections, and in 1997 she filed suit alleging that she had been subjected to a racially hostile work environment.[6] In addition to evidence that her subordinates refused to follow her orders and that her supervisors refused to back her up, she presented evidence of harassment by a subordinate officer, Wayne Allen. In one incident, Allen saw Sweezer at a local restaurant and called out, "Hey, there's a new colored woman in town." Back at the workplace, Allen recounted this incident in Sweezer's presence to officers who were supervised by Sweezer. Several months later, Sweezer took disciplinary action against Allen for abusing an inmate. After a hearing on the disciplinary action, Allen and others harassed Sweezer by calling her "bitch" and "nigger" and "making other remarks." Allen also blocked Sweezer in the parking lot with his truck and spit at her several times when she walked by. When Sweezer arrived at work, Allen would "follow her to where she parked her car, block her in with his car, display weapons, and follow her or try to hit her with his vehicle."[7]

The trial court granted summary judgment to the employer. The court thought that the evidence presented by the plaintiff was insufficient to get to a jury. Sweezer appealed, and the Sixth Circuit Court of Appeals affirmed. In affirming, the court explained that while "indisputably improper, Allen's comments were brief and isolated, and [were] more indicative of a personality conflict than of racial animus."[8]

Courts also tend to require racial incidents to "permeate" the workplace before finding a racially hostile work environment. Hostile work environment law requires that harassment be perceived by the victim as severe or pervasive and also that the victim's perception be "reasonable."[9] Some judges tend to tolerate a high level of racially offensive conduct before declaring it objectively severe or pervasive enough to amount to a hostile work environment in violation of Title VII. In one case, for example, decided in 2011, Rahman Pratt, a black man, who worked at a shipbuilding company in Mobile, Alabama, testified that he overheard three white co-workers saying "[h]ow him and the nigger got into it yesterday, and he'll hang that nigger and shoot that nigger, and all that kind of stuff. Just going on and on. And ... calling them 'monkeys' and stuff like that."[10] He also presented evidence that several white workers wore T-shirts and bandanas bearing the Confederate flag to work and that he saw racial epithets regularly in graffiti on the bathroom walls and stalls and on toolboxes. The judge granted summary judgment for the defendant. According to the judge, a jury could not conclude that a reasonable person would have found the environment racially hostile. It was important to the judge that Pratt "only overheard racial comments (not directed to him)" and that when he complained about the graffiti, it was painted over, although Pratt did testify that it was painted only after racial graffiti had "piled up" and others also testified that the walls would soon be filled again with racial graffiti. When Pratt complained to his supervisor about the continuing graffiti, the supervisor responded that it had been going on "for so long. We can't do nothing but paint the walls."

In another case, *White* v. *Government Employees Insurance Company,* Tricia White, a black woman, alleged racial harassment, pointing to several incidents: she overheard Gene Allgood, the branch manager in the GEICO office in which she worked, refer to an African-American customer as "nigger"; she heard from someone else than when white paint fell on or near Cynthia Johnson, a black woman, the manager said that he "always knew that [she] wanted to be a white female"; the same manager referred to the office where White worked as the "ghetto" and a "FEMA trailer."[11] The trial court granted summary judgment to GEICO on White's harassment claim, and the court of appeals affirmed, providing this reasoning:

> Most of the incidents alleged by White, while they might cause offense or indicate strife between White and her coworkers or supervisors, are not evidence of race-based harassment. The record contains only a few incidents that reasonably could be characterized as race-based: [reciting the three incidents described above]. Those incidents do not rise to the level of severity or pervasiveness required to support a hostile work environment claim. None of them involved physically threatening or humiliating conduct, as opposed to mere offensive utterances; Allgood's alleged use of the term "nigger" and his comment to Johnson were isolated remarks; the "nigger" comment was not directed at White and White only heard about the remark to Johnson; and while Allgood's use of the terms "ghetto" and "FEMA trailer" may have been "racially inappropriate," the record does not indicate when Allgood used those terms or how often White heard him describe the Metairie office set-up in that way.[12]

The race-based comments alleged by White, said the court, "pale in comparison, both in severity and frequency, to the kinds of verbal harassment that this court and other circuits have held would support a Title VII claim." Here, the court cited for comparison to three cases: a case in which the plaintiff submitted evidence of, as the court put it, "years of inflammatory racial epithets, including 'nigger' and 'dumb monkey'"; a case in which the plaintiff "was subjected to 'nigger jokes' for a ten-year period and the plaintiff's work-station was adorned with 'a human-sized dummy with a black head'"; and a case "where the plaintiff suffered 'incessant racial slurs' including 'nigger' and 'dumb monkey.'"[13]

Racial harassment also gets placed outside Title VII through disaggregation. Courts will take each encounter one by one, rather than looking at the environment as a whole. *White* is an example of this, as is *Vance*, where the trial court examined the alleged harassment by each of Maetta Vance's co-workers independently of the others and found reasons why each did not amount to racial harassment in violation of Title VII.[14]

These kinds of cases are not new. Individualizing and personalizing racial and also gendered encounters have long served to remove those encounters – and the environments that they create – from Title VII purview.[15] What is new is the underlying tone of many of these cases, the sense that extreme racial and gendered encounters are part of a way of work that should be tolerated, even preserved. These cases illustrate judicial perceptions about the limitations of antidiscrimination law in changing culture. They are part of a larger movement toward not just protecting employers, but toward establishing the workplace as a space where work cultures, even racialized and gendered ones, are considered outside antidiscrimination concern.

SAVING THE MAN CAVE: CONSTRUING "BECAUSE OF SEX"

Courts once considered sexualized harassment – the male supervisor repeatedly commenting on a female subordinate's dress or appearance and asking her out on dates or for sexual encounters – as "personal," as stemming from emotions related to sexual desire and attraction rather than as something giving rise to antidiscrimination concern. Today, courts tend to accept sexualized harassment as a form of sex-based discrimination, at least when it is severe or pervasive enough to alter the terms and conditions of work. After all, the Supreme Court has instructed as much. But courts still struggle to make sense of hostile work environment claims. Research shows that judges disaggregate relational encounters in cases involving allegations of sex-based harassment, much as they do in the race context, but with particular attention to sexual conduct, which is more likely to give rise to a finding of discrimination than nonsexual conduct. Like in the race context, courts also tend to require that harassing behavior be relatively extreme to be considered conduct that a reasonable person would find severe or pervasive.

Judicial resistance to Title VII as a tool for work culture change, though, can be seen most starkly in several recent cases involving all-male work environments. The "because of sex" requirement in harassment law is understood to provide something of a Title VII anchor. If harassment is not "because of sex" (or some other protected characteristic), then maybe it is bullying or even assault actionable under tort or criminal law, but it is not discrimination in violation of Title VII. Nonetheless, courts have struggled with what "because of sex" means when it comes to harassment in all-male work environments, and this particular struggle has come to mark a special place of judicial resistance. Some judges openly resist using the law for work culture change in all-male work environments. And they do so for some of the same reasons that they have been reworking individual discrimination law to protect employers. They see the cultures that develop in these workplaces as personal and private and beyond the purview of Title VII.

In 2007, Kerry Woods, a male iron worker and structural welder, brought a hostile work environment claim against Boh Brothers Construction.[16] Woods worked on an all-male crew assigned to repair and maintain the twin Spans Bridge between New Orleans and Slidell, Louisiana, starting in 2005 and through 2006. For much of this time, he worked under the supervision of superintendent Chuck Wolfe. As the courts described it, workers on the crew regularly "used very foul language" and "locker room talk." Wolfe in particular was "rough" and "mouthy" with the workers, and Woods became Wolfe's most frequent target. As the appellate court describes:

> Wolfe referred to Woods as "pu-y," "princess," and "fa-ot," often "two to three times a day." About two to three times per week while Woods was bent over to perform a task-Wolfe approached him from behind and simulated anal intercourse with him. Woods felt "embarrassed and humiliated" by the name-calling and began to look over his shoulder before bending down. In addition, Wolfe exposed his penis to Woods about ten times while urinating, sometimes waving at Woods and smiling.
>
> One time, Wolfe approached Woods while Woods was napping in his locked car during a break. According to Woods, Wolfe "looked like he was zipping his pants" and said, "[i]f your door wouldn't have been locked, my d-ck probably would have been in your mouth."[17]

Woods won his case at the trial level. Boh Brothers appealed, and a panel of the Court of Appeals for the Fifth Circuit overturned the jury verdict on the ground that there was not enough evidence from which the jury could have reasonably found that the harassment was "because of sex." The court framed the requirement narrowly, focusing on Wolfe's state of mind and in this case requiring evidence that Wolfe harassed Woods because Wolfe perceived Woods to be feminine.[18] The Fifth Circuit court then heard the case en banc (sixteen judges), and reversed, reinstituting the verdict.

The ten judges in the majority en banc did not reframe the "because of sex" requirement in reversing the panel. Instead, like the district court and the panel below, they focused on "the alleged harasser's subjective perception of the victim."[19] The majority simply concluded that the evidence presented was sufficient to meet that requirement. It pointed specifically to the sex-based nature of Wolfe's behavior, his flashing and humping, and of the epithets used, "fa-ot," "pu-y," and "princess," and also to Wolfe's admission that he thought that Woods's use of Wet Wipes was "kind of gay," which Wolfe explained meant that Woods was not manly.[20] The dissenting judges (six judges), two of whom were on the earlier panel overturning the verdict, insisted that this evidence was not enough to show that Wolfe singled out Woods because he believed Woods to be feminine or unmanly.

The dissenting opinions in the *Boh Brothers* case are particularly important for understanding judicial resistance to plaintiffs' use of Title VII to disrupt work cultures. In dissent, the judges attempt to explain why Woods (or the EEOC) should have to show that Wolfe harassed him because Wolfe perceived him as effeminate. This is the screening work that these judges think the "because of sex" requirement in Title VII should do.

More than anything else, the dissenting judges in *Boh Brothers* insist that the all-male makeup of the work environment makes a difference.[21] They each refer in various ways to concerns about over-breadth, stating, for example, that if the law does not require evidence that Wolfe chose to harass Woods because he perceived Woods to be effeminate, then "every one of Woods's co-workers could have filed suit against Boh Brothers."[22] At bottom, the judges seem most concerned that Title VII will intrude into the men's workspace. They are worried that Boh Brothers (under threat of litigation) will demand that the men behave differently, and will police them to make sure that they do. To these judges, the "because of sex" requirement keeps harassment law focused on the motivation of specific harassers so that wholly male cultures, particularly in blue-collar jobs that are historically male dominated, such as construction, need not change. As Judge Jolly (joined by five others) begins his dissenting opinion:

> Let me first acknowledge that the facts and language in this case, which occurred in an all-male workforce on an ironworker construction site, are not for tender ears. The vulgarities can cast turmoil in a strong stomach, but that does not mean that the laws of the United States have been violated, and it does not require Title VII and the EEOC to serve as federal enforcer of clean talk in a single sex workforce.[23]

In his earlier panel opinion, Judge Jolly put it this way: "It bears repeating that Title VII is not a 'general civility code for the American workplace.' Nor is it the business of federal courts generally to clean up the language and conduct of construction sites."[24]

Judge Jones is even more direct about her concerns about employer policing. She says, "What the [EEOC] has persuaded the majority to adopt is the disturbing proposition that, to avoid exposure to Title VII liability, employers must purge every workplace of speech and gestures that might be viewed in any way as tokens of sex discrimination."[25] She provides a hypothetical memorandum titled "Etiquette for Ironworkers" in which she details the behavior that she expects to be policed, including what she calls "school yard humor" and "locker room" behavior.[26] She obviously intends the memorandum in the spirit of humorous derision, but her point is that without a narrow construction of "because of sex," Title VII will become a law that unduly intrudes upon the private space for men working in all-male worksites.[27]

According to these judges, Title VII should not interfere with an "all-male workforce where rowdy language is commonplace." Instead, as Judge Jolly puts it, we should "call it for what it is: immature and gutter behavior between and among male coworkers. And then drop it."[28]

NOT JUST ALL-MALE ENVIRONMENTS: THE THEORY SWITCH

From Hostile Work Environment to Disparate Impact

Audrey Jo DeClue worked for the Central Illinois Light Company as a lineworker.[29] Over the course of several years, she worked out in the field where Central Illinois provided no bathroom facilities and men would regularly urinate out in the open in her and the other workers' presence. DeClue would try to hold her urine until the crew arrived at a public restroom. Her crew leader made remarks like, "You're just like my damn kids. I'm ready to leave and I have to wait for them to go to the bathroom"; "You've got the bladder of a three-year-old"; and "We'll never get to the job 'cause I'm sure we'll have to stop in Edwards for you to piss there too."[30] DeClue also experienced a co-worker deliberately urinating on the floor near where she was working, as well one or more men shoving, pushing, and hitting her, engaging in sexually offensive touching, and exposing her to pornographic magazines.[31]

After several years of this, DeClue sued, alleging a hostile work environment in violation of Title VII. The trial court dismissed her case, and a panel of the Seventh Circuit Court of Appeals affirmed. The panel was unanimous in holding that most of the incidents that DeClue experienced at Central Illinois Light occurred outside the time period within which DeClue had to complain to the EEOC, and that the only thing she complained about in time was the company's failure to provide bathroom facilities. Here, the judges diverged. Writing for himself and Judge William Bauer, Judge Richard Posner held that the "defendant's failure to respond to the plaintiff's request for civilized bathroom facilities can[not] be thought a form of sexual harassment." Instead, these judges thought DeClue's claim was best framed under disparate impact theory, and they dismissed her case for failing to mention disparate impact and for pushing only a harassment theory.

Audrey Jo DeClue, says Judge Posner, could have framed her case as a disparate impact, as Posner frames it before dismissing it, but she did not. Instead, she alleged that the conditions around urinating amounted to a hostile work environment. How could this be? How could simple failure to provide toilets to all, men and women alike, amount to a hostile work environment "because of sex" and not just have a disparate impact on women? Judge Rovner in dissent in the Seventh Circuit decision argued that Central Illinois Light's failure to provide bathrooms became a hostile work environment when DeClue complained about it and nothing was done.[32] Maybe. But there is also something else at play: the hostile environment that DeClue experienced resulted not merely from the lack of toilet facilities, but from the gendered behavior of her male co-workers around urination. Her crew leader, after all, when asked to wait for her to use a public restroom, told her: "You've got the bladder of a three-year-old" and "We'll never get to the job 'cause I'm sure we'll have to stop in Edwards for you to piss there too."[33] She was ridiculed for her reticence to urinate out in the open in front of the men, and yet surely made to feel uncomfortable if she did.

Why, then, does Posner think it crucial to frame DeClue's claim through the lens of disparate impact? In short, he wants to provide Central Illinois Light (and the defendant next faced with this kind of claim) with an opportunity to show that "it would be infeasible or unduly burdensome to equip its linemen's trucks with toilet facilities sufficiently private to meet the plaintiff's needs."[34] This is a defense that is available in disparate impact cases, but not in harassment cases. So in this sense Judge Posner's move is pragmatic.

It is also quite possible, however, that the defendant company could have remedied the situation in other ways, including by changing the work culture in which men harass women who urinate in the open in front of their male colleagues. Judge Posner's re-framing misses this entirely. Posner's framing, after all, removes this from the realm of inquiry.

Indeed, Posner's re-framing of the case under disparate impact does several things. First, it sanitizes the claim. It focuses the claim on a "neutral" employment practice used by the employer rather than on employee behavior (and workplace culture) built up around this and other practices. DeClue was not experiencing behavior or environment that was "because of [her] sex" in this view; she was merely disadvantaged by the use of the employer's business practice. The re-framing also triggers a distinct causation inquiry, which paints the plaintiff as the odd one out, butting up against a generally used, again "neutral" practice.[35] Finally, as Posner points out, it provides the employer with a defense that focuses on business needs. And this allows the courts an entirely unemotional, antiseptic weighing of the costs and benefits of providing toilets from the perspective of a business owner.[36]

Posner is so deft with his move that it might even be thought favorable to plaintiffs. DeClue *could* have chosen to frame her case as one of disparate impact, after all, but she chose not to. In *DeClue*, Judge Rovner suspects that something is up, though she cannot quite put her finger quite on it. But in other cases where Posner (and others) have made a similar move, the implications have gone almost entirely unnoticed.

The debate over pornography in the workplace is one example. Pornography is sometimes depicted as if it is just hanging out there, tucked away from view, or at most hanging on the wall or laying on the back of the toilet for interested people to peruse.[37] In reality, though, like urination, it is almost always part of a broader environment of behavior, including sexually explicit language and touching as well as nonsexual acts of job sabotage and ridicule.[38] Courts for the most part have come to recognize this,[39] but they continue to struggle with arguments that gender-specific sexually explicit language and behavior is not "because of sex" unless it is targeted at a specific woman. In *Ocheltree v. Scollon Productions, Inc.*, for example, the defendant argued that sexually explicit talk about women in subordinated positions and repeated sexual activity with female mannequins (including simulated oral sex and fondling) in the plaintiff's presence was not "because of sex" because the conduct "could have been heard [or seen] by anyone present in the shop" and it "was equally offensive to some of the men."[40] The en banc court rejected the argument (the panel majority had accepted it), but in doing so the court went out of its way to explain how a jury could have reasonably concluded that the men "behaved as they did to make [the plaintiff] uncomfortable and self-conscious as the only woman in the workplace."[41] The court understood this to be a legal requirement, as did the dissent, which argued that because the conduct went on before the plaintiff came to the workplace, it should be allowed to continue because the behavior *a fortiori* could not have been motivated by the plaintiff's sex.[42]

This requirement of targeted behavior harkens back to the debate surrounding the early *Robinson v. Jacksonville Shipyards* case, and the ACLU positions discussed in Chapter 1.[43] The *Robinson* case was brought in the 1980s by a female welder who worked at a male-dominated shipyard in Jacksonville, Florida. She alleged a hostile work environment after she was subjected to pornography depicting women and verbal, sexually explicit comments from co-workers and supervisors. The ACLU brief to the court argued that the men's expressive activity must be clearly directed at a particular employee (as did ACLU policy at the time) in order to amount to harassment. The concern was the same as that trumpeted throughout the development of harassment law in the United States: that the law should not infringe on male-dominated workplaces; it should not require an employer to "re-decorat[e] an office."[44]

From Systemic Disparate Treatment to Disparate Impact

The theory switch also occurs in systemic discrimination cases, cases in which private plaintiffs seek class certification after *Wal-Mart*. Judge Posner here, too, has led the way. In 2011, in *McReynolds* v. *Merrill Lynch*, the Seventh Circuit Court of Appeals, Judge Posner writing the opinion for a unanimous three-judge panel, reversed a district court's denial of class certification in a race-based discrimination case.[45] The decision was hailed by some as "the first major victory for civil rights plaintiffs after [*Wal-Mart* v. *Dukes*]."[46] In a recent search of the news and legal commentary, I found not a single word of criticism of the decision (other than from the defense bar, preferring that the court denied certification).[47]

The plaintiffs in the *McReynolds* case were black brokers working at Merrill Lynch, the investment powerhouse. They filed suit in 2005 alleging that disparities in pay between white and black brokers (and a dearth of black brokers in many states; there were no African American brokers in twenty-five states, from Illinois to California) resulted from differential treatment of black and white brokers in the firm. They alleged a racially discriminatory culture, citing anecdotal incidents involving offensive racial comments, and specifically alleged that stereotypes and biases exercised by white brokers restricted black brokers' access to resources, including membership on lucrative teams, and reduced black brokers' receipt of accounts distributed when brokers left the firm.

The plaintiffs sought class certification, and the trial court held that the Court's holding in *Wal-Mart* required denial of certification. Instead of focusing on the plaintiffs' claim under systemic disparate treatment law, however, Judge Posner at the appellate level isolated two elements of Merrill Lynch's employment practices for disparate impact review: (1) the company's teaming policy (a policy of allowing brokers to form their own teams); and (2) its account distribution policy (a policy of distributing accounts in a way that rewarded the most successful teams). According to the court, by isolating these specific practices for disparate impact review, the plaintiffs could establish commonality and obtain class certification.

It is easy to see why *McReynolds* has been lauded as a pro-plaintiff employment discrimination decision. The appellate judges seemed to understand the subtle, relational way that racial preference might be operating at Merrill Lynch, and to see how racial preference might result in pay disparities between white and black brokers under the organization's team and pay practices. Judge Posner described the teams as "little fraternities" and acknowledged how racial biases of white brokers and their perceptions about black brokers' access to wealthy clients might affect the makeup of the teams.[48] But in shifting the plaintiffs' case from one of systemic disparate treatment to one of disparate impact, the court also reduced substantially the law's pressure on firms like Merrill Lynch to examine the ways in which their structures and systems are inciting discrimination in those relations, and not just providing a neutral "conduit" for those relations.[49]

The shift to disparate impact does not eliminate the need to consider the context in which the practices are being used. Just like with a highly subjective decision-making system, we can only know whether that system is resulting in disparities in job success by looking at the practice in the particular context in which it is being used, including the employer's pay and promotion practices as a whole and the work culture in which the practice is being carried out. As a practical matter, what the shift does do, however, is push claims into a legal framework in which plaintiffs must isolate specific employment practices and prove that those practices have a disparate impact on members of a protected group. This is not easy to do. In *Wal-Mart*, the Court made clear its intention to continue to hold plaintiffs in disparate impact cases to stiff proof of causation.[50] And, of course, the shift gives rise to the business necessity defense for the employer. But perhaps most troubling is that success in a disparate impact case like the one envisioned by the court in *McReynolds* is likely to cabin employer action quite narrowly to changing the team and account distribution systems without any attention paid to the larger patterns of discrimination that may be operating within the firm.

The theory switch, whether from hostile work environment to disparate impact or from systemic disparate treatment to disparate impact, is likely a very pragmatic one, at least in Posner's view. It neutralizes the legal inquiry (positions the employer practice as "neutral" and the plaintiff as an outsider), gives employers a way out of liability based on considerations of cost and perceived importance to business, and limits remedial efforts to the very narrow and targeted adjustment of specific, identified practices. It is a form of judicial resistance to Title VII as a tool for disrupting the work cultures themselves, or of recognizing the ways in which an organization like Merrill Lynch may be shaping that culture to the detriment of women and racial minorities.

Together, the cases in this chapter show various sides of the same project. The judges here are saying that work culture is not within the purview of Title VII, even when racialized or gendered. Beneath this common thread, the judges reveal various reasons for their limit on Title VII. Tinged as it is with romanticism for the male locker room, for example, some of the judicial resistance to Title VII as a tool for work culture change may stem from sympathy for blue-collar workers, men like those working on the bridges in New Orleans, oil rigs in the Gulf, and used car lots across America. The idea seems to be "at least let these men have their locker room." The dissenting judges in *Boh Brothers* stress the "social context" in which the behavior occurred, for example. By "social context" they mean the all-male environment but also the long history of highly masculinized behavior in that environment. "This setting is customarily vulgar and crude," says Judge Jolly.[51]

But even apart from the many reasons why these cases are better understood through the lens of bias and organizational context, there is also reason to believe that the lives of the country's low-wage and blue-collar workers will be better improved by desegregation than by preserving all-male, locker room work cultures or tolerating extreme racialized conduct. Good, stable jobs are increasingly hard to come by as part-time jobs with low pay and employer-controlled flexible hours continue to rise. What working families in this environment need more than anything is working options –with families having a choice of who works which job at what point in their careers – and cultures like the one at Boh Brothers only serve to close those options by leaving in place extreme gendered work environments and segregation.[52]

PART II

What is Wrong with Discrimination Laundering

5

The Laundered Workplace

In the laundered workplace, organizations can focus their attention on providing written nondiscrimination policies and systems for complaint, and on responding to complaints with investigation and discipline, where appropriate. The law misses entirely discrimination that accrues over time or is otherwise difficult to identify in a precise moment. Organizations are under no pressure to do more than take very narrow efforts to reduce discrimination. In this chapter, I show what the law today is missing, and why it is important. I identify and examine the measures currently being taken by organizations to avoid or reduce discrimination. These measures are narrowly focused on complaint and discipline and on insulating key decisions from bias. Research suggests, however, that these measures are unlikely to reduce discrimination, and may actually hinder progress, punishing individuals while failing to get at the root of the problem.[1]

THE DISCRIMINATION BEING MISSED

Discrimination laundering leaves large swaths of discrimination unaddressed. It does this by shaping the law to remove any legal pressure on organizations to avoid discriminating. Discrimination laundering narrows the lens of the law to focus discretely on specific, observable moments of discrimination, putting pressure on victims to identify those moments and narrowing employer responsibility to responding to those moments with discipline, where appropriate.

Discrimination, however, is not so limited. It is not confined to specific, observable employment decisions. Instead, it often builds subtly over time so that an identified moment of decision making – such as the manager's decision not to promote – may appear perfectly neutral even when it is in fact the product of biased perceptions, judgments, and behaviors of the manager and also of others. The Court's decision in *Staub*, discussed in Chapter 2, reflects some understanding of this reality, that differences in treatment in key employment decisions, like hiring, firing, and promotions, can result from earlier biased decisions, but the understanding does not go far enough. The practical difficulties inherent in identifying and proving discrimination in individual instances mean that individual discrimination law necessarily falls short of addressing the problem of employment discrimination in the United States today.

Cognitive bias comes back into the story here, but the breadth of cognitive bias research reveals much more than the usual account lets on. Research shows that cognitive bias is not a matter of an isolated mind state, turned on or off at specific moments in time. Rather, biases operate and are reproduced relationally, often through ongoing interactions.[2] The visibility and cultural importance of race and sex in our society make them immediate salient categories in most interactions. Once we categorize others, we tend to evaluate their behaviors according to those categories and to alter our own behaviors in subtle ways that reinforce, build, and shape our racial and gender identities. Sociologist Barbara Reskin explains the role of cognitive bias in this way:

> Having categorized others, people tend to automatically "feel, think, and behave [toward particular members of the category] the same way they feel, think, and behave toward members of that social category more generally." Importantly, categorization is accompanied by stereotyping, attribution bias, and evaluation bias. These, in turn, introduce sex, race, and ethnic biases into our perceptions, interpretations, recollections, and evaluations of others.[3]

Social interactions and relations at work continuously shape actors' interpretations, perceptions and judgments, emotions, and behaviors toward each other. Think of Randall Kingsley and his experience at Large Company X, for example. In-group favoritism is also part of the full discrimination picture. A large body of research shows that people tend to help others who are similar to them, and to attribute failings of in-group members as situationally caused rather than caused by personal limitations or mistakes while attributing failings of out-group members to personal limitations.[4]

Understanding that discrimination is relational brings with it an awareness of the ways in which our behaviors and actions can be affected by the situation of the interaction itself, with whom we are interacting (e.g., how salient is the race and gender of the actors, and what is their degree of organizational status?), the context for the interaction (is the interaction an important meeting, lunch with clients, or a brief water-cooler chat?), and our expectations and perceptions (is this person likely to give me the benefit of the doubt?). Social psychologist Claude Steele and his colleagues, for example, show us that stereotype threat – concern about being judged according to negative group stereotypes or performing in ways that confirm those stereotypes – can affect performance by creating mental distraction.[5] Women taking difficult math tests underperformed as compared to men, except when they were told that the test did not reveal gender differences. The same was true for black students taking difficult verbal reasoning tests at Stanford University. White students did a lot better than black students on the tests when the test was assumed by the students to measure their intellectual ability. When the students were told that the test was merely a "task" for studying problem solving and did not measure a person's intellectual ability, black students performed at the same higher mark as white test takers with equal skills and knowledge.[6]

As with the research on cognitive bias, though, Steele's research on stigma threat tends to give rise to an image of a sole, isolated individual, like that of someone taking a test in an empty, silent room, when in reality most of the incidents involving stereotype threat in the workplace are relational moments. We interact with the people sitting around the meeting table outside the room as well as inside it, and this means that our perceptions of ourselves and of others build and shift over time.

In fact, the research on stereotype threat shows that identity threats often work both ways. Whites tend to worry about appearing racist. This makes them ruminate during interracial interactions about whether they are appearing racist and about how people will react if they think that they are racist.[7] "Will I have a chance to show him that I am a good person, that I really am not an insensitive white person?" This kind of thinking, just as the thinking associated with stereotypes related to being a woman in a math-related field, hinders not just mental processing and performance on exams, but interactions as well. Whites tend to sit farther back from blacks when they are told that the subject of conversation will be race-sensitive, such as racial profiling.[8] They also fidget more, exhibit decreased eye contact, smile less often, and use more hesitant speech when they are anxious about an interaction.[9] These behaviors are often mirrored by relational partners, and, ironically, perceived as biased by minority interactional partners.[10]

Knowing the ways that discrimination really operates helps us to see how seemingly small relational moments at work can affect outcomes down the road. Take Ellen Pao and her experience at Kleiner Perkins. Whether Pao and her female colleagues were seated at the table with the rest of the partners, almost all men, matters. It matters not just because asking women to sit on the outskirts of the room (or asking them to take notes) is consistent with stereotypes about the value and activities best suited to women, and therefore may be evidence of biased action by those who did the asking. This is how the lawyers and the media mostly construed the incidents. Kleiner Perkins's lawyer asked one of the top male partners, Ted Schlein, about the seating. He responded that "it was a woman from outside the firm who had set up the seating chart for [the] meeting," and he added "I really don't think it was a very big deal to us who sits at a table or who does not."[11]

Significantly, though, the seating arrangements may have mattered in another way as well: the interactions between Ellen Pao and her colleagues in that room were part of a longer relational history leading up to her performance reviews and ultimately to the decision not to promote her. Perceptions of Pao may have been skewed in stereotyped ways by Pao's seat around the edge of the table on that day (the seating arrangements mirrored stereotypes about gender roles and thus strengthened them), and those perceptions may have influenced interactions in the room that day as well as later decisions. These decisions would include not just performance evaluations, which critiqued Pao for being "passive and reticent" and a "support role player," but also other decisions like giving a good client lead to another colleague who was perceived as more able to "own the room," as a partner at Kleiner Perkins might say.[12]

We can expect that repeated small incidents of biased treatment by multiple people, or even a single person, will be difficult to detect in isolation. If we know that cognitive bias is prevalent, as we do, we also know that women and minorities are likely to experience biased interactions and decisions at various points in a career within an organization. Bias might influence a partner's decision about whom to invite to a client dinner, a co-worker's recommendation of whom to place on an important team, and a supervisor's performance review. Yet, because each incident is likely to be considered minor (and unlikely to involve express bias), it will be difficult to identify any specific treatment of women and minorities as discrimination.

An interview with one of the jurors in the Pao case reveals this difficulty. The juror described his impression of Ray Lane, the partner who asked Pao and another woman to take notes at a meeting. The juror says, "Here's my problem with Ray Lane – he was a fish out of water. Old guy, army training, [former president] of Oracle, this is a guy who gets whatever he wants, and I think he meant well but it didn't come out well." The jurors even joked about the note-taking incident in the deliberation room. When a woman volunteered to take notes, "we were like 'don't sue me!'"[13]

The jurors' reaction to the note-taking request is not surprising, and here is where it gets really interesting: it is not necessarily wrong either. The jurors did not want to label Ray Lane as a bad actor just because he asked the two women to take notes (or because he was less politically correct than he should have been). And, more importantly, they did not see how his asking the women to take notes should lead them to conclude that Pao's being a woman was a "substantial motivating factor" in the later decision denying her a promotion, as the California law of individual discrimination requires. The note-taking request suggests that at least one partner may have had stereotypic ideas of who does the "housekeeping" (although sometimes women should be asked to take notes, so long as men are asked to take them as well). And, as I described earlier, it might tell us something about Pao's experience at the firm, but as the juror's comments reveal, it can still be difficult to link the incident concretely to Pao's denial of promotion.

Pao was seeking past and future lost earnings, the money that she would have earned had she been granted the promotion. Had she wanted to, she might have also sought the promotion, to be put into the position that she was wrongfully denied. Without evidence that her sex was a "substantial motivating factor" in the denial of the promotion, as California law requires (or a "motivating factor" as Title VII law would require), then it seems right for the jurors to be reluctant to give Pao the money (and the promotion). After all, she has to prove that *she* was discriminated against, not that Kleiner Perkins was discriminating against women generally. This was why the jurors, even the ones that found for Pao, focused closely on the evaluations. The airplane conversation involving women as sex objects, the dinner and ski trip from which women were excluded because they would "kill the buzz," Ray Lane's response when Pao told him that she was experiencing retaliation from Nazre. These incidents, together with the note-taking request, might be evidence that stereotyping, even sexism, was common within the firm, but do they show that Pao in particular was treated differently in the promotion decision because she was a woman?

Indeed, courts have developed various doctrinal and evidentiary rules in the law of individual discrimination aimed at reining in judge and juror discretion in just this way, at focusing the legal inquiry on key employment decisions, those that indicate material job success, like pay and promotion, hiring, discipline, and discharge. The adverse employment action requirement does some of this work,[14] but many doctrinal rules also limit the evidence that is considered relevant or sufficiently persuasive in proving individual discrimination. In 2008, the Supreme Court gave implicit approval to trial courts to exclude evidence of discrimination experienced by employees other than the plaintiff (sometimes called "me, too" evidence) except in unusual circumstances, when the employees share the same allegedly biased supervisor, for example.[15]

Along similar lines, courts have developed what is known as the "stray remarks doctrine" whereby they will disallow evidence consisting of statements reflecting bias by a key decision maker when the statements are made in the court's view too far away in time or context from the decision in question.[16]

These kinds of rules, together with the practical reality that evidence of bias in a precise moment of decision (the proverbial smoking gun) is hard to come by, make it difficult for plaintiffs to prove individual discrimination, even when they may have suffered it. One can debate whether the rules are appropriate in some or all cases,[17] but what the rules legitimately do on the whole is keep Title VII focused on those decisions that affect individuals' success in work (rather than on decisions that might or might not later affect individuals' success), and on whether discriminatory bias affected those decisions (rather than on whether bias was generally present in the workplace or in a particular decision maker's mind at other moments in time).[18]

To say that it is difficult to identify and prove discrimination for specific individuals, like Ellen Pao or Randall Kingsley, though, is not to say that those individuals have not suffered discrimination, or that discrimination no longer remains a problem in American workplaces. The substantial body of research on bias and stereotyping gives us more reason than ever to believe quite the opposite: that discrimination continues to occur, and that it operates to the disadvantage of women and racial minorities. We know that seemingly "minor" biased moments (including many that we may not even notice) can add up over time to affect an individual, even if that individual will not be able to prove discrimination in her specific instance.

One way to get at the remaining problem is to step back from individuals and to look instead for the cumulative effect of bias on groups. We might not be able to readily see (or prove) racial or gender bias and stereotyping operating to the disadvantage of any specific individual, and yet nonetheless be able to see the cumulative effect of biases operating against multiple individuals over time. This wider vantage point is sometimes called looking to the "aggregate." In employment discrimination law, looking to the "aggregate" is an effort to see whether discrimination is a likely explanation for an observed group disparity in success outcome, such as pay or promotion.

Notice that looking to the "aggregate" shifts the inquiry from individualized discrimination to systemic discrimination. Simply put, systemic disparate treatment law asks a different question than individual disparate treatment law. Individual discrimination law asks whether a specific individual suffered discrimination. Systemic disparate treatment law asks whether discrimination is the "regular rather than the unusual practice,"[19] whether discrimination is widespread within the organization and resulting in disparate outcomes for members of different groups.

This is what the plaintiffs' evidence in *Wal-Mart* was trying to getting at. The statistical analyses and anecdotal and expert testimony presented in *Wal-Mart* and cases like it do not tell us the likelihood that any particular decision was the result of discrimination (or that any particular individual was the victim of discrimination).[20] The statistical analyses can, however, tell us something about whether discrimination is widespread within an organization, resulting in substantial differences in pay and promotion between men and women.

Of course, shifting the inquiry to the entity raises several important questions. The first question is one of proof: how can we know whether it is discrimination or something else that explains observed disparities in outcome between, say, women and men at a place like Wal-Mart? Maybe women do not earn as much as men because they do not try as hard as men. Or maybe they come in with less education or fewer skills than their male counterparts. We might call these "external" factors, factors other than internal discrimination (discrimination within the organization) that might explain observed disparities.

No statistical analysis alone can tell us whether discrimination explains an observed disparity. Rather, as described in Chapter 3, by controlling for external factors, what sophisticated statistical techniques can tell us is whether certain common explanations (such as years of experience or education or time on the job) explain away a disparity, and they can tell us whether an observed disparity is likely due to chance or some other unobserved factors. From there, we can only draw inferences. The Supreme Court in *Teamsters* and *Hazelwood* said that one reasonable inference to be drawn from statistical analyses showing that observed disparities are unlikely due to chance, without an alternative explanation by the employer, is that discrimination explains the disparity. This is a legal holding by the Supreme Court about the use of statistics to prove employer liability in a systemic discrimination case.

Statistics alone, though, are rarely used to make this showing of internal causation, that discrimination, in other words, rather than some other cause explains an observed disparity. As described earlier, in the early days after Title VII was enacted, plaintiffs regularly presented anecdotal evidence, testimony of individual instances of discrimination often involving overtly biased statements by supervisors, to "bolster" their statistical evidence. This was relatively easy to do in an era when people were still used to and willing to express their biases. A personnel officer at the trucking company involved in the *Teamsters* case described earlier, for example, told an applicant that he had one strike against him, and when the applicant asked why, the officer replied: "You're a Chicano, and as far as we know, there isn't a Chicano driver in the system."[21] The anecdotal testimony bolstered the statistical evidence in these cases by providing some reason to believe that discrimination within the organization rather than some nondiscriminatory or external cause explained the observed disparities.

Today, with overtly biased statements at the moment of key employment decisions much less common, plaintiffs tend to rely more on social science expert testimony to the effect that particular structures, systems, and cultures in place at the defendant organization are likely to result in regular, widespread discrimination. Like the anecdotal evidence in early cases, the expert social science testimony in these cases contributes to an inference that an internal explanation for the observed disparity (discrimination within the defendant organization) is more likely than an external one (such as lack of interest, discrimination in education, poverty, etc.). Social science testimony is useful in these cases not to prove that high-level policy makers acted with a purpose of keeping women or minorities down, or to show, as the Court in *Wal-Mart* expected, the precise likelihood that individual managers were acting on bias in pay and promotion decisions, but instead to support a finding of internal causation, that discrimination within the organization rather than some other factor resulted in the observed disparities in pay or promotion between identified groups.

The second question, of course, is the more normative liability question: what is it about this finding that makes (or should make) organizations responsible? We may agree that discrimination is occurring within an organization and resulting in disparities in pay and promotion between groups and still decide that the organization should not be held responsible for that discrimination. I will turn to this question in the remaining chapters. My aim at this point is merely to show that the lens of employment discrimination law is narrowing substantially when it erases the aggregate – and with serious consequences. If the law requires that plaintiffs prove that each manager at Wal-Mart acted on bias in a managerial decision regarding pay or promotion, then the law will be missing a large swath of discrimination that may actually be taking place. Looking to the aggregate, for disparities in outcomes, like pay and promotion, is the means for getting at everyday relational discrimination.

Wal-Mart can easily be seen in this way, not as a case about managers acting with bias, as the Court saw it, but as a case about bias pervading the workplace and resulting in differences in treatment, and in disparities in pay and promotion between men and women over time. Some managers may have acted with bias; others on a combination of biased performance reviews and perceptions/judgments of their own and of others who work with them and with female workers at Wal-Mart. Still other managers may have acted on nonbiased reviews of the performance of women who were placed in positions for discriminatory reasons or in positions where they were offered little support while their male counterparts were encouraged, mentored, even groomed for success. And, of course, some decisions may have been entirely nondiscriminatory, involving legitimate factors and no bias in the process at all. When many moments of different treatment – whether by managers or others – result in disparities in success outcomes for groups, though, we should see it for what it is: discrimination operating widely within an organization.

The pressure that the law puts on organizations is substantially altered by a law that focuses only on specific incidents and identifiable victims. Organizations in an environment of discrimination laundering – where the "aggregate" view is erased – experience no legal pressure to consider the ways in which they might be inciting discrimination and contributing to outcomes that are skewed along racial and gender lines. This is true even when there is evidence to suggest that discriminatory biases operating within the organization are driving the disparate outcomes.

WHAT ORGANIZATIONS ARE DOING AND WHETHER IT WORKS

The combination of narrowing the law to focus on discrete, observable incidents (erasing the aggregate) and corresponding construal of employer obligation around response to complaint narrows pressure on organizations. What are organizations actually doing in the face of this legal pressure? Organizations resist identifying their own actions as part of the problem of employment discrimination. This is, after all, the story of organizational innocence, and the same story is naturally reflected in and reinforced by talk about measures taken by organizations to reduce discrimination. Any measures taken by organizations are perceived to be taken on a blank slate; they are considered affirmative measures (triggered by law or otherwise) that organizations take if they are seeking to reduce what must be seen as societally fueled discrimination that may be occurring in their workplaces. The same story is also reflected in the sharp division in most organizations between equal opportunity measures and diversity management.

Not surprisingly, the measures that organizations in the laundered workplace do take to reduce discrimination (and "manage" diversity) tend to focus directly on individuals, seeking to alter or squelch biases through diversity training and policing and to insulate key decisions and information paths from the individuals' biases that might creep in. Indeed, these are the same remedies often sought by plaintiffs in settlement decrees and also by the EEOC.[22] Research shows, however, that many of these measures are likely to be ineffective, even counterproductive to the goal of reducing discrimination at work.

Nondiscrimination Policies

Nondiscrimination policies once served to publicly pledge nondiscrimination on the edge of an era of overt segregation, including race- and sex-specific job descriptions and advertisements. But formal nondiscrimination policies have been commonplace since the 1980s and today we would be hard pressed to find an organization that lacked one. Moreover, despite the *Wal-Mart* Court's favorable nod to Wal-Mart's nondiscrimination policy as evidence that the company was not discriminating,[23] a nondiscrimination policy tells us almost nothing about the prevalence of discrimination within any particular organization. Instead, the question is one of implementation. This is true for all organizational policies, but it is particularly true for those policies that are broad and loose – like one that says: "Employees should not discriminate" – and that do not translate concretely to daily behavior of employees who are carrying out those policies.[24]

Formal Complaint/Grievance Procedures

The idea behind formal grievance procedures as a discrimination-reducing measure is that they will allow, even require, victims of discrimination to complain, often early on, so that an employer can investigate and take disciplinary action against any individuals who are found to be discriminating. In this way, complaint and investigation processes are a form of policing, a method of quashing bias and biased actions through discipline and threat of discipline.

Research shows that requiring victims of discrimination to complain early on, as most grievance procedures do, is unrealistic and overly harsh. Individuals are actually unlikely to attribute negative behaviors and interactions to bias or discrimination, including harassment.[25] Moreover, many people are reluctant to complain about conduct that they do perceive as discriminatory out of fear of reprisals and concern about what complaining will do to their reputation.[26] Retaliation law offers little comfort to would-be complainants because, among other things, it protects only those employees who at least reasonably believe the conduct to which they object violates the law, a high standard, particularly for most lay people who know little about the law.[27]

Even putting aside the drawbacks of requiring complaint, however, grievance procedures as currently implemented by most organizations are a poor mechanism for reducing discrimination, and they may even be inciting it.

The process of investigating complaints focuses closely on specific individuals and discrete incidents, on "resolving" what is often seen as personal conflict, unrelated to discrimination. The search is usually for "bad actors," and those actors are rarely found. As one in-house counsel for a large transportation company described his experience investigating complaints: "I've never seen overt discrimination. I think it is something that does still happen, but I think it's pretty unusual, pretty rare. I've questioned managers at times … 'Are you sure [that discrimination did not occur]? … I think that 98, 99 percent of the time, [discrimination did not occur]."[28]

Seeing complaints of bias as complaints about personal, momentary conflict, the common solution is for organizations to seek to resolve the conflict as quickly and seamlessly as possible, and then to move on. Human resources professionals might transfer individuals away from each other, or sometimes simply counsel them in the hope that they will resolve their differences. These common responses fail to link individual encounters with broader environments, or to monitor for patterns of behavior (or outcomes) that might signal that discrimination is operating within an organization.

This individualizing of the problem trickles down in a grievance-focused system to the individuals who experience discrimination. In a world dominated by grievance procedures and individualized solutions, employees tend to frame their complaints around individual moments, even when what they are really concerned about are the broader structures and environments in which they work.[29]

It is not that policing is all bad. Policing can be useful for extreme racial or gendered conduct. Overt racists might respond to discipline or the sincere threat of discipline, and policing can reduce some of the more extreme forms of harassment, at least when the policing is consistent and followed as a matter of practice, and not just policy. The extreme gendered behavior prevalent on the construction sites of Boh Brothers, for example, or in some of the racial harassment cases involving racial slurs and nooses might be reduced through relatively minimal policing efforts.

But, on the whole, the idea of policing as the principal measure for reducing discrimination – particularly discrimination that is less overtly racial or gendered and hostile – is deeply problematic. Knowing about the prevalence of cognitive biases and how they operate can help us see where we need to work more to avoid or offset them, but research shows that our more subtle biases are difficult to self-correct. Just telling ourselves not to discriminate does not do the trick. Self-correction requires us to know exactly when our biases are in play, to be able to discern the direction and magnitude of the bias, and to have sufficient control over our decision making that we can accurately control for that bias.[30]

All of this is difficult to do, particularly in quick social encounters and other interactions that may not have job outcome significance to us at the time.

Even more alarming is that people tend to react negatively to policing, responding in ways that can heighten biases and result in more, not fewer, biased decisions. Recent research suggests that grievance procedures and other initiatives that limit managerial discretion in hiring and promotion decisions can actually spark managerial rebellion and lead to decreased diversity in outcomes. Sociologists Frank Dobbin, Daniel Schrage, and Alexandra Kalev examined how various diversity initiatives affected the shares of white, black, Hispanic, and Asian men and women in management, following 816 private-sector workplaces over 32 years. Grievance procedures in their study showed negative effects on all underrepresented groups, except Latino men.[31]

Policing can also more subtly undermine important inter-group relational ties. People tend to avoid interactions that they expect will trigger negative emotions, such as anxiety and fear of being labeled racist.[32] Most people already experience some anxiety in intergroup encounters, and this anxiety is heightened by a sense that any wrong step could be the basis for formal discipline. Indeed, some research suggests that harassment law makes some men apprehensive about creating relational ties with female colleagues out of fear that they might be accused of sexual harassment.[33]

Training

Training was first introduced as an equal opportunity measure in the 1960s when some employers added race relations sessions to their management training curricula, but it really took off in the 1980s with the rise of diversity management.[34] By 1991, one survey found that 63 percent of large employers offered diversity training for managers and 40 percent trained all employees.[35] Much of this diversity training focuses on making employees aware of what counts as discrimination under the law, often with an emphasis on sexual harassment, which should not be surprising given that the Supreme Court created legal protection in harassment cases for employers who make these kinds of efforts. Other programs focus on making employees aware of cultural differences and of their own biases.

Despite the prevalence of these kinds of diversity training, however, very little research suggests that they are effective, at least as currently administered, and some research indicates that they can even have negative effects. Some diversity trainings can reinforce stereotypes, and can trivialize discrimination by widening diversity to include styles of learning and whether someone is a daytime or nighttime person, for example.[36] Diversity trainings can also engender anger and resistance on the part of white employees and trigger negative reactions and retaliation toward people who complain about discrimination. One recent quantitative study found that diversity training, particularly when it is mandatory and focuses on legal liability, as many programs do, led to fewer women and racial minorities being promoted into management than when there was no diversity training program at all.[37] In another recent study by sociologist Justine Tinkler and colleagues, men and women interviewed after undergoing policy training on sexual harassment reacted negatively to the training and to people who complained about discrimination.[38] After the training, they perceived harassment law as over-policing employee behavior, and criticized women who brought harassment complaints. Two of the men interviewed went so far as to say that they thought a woman who obtained a large settlement after suing her employer for allowing pornographic emails and jokes at work ought to be put in jail: "Lock her up," said one.[39]

If the happenings in Silicon Valley are any indication, trainings on unconscious bias are the new wave of diversity training. Google put together a workshop in 2014 to raise awareness of bias among its employees, shortly after the company released its dismal diversity numbers. This past summer after the trial in the case brought by Ellen Pao, Kleiner Perkins brought in Brian Welle, the developer of the workshop at Google, to train 150 of its portfolio CEOs. The Stanford Clayman Institute for Gender Studies, which does similar trainings, has seen requests skyrocket, as companies like Pinterest and Pandora and a host of others join in the frenzy around "bias busting."[40] There is research that supports unconscious bias training, particularly the idea that raising individuals' awareness of their unconscious biases is important to their ability to control those biases.[41] Moreover, raising individuals' awareness of unconscious biases and stereotypes can help to change work cultures, making people more willing to call out bias when they see it operating and increasing conversation and learning across difference.[42] But there is little reason to believe that unconscious bias training alone will be sufficient, or even that it will always be productive, particularly if it is not done well.

Formalization: Insulating Key Decisions and Systems from Bias

Formalization, including written job criteria, performance rating systems, and job tests, have been popular since at least the 1950s, but grew exponentially in the 1960s, 70s, and 80s. Today, some studies put performance ratings systems at 90 percent of firms.[43] Standardized rules and procedures for key decisions such as promotion and layoff decisions do have some support in the sociological literature as a promising mechanism for reducing inequalities. Studies show that formalized personnel procedures can mitigate gender and racial inequalities by insulating key decisions from biases, both reliance on stereotypes and also favoritism that can creep into loose, more subjective processes.[44] Without stated criteria, studies show that decision makers are likely to shift job criteria to fit the qualifications of the candidate who best fits gendered (or racial) expectations for a job. In a laboratory study where participants were asked to rate candidate resumes with male and female names for the job of police chief, for example, the participants tended to shift the definition of merit to advantage male applicants, inflating the importance of qualities that a male applicant had for success on the job, but devaluing the importance of those qualities when a male applicant lacked those qualities.[45] Listing job requirements prior to selecting a candidate can constrain these biases.[46] Formalization can also increase individual accountability, which is thought to reduce bias by increasing attention to detail and motivation to correct for bias.[47]

Other research, however, shows that formalization does not always reduce inequality. Some studies suggest that this failure is sometimes due to lack of implementation, or to only partial implementation.[48] Still others show that even with full implementation, formalization can work against equality. The study by Dobbin and colleagues, for example, shows that formalization that seeks to constrain managers' discretion, such as using job tests for choosing workers and requiring supervisors to rely on detailed rubrics for selecting promotion candidates, can backfire as managers rebel against perceived bureaucratic control.[49] Other studies show that the effects of formalization can vary depending upon the broader organizational emphasis. When formalization is implemented alongside claims of meritocracy, participants in the study favored men over women, while formalization implemented without claims of meritocracy resulted in no disadvantage to women.[50]

Even with the promise of formalizing criteria for key decisions, moreover, formalizing personnel procedures can only go so far. As research discussed earlier in this chapter shows, discrimination is often the product not of bias in a key employment decision, such as a decision whether to promote, but rather has already built over time in much more informal opportunities to judge, perceive, help, and evaluate. These micro-interactions cannot be formalized in the way that key decisions such as promotion or hiring or pay can be, and yet they often form the basis for those decisions.

THE BOTTOM LINE

What is wrong with discrimination laundering? It leaves us with a workplace where a small number of individuals are targeted for investigations and punishment, and where nondiscrimination measures, generally taken without attention to broader patterns and cultures, are likely to be ineffective, even harmful. The discrimination that plays out without overt expressions of bias by individuals, more widely and over time, is completely missed by the law. And this means that organizations have little to no incentive to take the kind of steps that are actually likely to reduce discrimination within their walls.

6

How Organizations Discriminate – and
What They Can Do To Stop

This chapter draws out the remaining piece of the empirical story, of what is wrong with the discrimination laundering that is taking place on our watch. Discrimination, it turns out, is situational as much as it is relational and experienced over time. Bias even in a precise moment is influenced in multiple ways by the context in which individuals and groups interact. And organizations create that context.

This chapter challenges organizational innocence by bringing organizations back in. First, it shows that to varying degrees most organizations today consciously capitalize on race and sex. Organizations' leaders see the race and sex of their employees as key to their success, in various ways. This is true even as they profess not to discriminate.

But understanding the role of organizations in employment discrimination requires going deeper than just an increased awareness of the ways that race and sex are perceived as relevant to business success. The second part of the chapter presents some of the empirical research on how context influences bias, context such as demographics, structures organizing work, management regimes, and work cultures. These are the core conditions of interaction and decision making that organizations actively create and continually shape – the space in which organizations can incite discrimination even when they publicly (and honestly) proclaim adherence to a nondiscrimination norm.

The chapter then turns back to mechanisms for reducing discrimination. It looks at what organizations can and should be doing (and what they should be incentivized by the law to do). One of the reasons why discrimination laundering is so troubling is that it stifles research and experimentation around what organizations can do to minimize discrimination, but the research that we do have shows that attention to organizational context – the structures, systems, practices, and cultures of work and workplace interaction – is key.

CONSCIOUSLY CONSIDERING RACE AND SEX

Several years ago the NAACP Legal Defense Fund filed a lawsuit on behalf of African American managers at Wet Seal, the national teenage girls' clothing retailer. In the complaint, plaintiffs alleged that the Senior Vice President of Wet Seal, after visiting several stores, had sent an email to the Vice President of Store Operations stating "Store Teams need diversity – African American dominate – huge issue."[1] Another senior executive was said to have ordered a district manager to "clean the entire store out" after observing numerous African American employees working there. Nicole Cogdell, a black woman, described her experience when she was promoted from a store in Springfield, Pennsylvania, where there was a large black clientele, to a store in the upscale King of Prussia mall, where clients were mostly white. According to Cogdell, when the Vice President showed up at the King of Prussia store and saw Cogdell, she said to the District Manager, "That's the store manager? I wanted someone with blonde hair and blue eyes."[2] Cogdell was fired four days later.

Overt discrimination by high-level directive still occurs in the United States. If we asked executives in these organizations – and if they answered honestly – they would admit to thinking that race and sex are relevant to management decisions in their workplaces. Sociologist John Skrentny calls this "racial realism," a management strategy that sees race as having both significance and usefulness to business.[3] He contrasts the management strategy of racial realism to that of colorblindness, which maintains that race and sex are irrelevant to business, and to one that marks race as relevant for equal opportunity or affirmative action purposes but denies any usefulness of race for business ends.[4]

In his book, *After Civil Rights*, Skrentny documents racial realism today in the United States across various sectors of work. Some of this racial realism looks a lot like old-fashioned race and sex management.[5] Particularly at the low end of the job market, employers today continue to manage through and by race and sex much like the factories, railroads, and mines of the 1800s and 1900s did. From contractors hiring labor to rebuild New Orleans after Hurricane Katrina to factories building products or packaging chicken and meat, Latino (often undocumented) workers are in demand, and black workers are not.

In an industrial equipment manufacturing plant in the mid-2000s, sociologist Laura López-Sanders documented the "Project," as the plant managers called it, of replacing black workers with Latinos, who were perceived as harder workers. Over the course of just two months, the graveyard shift went from being 60 percent black and 40 percent white to being almost

70 percent Latino, 20 percent black, and 10 percent white.[6] To get rid of permanent black workers (who had more job security), the company implemented strategies to motivate the black workers to quit. The assembly line was sped up and tasks were added to existing jobs. Managers transferred workers to break up social groups and assigned black workers to unpleasant tasks.

Racial (and gender) realism also occurs in some of the low-wage areas of work that tend to slide under the public radar. Women in factories and in agricultural fields hold different jobs than men, working almost exclusively under male bosses. Women dominate low-wage, service-sector jobs, particularly in stores that cater to female clients, such as clothing and department stores.[7] Workers in the garment industry are mostly Chinese, Korean, and Hispanic women.[8] Workers in caregiving are also mostly women, and sex- and race-based requests made to agencies are regularly honored.[9] Nail salons employ almost exclusively women and in some areas are known to have a strict racial caste. New York City nail salons, for example, are dominated by Korean women, and Korean manicurists are paid much more than other Asians and non-Asians.[10]

Although there is plenty of reason to believe that this kind of conscious willingness to make employment decisions based on race and sex is widespread, you would be hard pressed to find any mention of it today in the business literature. The business literature, instead, talks loosely about the benefits of diversity. It also tends to focus more on higher-paying jobs than on the meat packers, construction workers, and nannies. As I described in Chapter 1, the business case for diversity prominent in the literature nonetheless makes a targeted case to organizations and their leaders: that the makeup of their workforce – the race and sex (the "diversity") of their workers – is relevant to the bottom line. The idea here is that a diverse workforce is not just unavoidable; it is desirable. If managed well, it will produce better decisions, make possible more fine-tuned market reach, and provide greater institutional flexibility in an increasingly globalized business world.

The Wet Seal case represents a specific flavor of this diversity-business pitch: the idea that race (and sex) are relevant to reaching markets. The Vice President at Wet Seal did not think that Nicole Cogdell was unprepared or not smart enough to be a good store manager (as we might expect if she were relying on longstanding negative stereotypes about black workers). Instead, she was concerned about reaching markets and building a brand name, and race to her was relevant to that enterprise. Having African Americans "dominate" at Wet Seal stores presumably worried high-level executives at the firm because of the signal that it would send to the shoppers about the brand. Having too many blacks – or a black store manager – might send a signal about the brand that made it less appealing to the white teenager market.[11]

Nicole Cogdell's story suggests that in addition to a broader branding concern, there was also an element of matching race to narrower markets going on at Wet Seal. The Vice President may have approved of (or at least tolerated) Cogdell managing the Springfield store, where much of the clientele was black, but not the King of Prussia store, where much of the clientele was white. This kind of race matching traces back long into American history. In the 1940s, companies began to hire African American marketing consultants and sales associates with the specific goal of developing marketing materials and targeting the black market. Today, race matching like this extends to Asian and Latino markets as well. One study of retail stores in four major cities found that seven out of ten surveyed managers admitted to race matching their employees to their client base.[12]

The business case for diversity has led firms to race and sex match much more openly than we might have imagined. Often the business literature emphasizes cultural knowledge, the idea that racial minorities have insider knowledge that is relevant to reaching markets and connecting with clients in an increasingly globalized world.[13] And major corporations seem to have heeded the call. As described in the Introduction, several companies submitted amicus curiae briefs in favor of affirmative action in higher education in the Supreme Court case, *Grutter* v. *Bollinger*, asserting just these grounds. As the brief submitted by MTV Networks put it, "a diverse workforce is critical to the development and marketing of programming targeted at specific racial and cultural communities."[14] The case for bringing women into the technology sector similarly tends to emphasize women as consumers, and the benefits of matching workers to the consumer base.[15]

Another reason that race and sex matching is more overt than we might expect is that it is often framed as a benefit to racial minorities and women. It is touted as opening up new markets and thereby also bringing members of historically subordinated groups into the key positions within organizations trying to reach those new markets. Race and sex matching can indeed open up opportunities for women and minorities. In the late 1970s and 1980s, for example, major corporations turned to minority-owned advertising agencies to target the African American market, and mainstream firms created in-house units for "special markets," hiring African Americans into those units.[16] Research also suggests that the rise of women in management in the service sector is tied to demand: Women are wanted to serve others, which can lead to economic benefit.[17]

But racial minorities and women often end up in jobs that earn less than the jobs that their white, male counterparts occupy. The overrepresentation of women and racial minorities in a job has been shown to trigger a process of gender and racial priming, which activates gender and racial stereotypes. Jobs that are identified as "women's work" or a "minority position" tend to be devalued, and the low status of the jobs further perpetuates the activation of stereotypes and biases against women and racial minorities who fill the positions in their interactions with others.[18]

In 2007, the EEOC sued the national pharmacy chain Walgreens for its race-matching practices and the income disparities that resulted. The company had an excellent record of hiring African Americans as store and district managers, much better than the rest of the industry.[19] But it allegedly assigned black managers almost exclusively to stores located in black neighborhoods, apparently both because community groups in those neighborhoods asked for black managers and because the company's leaders thought that black managers would be better able to tailor sales to a black clientele. A senior vice president of Walgreens at the time was accused of stating that the manager of one East Saint Louis store was making a mistake by stocking premium ice creams such as Häagen-Dazs rather than "ethnic products" like "cheap hair care and hot or spicy food" and that this failure to know her market meant that she was not "black enough."[20]

This kind of pigeonholing into certain jobs or tasks runs across industries. David Wilkins documents a similar phenomenon in corporate law, where black corporate lawyers struggle to specialize in practice areas in which being black is not seen as adding value. Wilkins found that black corporate lawyers at large law firms worked mostly in "labor and employment law" (which includes defending employment discrimination lawsuits) and other practice areas in which their race might be perceived as a valuable credential.[21] The black lawyers that he interviewed found themselves "trapped inside a 'black box' that severely limits their ability to broaden their horizons or, in many cases, to advance within the firm."[22]

The problem at Walgreens, moreover, was not just that Walgreens was race matching its managers to its stores, although that itself was problematic. The original plaintiff in the case testified that he lived in a mostly white, wealthy suburb but was assigned to manage an inner city, mostly black store where he experienced stress that resulted in a leave of absence.[23] But Walgreens was also tying promotion opportunities to sales revenue at the managers' stores, and stores located in black neighborhoods generally had much lower sales revenue than those located in white neighborhoods.[24] This meant that Walgreens was penalizing its black managers financially with its race-based store assignment system.

Organizations also use race and sex as a signal today that they are complying with equal opportunity laws and that they are genuinely committed to diversity. For this reason, women and racial minorities are often asked to appear in marketing and recruitment materials, to sit on diversity committees, and to generally serve as the face of diversity for the public. The Wet Seal settlement specifically required Wet Seal to put more African Americans in their hiring materials, presumably as a signal to African Americans that the company is open to hiring them and that it plans to treat them well.[25] Increasing the visibility of minority and female employees can be helpful for reducing bias and perceived bias.[26] This kind of diversity work, however, often places extra burdens on minority and female employees, taking their time and energy away from work-related tasks that are more closely tied to success within a firm.[27]

Unlike decisions about whom to hire in the first place, many of the race- and sex-based decisions discussed here are likely to be softer employment decisions, decisions about who does what tasks or who takes on which clients or market areas. These are decisions that can affect individual and group outcomes over time, but they can be difficult to challenge using individual discrimination law for the reasons discussed in Chapter 5.

CREATING CONTEXT, INCITING BIAS

John Doerr at Kleiner Perkins openly professed to care about getting more women into tech and venture capital, and there is some reason to believe that he really did take the issue seriously. He testified at trial that he backed twelve women-led companies during his time at Kleiner Perkins (more than most venture capital firms) and that he had a hand in hiring many of the female partners at the firm. He called the lack of women in the venture capital world "pathetic" and pointed out that Kleiner Perkins, which has 20 percent women in its workforce, sits well above the average for the industry.[28]

Of course, Doerr may still be biased against women who work in the world of high tech and venture capital. He was recorded in a May 2008 television appearance talking about his investment decisions. He said that if you look at the leaders of hugely successful, entrepreneurial companies, "they all seem to be white, male, nerds who've dropped out of Harvard or Stanford and they absolutely have no social life." He went on to say that when "I see that pattern coming in … it was very easy to decide to invest."[29] This is stereotyping, no doubt.

But if we believe John Doerr – and we can still believe him, even as we see that he might sometimes rely on race and gender stereotypes in his funding decisions – how could his firm nonetheless have been discriminating against women? When an internal investigator asked Eric Keller, the then Chief Operating Officer of Kleiner Perkins, to provide the firm's equal employment opportunity policy, Keller said he could not find it.[30] In fact, no one could. A new policy was created in 2012 after Pao and another woman complained about retaliation and harassment. One of the Pao jurors interviewed after the verdict said he wanted to see Kleiner Perkins "punished" for not being able to locate the policy, even though he did not think Pao herself had suffered discrimination.[31] Why punish the firm for not having a policy handy? More likely than not, the juror wanted to punish the firm because he saw that having equal employment opportunity policies and disseminating them – and caring enough about them to know what they say and where they are located – is the first order of business for a company interested in not discriminating.

But the dynamics at Kleiner Perkins – including the lost/nonexistent non-discrimination policy – are troubling for another reason, a reason that the juror probably did not have in mind. They are troubling because Kleiner Perkins (like all work organizations) was actively creating the conditions for work and interaction at the firm, conditions that can incite bias and lead to gender- and race-based disparities in outcome such as pay and promotion. Not being able to find the firm's policy may have been indicative of a lack of concern on the part of Keller and other high-level executives, but more importantly it may have been indicative of an organization that was stacking things against women, not necessarily with a purpose to harm women, but stacking it against women nonetheless.

Look again at some of what we know from the trial about the dynamics at Kleiner Perkins during this time:

- In 2011, all but one managing partner at Kleiner Perkins was a man. (The firm did promote several more women after Pao filed her suit).
- There was no disseminated nondiscrimination policy.
- When a woman complained to Ray Lane about sexual harassment by a partner (the same partner about whom Pao complained), Lane asked her if she really wanted to go public and if she had talked to her husband about it.[32]
- Lane asked two junior women to take notes at a meeting.
- At least one woman was seated around the outer edge of the room rather than at the table for meetings.
- Conversation in a private plane trip to a business conference in New York may have included talk of porn stars, "hot" female executives, a Victoria's Secret fashion show, and the Playboy mansion.

- Chi-Hua Chien, a male senior partner, organized an all-men ski trip for entrepreneurs. When asked in an email if a female entrepreneur from one of the companies that Kleiner Perkins had invested in could come along, he responded that because the trip involved shared accommodations, women probably would not feel comfortable.
- Chien also organized an all-men team dinner at the home of former vice president of the United States (and Kleiner Perkins partner) Al Gore. A female junior partner testified at trial that Chien had remarked that having women at the dinner would "kill the buzz." (Chien denied making this statement, though he admitted to organizing the events.).

Without knowing more (for example, the rate of women moving from junior partner to senior partner, the dynamics around sponsorship for investments, as well as mentorship generally in the firm), it might be difficult for us to conclude based on these facts that bias was operating against women in promotion decisions at Kleiner Perkins, but the failure to disseminate a nondiscrimination policy is part of the context in which interactions were occurring and decisions were being made. We know that a nondiscrimination policy alone is unlikely to translate into equality in treatment, implementation being the key, but by not having or disseminating a policy, the high-level men (acting on behalf of the firm) at Kleiner Perkins signaled to their employees that nondiscrimination did not matter much. What these men actually thought may be beside the point if what they did – the tone, culture, work environment that they created – incited bias against women at the firm.

This brings us quickly to the question of fault. It is hard to get away from the sense that in the entrepreneurial/tech industry of Silicon Valley we are going to naturally see businesses that become dominated by men. Like John Doerr, we all know the classic story of the nerdy, white men who do not know how to interact with women and who therefore tend to stay away from them in their entrepreneurial networks. We have this image of three or four computer or software visionaries sitting around a garage or a moldy Harvard dorm room deciding to drop out and start a business – and, as the story tends to go, "it just grew from there!"

But we do not let these growing businesses ignore environmental protection laws or securities laws or antitrust laws. What might be legally permissible (even if not ethically correct) in a garage or dorm room between three socially awkward young men is not necessarily legally permissible once they employ fifteen or more workers. This is the point at which antidiscrimination law kicks in.[33] Now these guys are really running a business, not just shucking around with their friends.

Similarly, Sam Walton and more recent high-level executives at Wal-Mart may not have structured their business with the purpose of keeping women down, but they may nonetheless have created and continue to shape a workplace that incites bias and produces widespread disparities in success between men and women. This is because our biases are affected by the context in which we think, perceive, feel, and interact. And organizations create and continually shape that context, the conditions for our interactions and decisions at work.

The organization can be at fault today for inciting biases and biased action against women and racial minorities in their firms, without our having to assign fault to the Sam Waltons and Eugene Kleiners who created the businesses in the first place or even to the John Doerrs and others who run the businesses today. This is not about static architecture; it is about ongoing business matters: structural choices, management regimes, and cultures that create conditions for interaction and can incite biased action against women and racial minorities.

WHAT CONDITIONS INCITE BIAS? — AND HOW DO ORGANIZATIONS CREATE AND SHAPE THOSE CONDITIONS?

Sexist and Racist Work Environments

One of the most obvious contextual influences on bias is the overtly sexist or racist work environment. The law tends to focus on the effect that racist or sexist work environments have on specific victims and their ability to do their jobs, but these environments also incite bias more broadly against members of the groups being targeted or denigrated and can lead therefore in multiple ways to disparities in outcome. Longstanding social science research – and common sense – teaches that stereotyping, hostility, and biased action against members of certain groups in an environment make it more likely that individuals acting within that environment will also rely on stereotypes and biases. What is more surprising to many, though, is that not only are individuals more likely to act on and express their *conscious* biases and stereotypes in an environment in which those biases and stereotypes are socially accepted; they are more likely to experience and act on even their *unconscious* biases and stereotypes when similar biases and stereotypes are prevalent in the environment.[34] This means that the environment that we work in can affect our biases and our actions, even without our being consciously aware of it.

Demographics

A long and robust line of research also shows that the demographics of a situation can affect biases and behaviors. One woman working among a group of men in a male-dominated field is more likely to be judged according to stereotypes and to be judged more harshly than a woman working in a group mixed with men and women. In her famous ethnology of the large, bureaucratic firm in the 1970s, sociologist Rosabeth Moss Kanter studied the dynamics of tokenism as it affected women in corporate America.[35] She documented the experiences of tokens, women working in environments in which the number of women was small (typically 15 percent or smaller) and the dominant group relatively homogeneous (white men). Her research showed that women experienced heightened performance pressures and stereotyping as a result of their numerical rarity.

Further studies have buttressed Kanter's account, and social scientists have developed more complex theories of how interaction in demographically skewed contexts can influence expectations, interactions, and performance.[36] This research shows that status plays a significant role, as low-status tokens, women and racial minorities, are much more likely to suffer negative outcomes than their white, male counterparts. Segregation also limits the visibility of low-status workers (giving them few opportunities to prove that they are competent and worthy of higher-status work), and it perpetuates negative stereotypes about women's and minorities' competence when interaction does take place.[37]

The segregated, low status of women's and minorities' jobs and job functions is also likely to activate gender and racial stereotypes and biases in interaction between workers across and within jobs. Men and women are more likely, for example, to enact gender-typical behavior during interactions in which men are perceived as having higher organizational status.[38] Men are more likely in these circumstances to interrupt in conversation, and women are more likely to qualify their statements. The kind of cooperative interdependence across racial and gender lines that can reduce the salience of demographic intergroup boundaries and minimize bias is rare in a segregated, stratified work environment.

Organizations influence the demographics in their firms in a variety of ways, both direct and indirect. The most obvious is by using race or sex as a factor in deciding what job to offer whom, or who gets what promotion, but firms affect demographics in many other ways, often without considering race or sex in specific employment decisions. The ways in which firms structure recruitment can have a substantial impact on demographics. Recruiting structures can affect the makeup of the labor pool (recruiting from predominately white colleges will yield a particular labor pool demographic, for example, as will using a word-of-mouth recruitment structure). Job descriptions and recruitment materials can also affect the interest levels of people within the pool.[39] The same is true for high-level jobs with internal labor pools.

But it would be a mistake to focus exclusively on demographics. Conditions for discrimination go well beyond sheer demographics, who from which group holds which job and at what hierarchical status, to include such matters as structural and system decisions about how work is organized and how people are evaluated, as well as softer elements of work culture that define the "ideal" worker and create everyday relational expectations.

How Work is Organized

How work is organized can have a significant effect on biases in intergroup interactions. In particular, structures for work-related interaction can incite biases in some circumstances and limit them in others. One study of teamwork in an engineering firm, for example, found patterns of intergroup interaction between more valued (mostly men) and less valued (mostly women) workers changed and were less demeaning when workers were placed on collaborative teams.[40] Researchers have also found that female and minority scientists have better career outcomes in organizations where work is arranged in network rather than hierarchical structures. In 2004, for example, sociologist Laurel Smith-Doerr compared the careers of more than 2,000 women scientists, some who worked in universities or pharmaceutical companies and others who worked in biotechnology firms.[41] Smith-Doerr's analysis showed that women in biotechnology firms, where scientists tend to interact on collaborative projects and are rewarded as a group and evaluated by their peers, were significantly more likely to attain supervisory positions than women who worked in academia, where scientists tend to adhere to rigid job categories, individual reward structures, and hierarchies.

The benefit of cross-boundary work teams extends beyond the scientific and technology community. Sociologist Alexandra Kalev conducted a nationwide study of firms across nine industries following the adoption of team and training programs between 1980 and 2002.[42] She found that women and racial minorities were more likely to be promoted into the managerial ranks in firms that adopted cross-boundary work teams – work teams that bring together workers from different jobs on a regular basis to share information and participate in decision making – than in firms that did not adopt those types of team. She also found that training programs that involved job rotation led to greater success for women and minorities than programs that focused on in-job training.

Work Culture

Work culture defines behavioral expectations on the job.[43] It establishes expectations of style in interacting and conversation boundaries (what we talk about and how), modes of dress and other appearance signals, and day-to-day displays of competence. In some workplaces, employees are expected to openly share information about themselves and their families; in others, they may be expected to talk only about work matters. In some workplaces, employees are expected to challenge each other and their superiors; in others, they are expected to defer to hierarchy and follow orders without questioning. In many workplaces, employees are expected to adhere to a relatively strict appearance code, even when not formally mandated. It is hard to know what amounts to "casual Friday" in most workplaces until you actually experience it. Even job competence is often a matter of work culture as employees (and employers) determine the interactional styles that define success and measure competence not just by output or end product, but by conformity with those styles.

Given the dynamic, social nature of culture, there is rarely just one work culture operating within an organization; instead, there are multiple work cultures that vary across professional and hierarchical divides as well as work group and informal socializing divides. Secretaries may adhere to a different work culture than engineers,[44] paralegals to a different work culture than attorneys. Similarly, work culture can develop differently in a small work group, or informal social groups, than it does organization-wide.

Work cultures can be explicitly racialized and gendered. Think of the classic sexist or racist environment. But they can also be more subtly racial and gendered, and they can interact with other organizational structures and systems in ways that trigger biases in interaction, perception, and performance. I provide here three examples drawn from the research on organizations and discrimination (including one example involving a legal case) that should help illustrate not only what work culture is, but also why it is an organizational source of employment discrimination (together with others) that we should be concerned about. My point here is not that any of the firms involved in these examples or any of the other organizations studied in the research on the interaction between structures, systems, and work cultures and human bias should necessarily be held legally liable for discrimination. Instead, my goal here is to show that the story of organizational innocence is wrong. It misses the many ways that organizations actively shape the conditions of work, conditions that can incite biases and result in unequal treatment.

Bravado, Tinkering, and "Fit"

Almost thirty years ago, sociologists Judith S. McIlwee and J. Gregg Robinson identified work culture as a central component of women's disadvantage in the traditionally male-dominated field of engineering.[45] The status and success of engineers in some workplaces, their research showed, depended not just on technical competence but also on the way that competence was displayed. Particularly in workplaces where engineers as a group were powerful, there was enormous pressure to conform to the image of a "good" engineer, an image characterized by displays of bravado and frequent demonstrations of technical, hands-on competence and a love of tinkering.

McIlwee and Robinson described one such firm. It was a well-respected firm that fostered an overall organizational culture of informality. The research showed that women could, and did, gain the technical competence required for excellent engineering at the firm, but that they had difficulty interacting in the requisite style, through frequent informal displays of technical know-how and demonstrations of a love of tinkering, of taking apart and fixing things for the sake of the project, whether it be bicycles, automobiles, or radios, computers, and other electronic devices.[46] In short, as McIlwee and Robinson put it, "one had to conform to the image of the 'technical jock,'" and women could not or did not want to do that.[47]

This tinkering work culture transfers today to computer programming. Some firms have considered requiring open-source coding for job applicants, and many use it to recruit and to compile an applicant pool. There is even a computer program that can measure the quality (and quantity) of a person's open-source coding.[48] The open-source community, however, is almost all white, and mostly male, which means that the labor pool is likely to be skewed in that direction in those firms using open-source coding as a signal of competence.[49]

Open-source coding can then become a part of the work culture defining the "ideal" worker. And, as with tinkering in engineering, as outsiders, women and racial minorities have to prove that they "code" when white men do not.[50] Women and minorities are not given the benefit of the doubt, are not assumed to be part of the in-group culture. One female software developer explained that she had to constantly prove herself. "'Do you code?' they always ask." "Of course I code; I am a coder," she responds.[51]

This is an example of biases operating in the workplace to women's disadvantage, not just the interaction of women's skills or interests with neutral practices used by the firm. And it is not just a matter of outsiders needing to work harder to fit in, or being turned off by a work culture that is not easy for them to navigate. It is true that work cultures can affect women's and racial minorities' decisions about whether to enter a field or job in the first place (or whether to stay once in), but those decisions are likely to be inextricably intertwined with racial and gender biases operating *within* the firm.[52] Research shows that insiders often use work culture as a means of social closure, even if not necessarily consciously conceived to keep outsiders out. Rigidly policing culture can be a way of maintaining comfort, and power.[53] Moreover, women in these environments are often held to a double bind. If they do not engage in the interaction style required in the workplace, they do not "fit in," but if they do, they are penalized for overstepping, for not being feminine enough, or for "trying too hard."[54]

A Culture of Commitment and Perceptions of Deviance

The tinkering work culture common in engineering may be obviously gendered, but work cultures can incite biases and disparate group outcomes even when the cultures themselves are not so obviously gendered or racialized. Several recent studies show how this can work.

Sociologist Catherine Turco studied work culture in leveraged buyout (LBO) firms, which use money raised from outside investors and debt borrowed against companies' future earnings to buy companies, hoping to then turn around and sell the companies at a profit.[55] The industry is overwhelmingly white and male (women are estimated at less than 10 percent; African Americans at much less that that). The typical LBO worker is highly compensated, with annual salaries in 2004 averaging $100,000 for new associates, $320,000 for mid-range principal/vice presidents, and $1,000,000 for general partners. Turco's study focused on the differences in experience between female associates and African American male associates at these firms. African American men reported feeling more comfortable performing in the sports-dominated culture at the firms, while women described not only feelings of exclusion from conversations, but also exclusion from events around sports, such as golf outings and basketball games.[56] This aspect of the work culture operated much like tinkering in the study of engineers by McIlwee and Robinson. LBO work culture has long revolved around highly masculinized interactional styles. LBO investors of the 1990s were characterized as "sharks" who went "big game hunting" to "ambush" and "rape" companies.[57]

Another part of Turco's study, though, involved a different aspect of the ideal worker norm in the LBO firms: commitment. Most participants in Turco's study described the ideal investor as not only aggressive, but also intensely committed to work. Indeed, when asked to describe the qualities of a good investor, participants' most common answer was dedication to work. Commitment seems like it might be a gender and race neutral expectation, but as it plays out biases enter the picture. The folks at the LBO firms saw women, particularly mothers, as less committed, across the board.[58] Indeed, a wealth of research shows that women suffer a motherhood penalty, a bias that disadvantages them at work.[59] Women who are mothers are generally perceived as less committed to work than their non-mother counterparts.

Sociologist Erin Reid's work adds to this research on the commitment norm by emphasizing the intersection between the organizational structures and systems that drive a firm's work culture and the identity management of individual employees.[60] Specifically, Reid chose a global consulting firm with a strong commitment norm (and a work culture built around it), and she studied how men and women managed their deviance from that norm. Her research is particularly helpful because it shows how systems can create and interact with work cultures (and biases) to produce discrimination and disadvantage.

Consulting is a notoriously demanding profession. Consulting firms like the one that Reid studied generally offer advisory services in multiple areas, for instance strategy, marketing, and finance, and they use small teams to complete projects over a period of time, usually weeks or months. At the firm that Reid studied, which she calls AGM, nearly all senior partners and leaders of the human resources group cited commitment and availability as attributes that distinguished successful from unsuccessful consultants. This norm was reinforced by the organization through the structure of work. Work at the firm was organized haphazardly, often around crisis situations with teams working late into the night. Partners would promise clients new work mid-project, and clients expected travel at short notice. Performance systems, too, enforced the norm. Consultants were evaluated based on multiple dimensions, including relational and analytical skills, but members of the HR department described what it takes to be a "good consultant" mostly around commitment and availability.

Reid found many men and women who thrived in the environment at AGM, who easily embraced the identity of the ideal worker committed to the firm, willing to work late, with harried hours, and to travel at a client's "whim." More than half of the people she interviewed, however, expressed conflict between the work culture (what Reid calls "expected professional identity") and their own professional identities. Moreover, men and women fell equally into this group. What differed between the men and women whom Reid interviewed was their willingness and ability to hide their deviance from the norm. Reid found that more women than men at the firm revealed their deviance to senior members of the firm, often by taking advantage of formal accommodations, like parental leave or part-time schedules. Eighty percent of women who strayed from the ideal (failed to perform work culture demands) ultimately revealed their deviance to senior members of the firm. The strategies of the men who "strayed," as Reid puts it, were more evenly split, with some hiding their deviance from senior management and others revealing it. Importantly, Reid notes that one reason for this difference "may be that mothers were targeted by AGM's formal accommodation policies and thus tended to gravitate toward these policies. Men, however, were not targeted and instead tended to experiment with informal strategies for straying."[61]

Similar dynamics may be in play in the creation of racial stratification in many low-wage work sectors, like poultry processing. There, Latino workers are perceived as the "good" workers, and black workers as the "bad" workers. Because the Latino population in these low-wage jobs is often undocumented, black workers may have more formal organizational rights (and perceive them-selves as having more rights), albeit mandated by law, which may contribute to the managers' racially skewed biases around complaint, "attitude," and what makes a good or bad worker.[62]

Professionals, Connections, and Acquiring Clients and Cases

We also know something of the difficulties that women and black professionals can experience in law firms and finance companies, high-paying fields historically dominated by white men. Like Randall Kingsley at Large Company X, they have difficulty getting help and mentors and are assigned work outside their field of expertise. Some of the partners thought Kingsley just did not "fit in." He was "too flashy" and "too demanding." Similar comments were made about Ellen Pao at Kleiner Perkins.

Of course, not all problems of individual fit are racial or gendered (just as not every woman who is called abrasive is necessarily being more harshly judged or judged according to stereotypes). But whether someone "fits" or is promotion material at a firm often depends on the pervading work cultures, and those cultures are affected by the structures, policies, and practices that are instituted by the organization. A closer look at the work dynamics at Merrill Lynch, the financial services firm sued in 2005 for race-based discrimination, sheds light on the ways in which these organization-created structures and cultures can operate together to disadvantage women and racial minorities.

Here, we can see that the culture is operating to define and shape not just how workers should act if they want to fit in (and succeed) at a firm, but how workers are treated and evaluated within a system for pay and promotion. Sociologist William Bielby served as an expert witness for the plaintiffs during the class certification stage of the *McReynolds* v. *Merrill Lynch* case, and in a subsequent academic article he described the pay systems, work structures, and other organizational practices that may have contributed to the substantial disparities in pay at the company.[63] He based his description on company documents, statistical reports, and testimony of some of the company's managers and executives obtained during the early stages of the litigation.[64]

Like other large brokerage firms in the United States, Merrill Lynch used a commission-based pay system for its financial advisors that was linked to the fees generated by client transactions. As a financial advisor's production increased, so did the rate of payout. Higher producing financial advisors also received greater access to training programs and other resources, which meant that the highest producers had the greatest firm support for improving their effectiveness and increasing their productivity even more.

Merrill Lynch also used a team-based structure for organizing work. It had formal policies authorizing the teams, and it had a corporate department supporting them. From 2000 to 2003, the percentage of financial advisors on teams went from 20 percent to more than 40 percent. As Bielby explains, "Under a team arrangement, multiple [financial advisors] pooled at least a third of their production under a single pool number, with a prearranged split of the production being allocated to the individual team. Teams could range from simple 50/50 partnerships between a pair of financial advisors to a larger and more structured arrangement in which a team head oversaw multiple financial advisors who covered particular clients and specialties."[65] Firm documents "showed that brokers who were part of teams were generally more successful than those working alone, especially for those financial advisors who were in the early years of their careers with the company."[66] A Merrill Lynch executive responsible for managing the financial advisor workforce explained that teams included benefits such as improvements in client service, client acquisition, production, assets under management and "lifestyle advantage," such as coverage for another team member when a financial advisor is away from the office.

Merrill Lynch did not require formation of teams. High-level executives at the firm considered the pay and team process race-neutral and meritocratic. Executives described the process by which teams were formed as analogous to the process of forming a marriage and insisted that it was not company policy to force "arranged marriages."[67]

At the same time, Merrill Lynch was implementing programs that tended to reinforce common assumptions about racial minorities and their value to the firm. In fall 2001, the brokerage division at Merrill Lynch launched its multicultural marketing project, which was to "partner" with the firm's broader diversity efforts. The head of each of the multicultural marketing groups was matched to the race of the group to be targeted. According to the head of the project, race-matching was used in part because "communities are usually more likely to embrace one of their own."[68] Around the same time, the firm also instituted a "virtual teams" initiative through which financial advisors in different offices could work together on a specific client relationship. As part of the multicultural marketing project, the "virtual teams" were pitched as a way of reaching minority markets and therefore a place for diversity. According to a document prepared for an African American Financial Advisor Symposium held by the firm in 2005, "Diverse [financial advisor] teams ... raise the profile of Merrill Lynch in diverse communities that previously have been under penetrated but represent significant business opportunities." Diverse virtual teams, according to the document, can bring business from "nontraditional markets (e.g., athletes, entertainers, casino operators, et al.)."[69]

Black financial advisors participated in teams at Merrill Lynch at a much lower rate than did other financial advisors. From 2001 through 2006, black financial advisors also earned on average about 35 to 40 percent less than their white counterparts. One explanation for this difference links the prevailing work environment valuing racial minorities mostly for reaching minority markets (which on average are made up of smaller financial accounts) and assumptions about race-based network connections with the pay system and team-based structure.[70] The social science research on racial isolation, tokenism, and perceptions of "fit" discussed earlier add further support for this explanation.

As these examples illustrate, organizations' work cultures (from expectations of tinkering behaviors to talk of sports, commitment norms and deviance strategies, and "marriage"-like teaming behaviors) can operate together with organizations' structures and systems for conducting and rewarding work in ways that make it likely that biases will be triggered and that members of different racial and gender groups will be treated differently than their white, male counterparts. With this in mind, it is easier to see how the lack of a bathroom on a pole worker truck is problematic in the broader context of a work culture (endorsed and shaped by the employer) in which urinating in the open was common and breaks in town to use restrooms were not. Audrey Jo DeClue's attorneys saw her experience as harassment not because the organization at a high level acted with purpose to humiliate her but because the work culture interacted with the no-bathroom practice to incite biases and biased action. DeClue was treated differently at work, even if not with respect to the availability of a bathroom.

Work cultures are clearly the product of human relations, individual- and group-level struggles to define social norms, but they are also the product of organizational structures, systems, and values. Indeed, many of those very same structures that are interacting with work culture to produce disadvantage may be driving the work culture to begin with. And organizational leaders already understand this.

ORGANIZATIONS ALREADY ARE WORKING THEIR CULTURES

If they learn anything in business schools, business leaders in this country today know a lot about work culture and its influence on decision making and relations at work. As firms literally merge and shift in response to changing markets, culture is constantly on the business radar, and is itself a big business. Harvard Business School has no fewer than twenty professors who teach under the heading of "organizational behavior." And the turn over the past several decades has been decidedly toward a cultural, context-based approach to managing over the rigid systems view of the 1960s. Often called "corporate culture" in the business literature, culture is understood today to be a valuable managerial tool.

As the business literature reveals, managing culture is managing people, with particular attention to the context that organizations create for individuals to interact, strive, and succeed. Here is how Harvard professor Linda Hill and her colleagues describe the role of culture and context in leading innovative companies:

> Great leaders of innovation don't fit the conventional mold of "good" leadership. They're not visionaries who set direction and inspire others to follow. Instead, they create the context in which others are both willing and able to innovate. As one leader said, "My job is to set the stage, not to perform on it."[71]

Hall knows that context often drives individual and group action within that context. One recent *Harvard Business Review* article outlines several principles to help organizations to manage (and change) work cultures for their competitive advantage.[72] The authors gives this advice:

> [I]magine how people would act if your company were at its best, especially if their behavior supported your business objectives … Say your organization

is a former utility or government agency interested in becoming a better service business. If it excelled at service, how would people treat customers differently? What kinds of interactions would be visible in any new offices you opened? How would employees propose new ideas or evaluate one another? How would they raise difficult issues or bring potential problems to others' attention? And how would employees react when they actually saw colleagues doing things differently?[73]

The authors include a sidebar with what they call "mechanisms for getting the most from your culture," and a list of formal and informal mechanisms relevant to building and changing culture. For example, "reporting structures," "decision rules and rights," "business processes and policies," "training, leadership," "internal communications," "councils and committees," and "company events" appear on the "formal" side, in addition to "performance management" and "compensation and rewards." The "informal" mechanisms side includes "behavior modeling by senior leaders," "internal, cross-organizational networks," "meaningful manager-employee connections," and "ad hoc gatherings."[74]

The recommendations of these business leaders focus on structural measures, measures that depend on organizational implementation, not on narrow complaint, policing, and discipline of individual employees. There may be a component that includes monitoring, but shaping culture goes well beyond individualized policing, and these business leaders know it.

Shaping culture is what executives at Wal-Mart were doing with their mandatory shift-break cheer, which still goes on in Wal-Marts across the world.[75] It is also what Home Depot did in the early to mid-2000s, when it hired and then instituted changes made by Bob Nardelli.[76] Nardelli is a former military, "command and control" guy who has used his culture tactics in several big companies, including General Electric, and he (with other high-level executives) made many changes at Home Depot, from hiring practices and management regimes to managerial slogans. He started hiring former soldiers, and putting them into leadership positions. In 2001, almost half of the people enrolled into Home Depot's store leadership program were junior military officers. Everyone at Home Depot is now ranked on the basis of specific performance metrics. Store managers were all given a booklet, dubbed "how to be orange every day," and were required to carry it in their apron at work.

We can debate whether Nardelli's culture work has been good for Home Depot, and for its employees as a whole, some of whom saw the new approach as creating a "culture of fear." Nor is it clear whether the new military-style management structures and systems will be better for women. A class of women sued Home Depot in 1994 alleging that the then decentralized, highly subjective management regime, together with pervasive stereotyping associated with women and certain floor and managerial positions, were resulting in discrimination in pay and promotion against female workers at Home Depot stores. In fact, one of the requirements of the settlement in the case was that Home Depot set up a more formal system for notifying workers of promotion and transfer opportunities.[77] There is less room for debate, though, over whether the structural and systemic moves implemented by Nardelli and others are changing the work culture at Home Depot. Surely they are, and they are changing it – and the organizational conditions as a whole – in ways that are likely to affect racial and gender biases and behavior, one way or another. Yet, given discrimination laundering, Nardelli and other executives at Home Depot are unlikely to have had equal opportunity and nondiscrimination on the table during strategic planning or assessment of the shift.

BEYOND POLICING: WHAT MEASURES SEEM TO WORK

There is not yet and probably will never be a list of ready-to-go, discrete measures that can be implemented across all organizations to reduce or minimize discrimination. We do know that, overall, organizational changes and efforts work best, not those that focus exclusively on changing individuals. Some policing of extreme behavior is necessary, and can be effective. A complaint system and meaningful investigation that includes monitoring for patterns and not just individualized inquiries can also be helpful, as can clear guidelines for certain easily identified and easily controlled types of behavior, like a ban on pornography and on the use of racial epithets. And a degree of formalization of key decisions, too, can be helpful. These types of individualized measures, however, should not be emphasized to the exclusion of larger organizational measures that shape the context for employee interaction and decision making on a day-to-day basis.

In addition to thinking about demographics, organizing work, and work cultures as organizational, contextual influences on biases and discrimination, several more specific context-focused measures emerge from the research as particularly promising for reducing or minimizing discrimination. Accountability and transparency are among them. Accountability in social psychology is usually defined as pressure to justify one's acts to other parties. A longstanding and growing body of research shows that when decision makers know that they will be held accountable – that they will have to justify their decisions as fair – bias is less likely to occur. This research offers support for some forms of formalization, as discussed in Chapter 5. Another kind of accountability, though, is more structural, aimed at linking a policy of nondis-crimination to practice more broadly within an organization. Research shows that structures establishing responsibility within an organization, such as diver-sity staff positions, diversity committees, and affirmative action plans, may be more successful than individually focused initiatives. Kalev and colleagues found, for example, significant increases in the share of women and racial minorities in management ranks after organizations instituted these kinds of structural responsibility measures.[78] Moreover, their study showed that these responsibility structures catalyzed the effectiveness of some of the other com-monly adopted, more individualized measures, such as training, performance evaluations, and networking and mentoring programs.

Along these lines, organizational reforms that engage managers in promot-ing diversity and that connect leaders with underrepresented groups are also promising. In another study, researchers showed that special recruitment out-reach programs and management-training programs had positive effects on the success of women and racial minorities, and they theorized that this was due to the fact that these measures are likely to foster management support for diversity.[79] Managers and high-level executives can become invested in the project that they have undertaken, leading to more earnest engagement and creativity in finding meaningful solutions as well as motivation to correct biases in individual decisions and behaviors.

Measures that increase transparency in systems and decision making also seem promising. Transparency in job openings and eligibility can operate as a shortcut around biased information networks. And transparency in decision making can also make managers accountable for their decisions, not through discretion control, but through knowledge that others will see their decisions and the effects of those decisions. The studies on accountability show that people tend to censor their own biases when they expect others to review their decisions. Transparency in pay can raise consciousness on the part of women and racial minorities while simultaneously creating accountability for those managers who are making the decisions.[80]

Recent research also suggests that integrated work teams in which peer-like collaboration is encouraged can reduce discrimination and lead to bet-ter career outcomes for women and racial minorities. As described earlier, the study by Laurel Smith-Doerr of the careers of women scientists found that women who worked in biotechnology firms, where scientists tended to interact on collaborative projects and were rewarded as a group and evaluated by their peers, were significantly more likely to attain supervisory positions than women who worked in academia, where scientists tended to adhere to rigid job categories, individual reward structures, and hierarchies.[81] And, as also mentioned, Smith-Doerr's findings are consistent with a recent nation-wide study across nine industries finding that women and minorities were more likely to be promoted into managerial ranks in firms that adopted cross-boundary work teams – work teams that bring together workers from different jobs on a regular basis to share information and participate in decision mak-ing – than in firms that did not adopt those types of team.[82] Training programs that involved job rotation also led to greater success for women and minorities than programs that focused on in-job training. Even physical environments – whether the open-room concept of a start-up technology firm, or the secretary cubicles of a law firm, or the location and availability of a lunch room in either – can affect patterns of interaction and interactions themselves.

An organization's overall approach to diversity – sometimes called its "diver-sity narrative" – makes a difference, too. Most organizations will frame their approach to diversity in a certain way, often in human resources materials and promotional materials. This diversity narrative is the firm's message about how best to approach and experience diversity in the workplace. It is a message sig-naled internally to employees and externally to clients and applicants, and it also serves as a guiding ideology for those people designing and implementing practices and policies. Research shows here that a narrative that focuses on "integration and learning" – valuing diversity as an avenue for thinking about how to organize and carry out work together – is more likely to enhance group functioning and to reduce stereotype threat than either of the more com-monly adopted narratives, colorblindness ("We don't see race and sex and our employees shouldn't either") or multiculturalism ("We celebrate difference and our employees should be tolerant of differences").[83] In an integration and learning environment, biases in interactions are more likely to be called out, and addressed, than ignored or reinforced.

None of this research tells organizations exactly what to do, which boxes to check to have successfully accomplished an end-goal of minimized dis-crimination in their workplaces, once and for all. The research simply does not reveal a list of specific, discrete measures that must (or can) be adopted and implemented in all organizations. We can glean from the research which measures are promising, and which are less so, and we can identify some that warrant particular concern. But we cannot devise a recipe for success for all employers, at least not yet, from the social science research alone.

This said, there are unquestionably success stories, some initiated in col-laboration with social scientists, others initiated by the private sector, such as the Women's Initiative begun in 1991 by Mike Cook, then Chairman and CEO of Deloitte & Touche, and still others initiated by settlement negoti-ations sparked by litigation, like the lawsuit against Home Depot in the early 1990s.[84] What all of these stories have in common is not a specific measure adopted – each firm adopted different measures – but an ongoing commitment to assessment and action.[85]

Take Deloitte & Touche as an example. Deloitte & Touche was hiring women at the same rate as men for ten years going into the early 1990s, but women were leaving at much higher rates than men, leaving women at just 10 percent of the candidates for partner in 1991, and projections for future years were no better.[86] The firm created a Task Force, with Mike Cook at the helm, and it hired an outside consultant, the nonprofit research organization Catalyst. Catalyst surveyed people at the firm and identified three problem areas, and at the top was a male-dominated work environment that skewed women's experiences toward the negative and affected women's ability to get the same opportunities as their male counterparts. One partner at the time explained it this way:

> The pervasive issue was people in leadership positions in our firm – then they were exclusively male – making assumptions about women, like "I wouldn't want to put her on that kind of client because it's a dirty manufacturing environment, and that's just not the right place for her," or "That client's in a really nasty part of town." Or making assumptions on behalf of the client, like "Well, that client's not really going to be comfortable with her." If you asked the people who were doing that if they were doing that, I think they'd say no. It was very subliminal and unconscious, but it was happening a lot. So women were deciding not to stay with the firm and then men were saying, "See, I told you so." It all sounds much more conscious and Machiavellian than it was, but that was going on.[87]

Another partner described some of the subtle differences in evaluations of men and women: "A woman was found a little bit short, and we [male partners] didn't see how she was going to get there. A man was found a little bit short, but we could figure out how he was going to get there ... because he looked like me, and I knew what I looked like five years ago and I grew into this."[88]

Concretely, the firm appointed an external advisory group, the "Council on Advancement of Women" Task Force, instituted a workshop aimed at exploring differences in perception between men and women in the workplace, required annual assignment reviews to see whether women were attaining some of the top assignments, and reviewed its policies and practices for gender bias, such as policies of reimbursing for lunches at all-male clubs and bending to client requests for male consultants. Over time, it also reorganized its work and travel expectations from a five-day-away to a three-day-away cycle. By 1995, the percentage of women admitted to partner rose from 8 percent in

1991 to 21 percent, and the turnover rate for female senior managers dropped from 26 percent in 1992 to 15 percent.[89]

Google and some of the other major tech firms in Silicon Valley might also turn out to be success stories for organizational nondiscrimination. Google put nondiscrimination squarely – and publicly – on its corporate agenda after it released data on the makeup of its workforce in May of 2014. The company released the data under intense public pressure after years of declaring the data a "trade secret." As predicted, the data revealed a dismal picture. It showed that men made up 83 percent of Google's global tech force and 79 percent of its managers. Overall, seven out of ten people who worked at Google in 2013 were male, and at Google U.S., 61 percent of employees were white, 30 percent were Asian, and only 3 percent and 2 percent were Hispanic and black, respectively.[90]

Google pledged to do better, and set out on a campaign to change its numbers, and specifically to change the organization in ways that would reduce the occurrence of discrimination within the firm. The bias-busting workshop put on by Brian Welle, Google's director of people analytics, was probably the most publicized move taken by Google, but even that workshop indicates that Google executives – or at least Welle – understand that shifting a culture to reduce discrimination is about organizational changes as much as it is about individual awareness and vigilance. In his workshop, a video of which was released to the public, Welle stresses that Google is focusing on organizational solutions, such as changes to the physical environment at Google (adding, for example, several women to the names of scientists adorning work rooms), changes to job interviewing practices and job descriptions, changes to social networks within Google, and changes to the Google work culture that all go beyond increased policing and self-cabining of bias.[91]

The Deloitte & Touche Initiative did not end in the 1990s, and nor should the Google effort, even once it has increased the numbers of women and racial minorities working at Google and rising to top positions. Indeed, success in nondiscrimination by organizations requires that nondiscrimination be constantly on the agenda, building in assessment and, if needed, more change. The quieter success stories, of course, involve organizations that have always made nondiscrimination a priority and have devised organizational structures and practices from the outset with nondiscrimination in mind. Even these organizations, though, will have to monitor and assess the efficacy of their practices, just as they assess the efficacy of the rest of their business practices. What all of these companies have in common – including those who have undertaken efforts in response to litigation, so long as the effort continues beyond the settlement agreement – is an ongoing commitment to addressing discrimination at a structural level into the future, to assessing, devising, and implementing measures aimed at systems and practices as well as cultures, assessing again, and revising.

Not all organizations are involved in consciously capitalizing on race and sex, just as not all organizations are inciting widespread discrimination. But organizations generally are active participants in discrimination and nondiscrimination – two sides of the same coin. The social science research provides no single solution for all organizations, no single recipe that all organizations can follow. Instead, organizations need to put nondiscrimination on the agenda, examine their own practices and policies, those practices and policies that create the conditions for workplace interaction, and then make changes so that they are minimizing discrimination rather than inciting it.

PART III

Reversing Discrimination Laundering

7

Reversing Discrimination Laundering

We often tell our stories of discrimination by recounting individual encounters and incidents: The time a boss or co-worker told a racial joke, or the time the guys took a client to a strip bar. Individuals and their stories bring the problem of discrimination to life. Randall Kingsley, Ellen Pao, Lilly Ledbetter, Maetta Vance, Audrey Jo DeClue, and Kerry Woods are some of the people that are likely to come to mind from the stories that I have told in this book. And their stories are told in part by recounting their interactions and relationships with other people in their workplaces. Lilly Ledbetter's supervisor who falsified deficiency reports about her work after she rejected his sexual advances, for example, or Ray Lane's request that Ellen Pao take notes during a meeting, and Chuck Wolfe's sexualized harassing of Kerry Woods.

The same is true of many of our personal encounters with and perceptions of discrimination. When people learn what I do – that I am a law professor – and what I specialize in – employment discrimination law – they tend to get self-conscious. "Can I use profanity?" they ask. Or, "Is it okay that I just referred to him as a cheap Jew if I am also Jewish?" And, "Do you object if I call a woman judge 'pretty'"? Most whites will not even mention race to me (a white woman), although research shows that individual behavior dominates whites' thinking there, too.

At the same time, researchers have identified a range of behaviors that are perceived by racial minorities as racially biased or discriminatory. Questions about hair, telling a black woman that she does not "seem black," mistaking a Latino man or Latina woman for a service worker or more subordinate employee, mistaking one black person for another, laughing at a racial joke. All of these behaviors might reasonably be perceived as racially biased.[1] A similar list for gender might include behaviors from the more obvious, like attending strip clubs during work hours, to the more subtle, like ignoring contributions in meetings and commenting on appearance. In addition, behaviors that "minimize the psychological thoughts, feelings, or experiences," such as suggesting that concerns expressed by racial minorities and women about perceived discrimination or bias are overblown or exaggerated (e.g., are "playing the race card"), can also be reasonably perceived by women and racial minorities as discriminatory.[2]

We *should* be concerned about our individual behaviors and how they are perceived by others, just as we *should* be alert to behaviors that we perceive as biased or discriminatory. But it is easy for us to lose the organizations in the telling of our stories and in the worrying about our behaviors. From sexualized dominance on segregated oil rigs and construction sites to subtle bias around "fit" across a broad range of jobs, we tend to isolate individuals in our stories of discrimination (as victims and as discriminators) to the exclusion of the organizations in which interactions take place. Organizations are seen as the innocent bystanders to discrimination. And when organizations are brought into these stories, they are seen as merely secondary actors – we talk of retaliation and cover ups, and organizations' failure to police and punish individual wrongdoers.

Neglecting the direct influence of organizations in our stories of employment discrimination – the ways in which organizations through their choices of systems, practices, rules, and cultures incite discrimination in day-to-day interactions as well as in key employment decisions – is a critical mistake. Discrimination laundering builds from the frame of organizational innocence, and also feeds it. The EEOC and private litigants alike tend to devise solutions in settlement decrees that focus on grievance procedures, training, and insulating key moments of managerial decision making from bias.[3] These solutions are all aimed at individuals and individual moments of decision making rather than at the organizational context in which day-to-day interactions take place. Diversity training in many of its common forms ratchets up resistance and emphasizes individual behavior over all else. The laundered workplace tamps down on individuals, as victims and as perpetrators of discrimination, and leaves vast swaths of discrimination largely unaddressed.

Indeed, tamping down on individuals makes bias-reducing intergroup interactions less rather than more likely. Avoidance and colorblindness are common coping strategies for whites who fear being labeled prejudiced, just as perceptions of bias drive racial minorities to avoid or minimize interactions with whites. Yet what we need is more conversation, not less. We need to talk about our perceptions, the ambiguities in our behaviors, and our discomfort.

We need to be open to making mistakes and to learning from difference in our interactions. As two social scientists recently put it:

> Perhaps the single most important problem facing us over time is that we are afraid to communicate. So many people are afraid to say "I don't know how to do it." They tell their friends about the difficulties they encounter, but they don't tell minority group members. Many minority group members are reluctant to educate majority group members. These are issues that we have to put on the table and try to work through as interaction partners if we are ultimately going to solve the problem of intergroup tension. Then we can learn, together, to navigate this rocky road.[4]

Organizationally, providing space for conversation and learning means going beyond individuals and individual policing. In an edition of the *Harvard Business Review*, authors presented a fictional case study involving a relational incident at an accounting firm.[5] A black man working at the firm had decided to go into the office to work on a Sunday morning, as did a white woman partner at the firm. He arrived at the parking garage just behind the woman, and he skirted through the gate behind her without pulling his access card. She explains that she was afraid when she saw a man entering without a card (as she says she would have been regardless of his race), so she stopped him and asked him to show his credentials. He perceived the request as racially biased and later called the managing partner. What came next went well beyond the two individuals involved in the incident. The company seemed to be "splitting into two angry camps" with some charging the company as racist and others outraged that the woman was made to feel unsafe.

The case study solicits responses from several experts, asking what the managing partner should do. Among the contributors is diversity scholar and Harvard Business School professor Robin Ely, who starts by pointing out that the response from others at the firm and even of the individuals involved reveals that "the incident in the parking lot is much larger than a conflict between two people."[6] She has this advice for the managing partner: meet with the individuals to hear their stories, and then implement an organizational intervention that facilitates conversations and data gathering more broadly about how members of different racial and ethnic groups experience their work and relationships in the firm, and, importantly, tie these efforts to the work of the organization, to creating a "more effective workforce" that advances the organization's mission. She goes on to explain:

> Let me be clear about this organizational effort. The primary goal is not for white people to learn how to be more sensitive in interactions with their colleagues of color. Nor is it for people of color to learn how to be less sensitive

to perceived slights so that they might be less likely to be derailed by them. Nor is it for [the organization] to ensure that such events never occur again – though there may be gains in all these areas. The goal is for all employees to learn how to discuss these events openly and constructively, with as little defensiveness, blame, and judgment as possible, when they do occur. Because in a culture such as ours, these kinds of events undoubtedly will occur, no matter how sensitized or desensitized people may become.[7]

Ely does not have all the answers for this firm, and she actually treads quite softly when it comes to any structural changes that might be necessary, too softly in my view. Her response nonetheless rightly emphasizes that nondiscrimination on the part of organizations requires an organizational effort, one aimed at structural sources, including organizational culture, not one focused narrowly on tamping down on individuals and eliminating unpleasant relational incidents.

We cannot and should not deny that discrimination is a human problem, a problem of cognitive biases, and also of individual and group-based insecurity and desire for power. Retaining a law that acknowledges context beyond policing of individuals, indeed accepting that race- and gender-based tensions can exist even in a nondiscriminatory work environment, is not an embrace of post-racialism/sexism, or an attempt to ignore the micro-relational aspects of discrimination. The idea instead is to pull our individual interactions into a broader awareness and conversation – to learn from our differences – and, yes, our biases – without triggering animosity and avoidance.

CONTEXT MATTERS

There is an alternate frame. Early thinking in employment discrimination law tended to see beyond individuals to the organizations in which those individuals acted. Over the past several decades, moreover, scholars of organizational misconduct have adopted an increasingly situationist approach to wrongdoing. This model acknowledges that wrongdoing can be driven by context and that it can occur even absent individual, amoral actors.[8]

Police brutality is one area receiving increasing attention to context..[9] Professor Erwin Chemerinsky, for example, took a situationist approach to organizational wrongdoing in his critique of efforts to reduce misconduct by officers in the Los Angeles Police Department (LAPD).[10] In his independent analysis of the Board of Inquiry Report, issued in response to a corruption scandal discovered in the late 1990s within the LAPD, Chemerinsky pointed to a lack of attention to the culture of the LAPD as an organization and its failure to identify structural solutions. Commentators (and the U.S. Justice

Department) have since followed Chemerinsky's lead with proposals for a new paradigm of police governance that focuses on contextual change. As law professor Samuel Walker describes the new approach, it emphasizes the systematic collection and analysis of data for identifying problems and "changing police organizations, as opposed to pursuing individual officers guilty of misconduct."[11]

After the 2014 police officer shooting of Michael Brown in Ferguson, Missouri, the U.S. Department of Justice released a report identifying broader contextual sources of the problem of bias and brutality in the Ferguson Police Department.[12] In addition to citing the department's failure to respond meaningfully to citizen complaints, the report cited the city's emphasis on revenue generation and the police department's culture in which officers were pressured to write tickets (to be "productive") regardless of public safety and in which officers expected and demanded compliance even when they lacked legal authority to do so.[13] Changes proposed by the report included the implementation of a "robust system of true community policing," and "[f]ocusing stop, search, ticketing and arrest practices on community protection" as well as the usual improvement of supervision and training of officers and response to citizen complaint.[14] Moreover, the proposed changes included some in other areas of city governance, including the courts and the city practices that contributed to a police culture that emphasized revenue generation over community service.[15]

We can do the same for employment discrimination by telling the larger story of how discrimination operates within organizations. Take two seemingly different scenarios. The first involves extreme sexual harassment, including rape and physical assault, of female workers in the American agriculture industry. The EEOC recently sued several large agriculture firms for this harassment and obtained consent decrees, which were hailed as a success against discrimination. The agriculture harassment cases brought by the EEOC, however, fit perfectly into a story of organizational innocence, where the organization's sole responsibility is to make complaints feasible for victims and to respond adequately to any individual complaints. In each of the lawsuits, the EEOC highlighted the high-level organizational actors who retaliated against the women who complained or who ignored women's complaints. The solutions identified in the settlement decrees mimic this story. They include employee training on employment discrimination laws and posting a notice of employees' rights to be free of harassment and retaliation.[16]

The law should require the basic measures being sought in these extreme harassment cases, but the framing of the cases as exclusively individualized sexual harassment (and of employer wrong lying solely in failure to adequately police individuals doing the harassing) misses the many possible structural sources of discrimination and harassment against women in the fields, such as the length of work hours, schedules, geographic isolation, and the work culture more generally. Given the kinds of extreme sexual assault taking place in some of these organizations, we might expect that the organizations are inciting discrimination and harassment – different treatment driven by bias and stereotyping – in other ways as well. Men hold the supervisory and high-level positions in most meat-packing and agricultural firms, while female and male immigrants cut the chickens and work the fields. Even at the lowest levels, men take home more pay than their female counterparts. One estimate puts the average income for female crop workers in 2011 at $11,250 per year, and for men at $16,250.[17] There is every reason to believe that these disparities are related to the high levels and extreme forms of harassment in the jobs, and our stories and solutions should be pushing change in these broader conditions, not just in systems for reporting and policing harassment that takes place.

The second scenario involves the more subtle discrimination of the type that women at Kleiner Perkins and other venture capital firms in Silicon Valley may be experiencing, or of the kind that Randall Kingsley and other black lawyers at Large Company X may have experienced. Here, too, the law of discrimination tends to focus on individual moments, when it should also (or instead) be looking for bigger patterns that indicate that biases are operating against women or racial minorities as a group. If Ellen Pao or Randall Kingsley can convince a jury that the relational moments that they experienced resulted in job detriment – the denial of a promotion, for example – then they should be provided individualized relief. But the inquiry should not end there, regardless of whether individualized discrimination is proved. The law should incentivize organizations to pay attention to patterns of success of women and racial minorities in their firms and to examine whether their organizational practices are inciting bias and discrimination.

In short, what we need is for the law to incentivize attention to primary organizational sources of discrimination. When we ask the question, "What can employers do to avoid discrimination?" we need to widen the lens of our response, while at the same time tempering our expectations for individuals who are struggling to overcome their biases and to interact in productive ways across group boundaries. Our goal should not be to avoid every instance of expressed bias, of misunderstanding, of discomfort around race and sex in daily interactions at work. Harassing behavior should be identified and addressed, but as a general rule employers need not install video surveillance, indeed should not be monitoring and policing every micro-social exchange. Instead, they should be monitoring for patterns – patterns of behavior, and of outcome – that signal that discrimination is operating within their workplaces and they should be devising and implementing structural and systemic measures that can reduce or avoid it.

HOW TO DO IT: A BETTER PATH FOR THE LAW

Knowing what we need is only part of the answer. Knowing how to do it – and understanding the role of law in incentivizing organizational behavior – is the other part. Bringing organizations back in does not solve all of the difficult questions about what the law should look like. It does, however, lead to several legal recommendations with an aim toward structuring the law to incentivize organizational attention to organizational causes of discrimination.

Individual Discrimination Law – Recommendations

Resist Efforts to Create a Second Layer of Liability Protection Around Complaint and Response

Individual discrimination law should hold employers strictly liable for proven discrimination. The law of complaint and response that has been building since well before *Faragher* and *Burlington Industries* can be easily and sensibly disrupted with this simple legal change. Employers can and should implement processes for victims' and others' complaints about discrimination and for investigating allegedly discriminatory incidents, but the law should not protect organizations from liability merely because these processes are in place. To do so puts too much emphasis on those systems of policing and not enough emphasis on other – often more effective – ways of reducing discrimination.

Reverting to a scheme of vicarious liability for individualized discrimination poses little in the way of practical difficulty. A system that imposes vicarious liability on employers for proven individual instances of discrimination makes sense in light of Title VII's goal of providing relief to victims of discrimination and putting pressure on employers to reduce discrimination. It is consistent with the statutory text of Title VII, the legislative and social history of Title VII, and also makes pragmatic sense.[18]

Acknowledge the Limits of Individual Discrimination Law

Individual discrimination law alone cannot adequately address discrimination in the U.S. workplace. Acknowledging this reality may help redirect some of the intense focus on individual discrimination law. Individual cases can be

difficult for plaintiffs to win, but not all of the doctrinal hurdles that plaintiffs face are misguided. Some of the hurdles are practical limits of litigation
seeking to address individualized discrimination. Of course, the hurdles that
plaintiffs face extend beyond the legal doctrine to availability and affordability
of legal representation and even judicial bias.[19] But these hurdles are unlikely
to change with small doctrinal changes in individual discrimination law.

Plaintiffs bringing individualized claims often talk of making an impact for
members of their group more broadly, of hoping, for example, that success in
an individualized lawsuit, as Lilly Ledbetter said, will mean that "the women
working at Goodyear and other places would be safe from being harassed and
underpaid."[20] Sometimes single plaintiffs suing for individualized justice do
make substantial headway for the nation as a whole. The private attorney general component of Title VII rightly buttresses this perception. But research
shows quite starkly that individualized adjudication is not likely to achieve
much for either individuals or groups. Individual claims have a very low likelihood of success in court, and individual plaintiffs report deep dissatisfaction
with their experiences, even when they win relatively large monetary awards.[21]

Taking the pressure off individual discrimination claims by acknowledging
the limits of those claims – and understanding them as a limited avenue for
substantial change – could result in greater satisfaction with the internal and
external processes of adjudicating individualized complaints (and also in
fewer individual discrimination claims being filed). Plaintiffs would continue
to seek individualized justice, of course, but they would go into individualized
litigation with a more realistic sense of their likelihood of success. Indeed, a
concerted focus on systemic claims over individual ones has the potential to
spark a reframing of not only what we hope to achieve from litigation, but
also of our personal stories and perceptions of how discrimination operates. It
could change our experience of discrimination to be less individualized.

Systemic Discrimination Law – Recommendations

Resist the Individualizing of Systemic Discrimination Law

A context model of organizational wrongdoing helps make clear why entity liability for systemic disparate treatment is direct rather than vicarious. The employer is being held responsible for something that *it* has done. Importantly,
moreover, the employer's responsibility under this model turns not on iden-
tification of a single instance or even multiple specific instances of discrimination; rather, responsibility turns on the employer's own role in producing
discrimination within its walls.

Instead of focusing directly on the question of whether the entity has produced or is producing discrimination, systemic disparate treatment law identifies those organizations in which discrimination is the regular rather than the unusual practice. When discrimination is not regular within the organization, then it is difficult to say that the employer is doing anything wrong apart from identifiable acts of discrimination by individuals (for which it should be held vicariously liable under individual discrimination law). But when discrimination becomes the regular rather than the unusual practice within an organization, then based on the vast social science research on contextual influence, it is reasonable to infer that the entity is doing something to produce decisions based on race or sex or other protected characteristics within its organization. A practice of regular, systemic disparate treatment, in other words, is unlikely to be the result of select rogue individuals acting on biases wholly uninfluenced by the work cultures, practices, and norms of the organization.

Systemic discrimination law is needed to identify those organizations in which discrimination is widespread – and to incentivize structural solutions. Systemic disparate treatment law (much more so than individual disparate treatment law) puts pressure on all organizations to place nondiscrimination on the business agenda. The people sitting around the table making policy and formulating mechanisms for culture change should have on their minds the firm's obligation not to discriminate. And they should be expected to consider the entire toolkit, structural, system, and culture change as mechanisms for reducing and minimizing discrimination, not just individual policing.

Resist the Theory Switch

Systemic disparate treatment law shares with disparate impact law the understanding that high-level executives need not intend to keep women and racial minorities down (or even act with bias) in order for an employer to be responsible for system-wide discrimination. Inciting widespread bias and discrimination that is resulting in disparate outcomes is enough. Disparate impact law, however, goes further, holding employers responsible for use of practices that have a disparate impact on a protected group even when bias is not operating within the organization. The bias may be operating outside the workplace, or there may be no bias at all. Imagine a height and weight requirement, for example, that screens out more women than men and that is adopted with genuine belief that larger people will be better able to do the job. Disparate impact law therefore requires isolation of a specific practice that the employer is using and proof that that practice is causing the impact. Disparate impact law also offers employers an affirmative defense, allowing them to continue to use a practice even when it has a disparate impact so long as the employer can show that the practice is job related and consistent with business necessity. In this way, disparate impact law homes in on a specific practice, both in requiring proof that a practice has a disparate impact and in deciding whether the use of the practice is unlawful, including whether there is another practice with a lesser impact that the employer refused to adopt.

Systemic disparate treatment law, on the other hand, asks whether discrimination is widespread within an organization, incentivizing a more holistic assessment of the relational dynamics and contextual causes of those dynamics. Some practices can be easily isolated from others in a workplace. A high-school diploma requirement, for example, or a pen-and-paper test can often be easily analyzed using disparate impact theory. But many practices cannot be so easily isolated. Take the team-forming and account distribution policies identified by Judge Posner in *McReynolds* v. *Merrill Lynch*. Framing that case as one of disparate impact, a court would have to decide whether the employer's reliance on the subjectivity exercised by brokers in forming teams is legally permissible, and to do this the court would have to look at the decision-making system as a whole and the workplace culture in which the practice is being carried out. The question, in other words, will not be whether a practice in isolation (e.g., allowing teams in Merrill Lynch or subjectivity in decision making generally) is job related and consistent with business necessity. Instead, the question will be one of whether the employer has instituted sufficient safeguards against bias and differential treatment as part of its use of the practice.

Framing the case as one of systemic disparate treatment, in contrast, a judge in the *McReynolds* case would be asked to decide whether discrimination (biased decision making against members of a protected group) is widespread within the organization. The judge would likely make her determination based on statistical analyses of pay and promotion and any other evidence (including social science expert testimony) tending to show or undermine a showing that any observed disparities are likely due to legitimate factors, or to chance.

Notice also the role that social science plays in each of these approaches.[22] Under disparate impact law, judges must rely on social scientists in order to come to a liability decision. Just as experts argue about pen-and-paper test validation, battling experts in a case like *McReynolds*, after examining the entirety of the organization's relevant practices, systems, and cultures in light of existing research, would testify as to what more the organization could do to reduce bias in its employment decisions. The final normative or legal question would remain for the court: If more can be done, then is the cost of doing more too much such that use of the existing practice "as is" is permissible, even given a disparate impact, or is the employer required to alter its use of the practice (or the context in which the practice is being used)? Without social science as an initial matter, however, it is difficult to see how a court could reliably discern the alternatives from which to make a final legal determination of permissibility/liability as to any particular practice.

A systemic disparate treatment approach, in contrast, does not embed social science testimony into a judge's fact finding. The judge might rely on social science testimony as evidence of whether widespread discrimination is a likely explanation for observed disparities, but the judge would not need to rely on social science testimony in every case.

Organizations seeking to avoid liability under threat of systemic disparate treatment law are also left with leeway to devise solutions that are best tailored to their organizational goals in addition to the Title VII nondiscrimination goal. Merrill Lynch, for example, might decide to retain its team-forming and account distribution policies but alter its multicultural marketing project and make changes to its corporate support structures for the teams and/or implement new mechanisms to generate stronger work-based lines between advisors of all racial groups. Indeed, this is exactly what the firm agreed to do in a settlement agreement approved by the court in 2013. Merrill Lynch did not agree to eliminate its practice of relying on teams.[23] Instead, it undertook measures to increase the numbers of black brokers on the teams (and changed its account distribution practice temporarily to allow them to join those teams and then more equitably share in the account distributions). It also hired experts to evaluate the team and account distribution practices, presumably as they operate in the context of specific offices and the firm as a whole. Wal-Mart similarly might decide to devise criteria for its manager's pay and promotion decisions but otherwise leave some subjectivity and institute mechanisms aimed at generating a work culture less rife with sex stereotypes.[24]

Organizations will have to self-monitor to determine if their measures and changes are working, but they retain flexibility in devising mechanisms for minimizing discrimination that are most in line with their broader business mission and practices. My point is not that there is a single or best answer for either of these organizations, or any others. Quite the opposite. Systemic disparate treatment law puts the project to the organizations and asks them to put nondiscrimination firmly on their agendas.

Proceed with Caution in Considering an Employer Defense in Systemic Disparate Treatment Law

Once we see that cases like *McReynolds* and *Wal-Mart* are likely to be better suited to systemic disparate treatment law than to disparate impact law, the

question often arises whether systemic disparate treatment law should build in
a defense or "safe harbor" for those employers who have "done enough" and
yet whose workplaces still exhibit widespread discrimination. Several legal
scholars have argued that an employer in a case such as *Wal-Mart* v. *Dukes*
should be free from liability if the employer can show that, as one author
puts it, "it made substantial compliance efforts, even if those efforts have not
eliminated inequalities."[25] Another author argues that "conscientious effort
to prevent discrimination might serve as an affirmative defense to liability"
for widespread discrimination, explaining that to meet this defense, "the
employer, at a minimum, should be required to show that it followed the best
practices in the industry to correct the vulnerability of its employment procedures to sexism."[26]

Putting aside the endorsement of organizational innocence that the framing "vulnerability of its employment procedures to sexism" implies, the
problem with this "done enough" or "best practices" defense is twofold. First,
and most fundamentally, it assumes that social scientists can provide generalized recommendations that apply easily across organizations and industries to
reduce discrimination. On the contrary, this expectation – at least at this point
in time – is unrealistic. The literature on bias and organizational behavior
suggests that mechanisms for reducing discrimination are inextricably intertwined with particular organizational context, including workplace culture,
and are dependent on effective implementation by each organization.[27]

This gets us to the second problem. If the law, whether through administrative agencies or judicial decision making, cannot identify specific, discrete
practices that will minimize discrimination across all organizations, then the
likely result of creating a "best practices" or "done enough" defense will insulate organizations from liability (and legal pressure) without any reduction in
discrimination on the ground. Organizations will do those things that they can
most easily and cheaply do as a signal of compliance, and courts will defer to
those organizational structures, leaving widespread discrimination in place.[28]
Indeed, recent research shows that judges – conservative and liberal alike –
tend to defer to "best practices" structures in employment discrimination
cases, including formal antidiscrimination policies, standardized personnel
practices, progressive discipline policies, and training programs, without scrutinizing whether those structures are effective as implemented.[29] A best practices defense would only exacerbate this judicial tendency by making it part of
the legal standard for whether the employer should be held liable.

This does not mean that the EEOC and other intermediaries – public
interest organizations, insurance companies, lawyers drafting settlement
terms – should not try to identify practices that are good practices for most

organizations or give guidance generally to organizations seeking to minimize discrimination in their workplaces. Of course they should (and we might ask the EEOC to play more of a role in this enterprise). It means only that organizations should be expected to consider this guidance in light of their own structures, cultures, and systems to devise a path that best suits their own discrimination problems.

The "done enough" or "best practices" defense also buys into an old – and false – ineptitude trope: Organizations are at a loss when it comes to discrimination; they cannot figure out which of their practices are inciting discrimination and do not have the tools to make changes when they do. This is the trope that leads to concern about employers relying on quotas, to hiring on the basis of race or sex just to improve their bottom-line numbers, which would itself be a violation of Title VII. According to this line of thinking, Title VII presents a "catch 22" for employers: either they leave their highly stratified workplaces as they are, violating Title VII by maintaining a workplace which makes it virtually impossible for women and racial minorities to get ahead, or they engage in quota-based hiring and promotion to change their racial and gender demographics.

Professor Richard Ford notably takes this position, recently arguing that we should release organizations from the bind by "giving employers an objective target and then leaving them to decide how to meet it."[30] What Ford misses, though, is that this is largely what systemic disparate treatment law already does. It gives employers a target – that is, avoid widespread discrimination that leads to statistically significant disparities in success outcomes among groups – and it "leaves them to decide how to meet it,"[31] although the constraints of Title VII still apply. Most employers cannot lawfully institute quotas to improve their bottom-line numbers, for instance, nor can they provide signing bonuses only to women or to black recruits.[32] But organizations nonetheless have a vast realm within which they can experiment in formulating and implementing a plan to minimize discrimination – and they have many tools at their disposal, tools that allow them to obtain a good synergy between their nondiscrimination practices and their business practices as a whole.

Indeed, Ford's "catch-22," as he calls it, wildly overstates the bind that employers are in. Yes, employers have to act within the law when they devise and implement systemic solutions to their discrimination problems, and perhaps the law should provide greater flexibility to organizations that are implementing solutions to widespread discrimination,[33] but the law even as currently structured gives them substantial leeway. It is not a violation of Title VII to expand recruitment practices, to alter team assignment practices, to create opportunities for cross-group collaboration, or to take measures to shape work cultures in new directions that are bias-reducing rather than bias-producing. Nor should it be. And efforts to shrink this realm of employer action should be met with strong resistance. Moreover, the law does not expect organizations to eliminate discrimination and bias within their walls altogether. Rather, they need only minimize it so that it does not result in statistically significant disparities in success outcomes, disparities that can be attributed to bias operating within the organization.

We need to shake off this idea that organizations cannot effectively structure and manage their workforces in ways that minimize rather than incite discrimination.[34] Organizations are actively engaged in meeting expectations that require change in work practices and cultures in a variety of areas, from pharmaceutical development to innovation and use of technology. There is every reason to believe that when organizations set their priorities to include nondiscrimination and include organizational sources within the lens, they can and do make meaningful change without resorting to quotas. Linking individual complaint systems to equal opportunity monitoring will help organizations see what is going on within their walls. Social scientists, including those housed in business schools across the country, consultants who regularly devise and implement mechanisms for organizational, including culture, change, even experts within the EEOC, can work together with each other and with business organizations to devise programs for reform. And business leaders can share their successes, and sometimes even their failures, learning from each other just as they do in many other areas of business concern.[35]

Nor is there – nor should there be – some sort of a right to retain or experience racial or gendered work cultures, as some of the judges reviewing harassment cases involving more blue-collar work seem to think. The legislative history of Title VII and the Civil Rights Act more generally makes clear that Title VII was intended to disrupt racialized and gendered work cultures, to alter our workplaces and our workplace relations. This is exactly why it was so hotly contested; it undertook to interfere with what were considered to many "private" business decisions and "personal" relationships and longstanding work cultures. The carve-outs for very small businesses (those with fewer than fifteen employees) and certain private associations were limited carve-outs necessary precisely because it was well understood that the law was changing the practices of businesses that had been defended for years on personal-choice grounds. The drafters of Title VII may not have envisioned the specific forms of discrimination today, but they did envision an Act that would put pressure on employers to change their practices in substantial ways and in ways that would alter workplace cultures.[36]

Acknowledge that Systemic Disparate Treatment Law Provides Only Rough Justice for Individuals

As I have maintained throughout, claims of systemic disparate treatment do not aim to identify individualized moments of discrimination. Proof that discrimination is widespread within an organization tells us something about whether individuals in a group generally are likely to have experienced discrimination. It does not tell us with any certainty or even level of confidence which individuals in the group – which female employees at Wal-Mart, for example – experienced discrimination. In the same way that failure to show widespread discrimination does not foreclose a finding of discrimination in an individualized instance, a showing of a pattern or practice of discrimination does not prove that any particular individual experienced discrimination. This was what the Court meant in *McDonnell Douglas* when it said that statistics "while helpful, may not be in and of themselves controlling as to an individualized hiring decision."[37]

Understanding that systemic disparate treatment law provides only rough justice for individuals resolves some pressing procedural and remedial questions, and raises others. The Court and Congress will have to work together to correct those procedural decisions in which the Court has misunderstood the nature of systemic disparate treatment law, just as they will have to work together to redirect the substance of individual discrimination law away from a system of complaint and response. One avenue, for example, would be for Congress to provide for statutory authorization of class treatment in systemic discrimination cases, laying out specific requirements that will sufficiently balance concerns about adequacy of representation and manageability, including the use of statistical formulas to determine monetary payments to individual class members.[38]

There is also the lingering problem of required arbitration and waiver of class adjudication, which I have not yet mentioned., Mandatory arbitration clauses in employment contracts, including those that restrict private class actions, have gained in popularity. The EEOC retains its power to sue regardless of any agreement between the employer and an employee on whose behalf the agency is suing, just as the agency can bring a systemic discrimination claim without obtaining class certification. At least one court has also blocked enforcement of an arbitration clause that would have prevented an employee from proceeding on a class basis because, in the court's words, the plaintiff would thereby "be foreclosed from bringing her pattern or practice claim."[39] Preserving a role for private litigants as this court did helps maintain enforcement even as the EEOC – a federal agency – struggles with focus and funding. Striking the right balance between private and public enforcement of Title VII is a complex undertaking, well beyond the scope of this book. Regardless of the end-balance between agency and private adjudication, though, leaving avenues of enforcement for systemic claims will be key to reversing discrimination laundering.

ADDITIONAL WORK

There are other ways, of course, to incentivize change, and the law often works in conjunction with nonlegal pressures, including the market, to push actors in the right direction. In fact, research suggests that lawsuits in the discrimination area tend to operate indirectly by shifting legal environments and norms as much as directly by threatening sanction and oversight.[40] Making an example of an employer that is violating Title VII, in other words, encourages change by other organizations, even if the directly targeted organization is not especially responsive to the lawsuit brought against it.[41] We should continue to work on devising legal incentives that are most promising for meaningful organizational change.

Indeed, there remains much work to do in thinking through the full contours of an effective nondiscrimination system: the role of the EEOC and public action generally, for example, in litigation as well as in research, counseling, and expert assistance; the role of private litigants and class action certification under Rule 23 or by statute; the effectiveness of specific mechanisms requested by plaintiffs and the EEOC in settlement or consent decrees or during the remedial stage of litigation; and the role of intermediaries, including insurers and the personnel profession. These are all issues needing more attention.

We should also continue with research in the social sciences on discrimination and how it operates, including organizational sources of discrimination, but also individual and relational sources as well. One of the problems with discrimination laundering, after all, is its power to stifle effort and research on what works and what does not work to minimize discrimination within organizations. As we learn more from the social sciences, we may decide that we need to make changes to the substantive laws – the doctrines and standards that govern employer liability – under Title VII. We may even decide, based on this research, that a "best practices" defense is practical and effective after all. Or perhaps EEOC Enforcement Guidance that adopts something along the lines of Title IX's idea of progress working toward reducing disparities could provide organizations with some cushion as they implement new programs for reform.[42] But we should make these changes based on data and research, not on exaggerated fears of organizational ineptitude.

I started this book by saying that equal opportunity – an ideal that Americans agreed upon in the 1960s and have valued ever since – is under threat. Several early readers pointed out to me that this may mischaracterize our current state. It implies that we as a society agree that equal opportunity is important, and is worth continuing to work toward. I do think that we have made progress toward a common goal of equal opportunity, and I hope that this book has the potential to reach readers across the political divide, many of whom will disagree with me in some, perhaps many respects. I hope readers – whether well-versed in the law or in lived experience as community and organizational leaders, teachers, and students – will come to see that organizations are active participants in discrimination and that the law needs to put nondiscrimination on the table in the executive suite, regardless of disagreement on how we might go about doing that. We need to put the brakes on discrimination laundering, and re-focus the law on organizational causes over individual ones.

Notes

INTRODUCTION

1   See Jacob S. Hacker, *The Great Risk Shift: The New Economic Insecurity and the Decline of the American Dream* (Oxford University Press, 2006).

2   See Elaine McCrate, Flexibility for Whom? Control over Work Schedule Variability in the US, 18 *Feminist Economics* 39 (2012). Variable "D-Schedules," as researchers call them, are often tied to hourly, low-wage work in the leisure and hospitality sector, jobs disproportionately held by rural single parents of color. See also Elaine McCrate, Parents' Work Time in Rural America: The Growth of Irregular Schedules, in *Economic Restructuring and Family Well-Being in Rural America* 182 (Kristin E. Smith and Ann R. Tickamyer eds., The Pennsylvania State University Press, 2011).

3   See David Harvey, *A Brief History of Neoliberalism* (Oxford University Press, 2005).

4   I use the term post-racialism here to refer to the idea that we are past making difference of any kind, whether race or sex or other, matter in broader policy. On post-racialism emphasizing race, see Eduardo Bonilla-Silva, *Racism without Racists: Color-Blind Racism and the Persistence of Racial Inequality in the United States* (Rowman & Littlefield Publishers, Inc., 2003). For recent analysis of survey data showing changes in racial attitudes, see Lawrence Bobo, Camille Z. Charles, Maria Krysan, and Alicia D. Simmons, The Real Record on Racial Attitudes, in *Social Trends in American Life: Findings from the General Social Survey since 1972* 38 (Peter V. Mardsen ed., Princeton University Press, 2012).

5   On the rise and importance of the discourse on diversity, see Frank Dobbin, *Inventing Equal Opportunity* (Princeton University Press, 2009); and Ellen Berrey, *The Enigma of Diversity: The Language of Race and the Limits of Racial Justice* (The University of Chicago Press, 2015). See also Chapter 1 for more discussion.

6   Kevin Stainback and Donald Tomaskovic-Devey, *Documenting Desegregation: Racial and Gender Segregation in Private-Sector Employment Since the Civil Rights Act* (Russell Sage Foundation Press, 2012). Almost one-third of the fifty-eight industries studied recently by sociologists Kevin Stainback and Donald Tomaskovic-Devey showed a trend toward racial re-segregation between 2000 and 2005.

7   Ariane Hegewisch and Heidi Hartmann, *Occupational Segregation and the Gender Wage Gap: A Job Half Done* (Institute for Women's Policy Research, January 2014).

8 Ariane Hegewisch and Emily Ellis, *The Gender Wage Gap by Occupation 2014 and by Race and Ethnicity* (Institute for Women's Policy Research, April 2015).

9 Margery Austin Turner, Michel E. Fix, and Raymond J. Struyk, *Opportunities Denied, Opportunities Diminished: Discrimination in Hiring* (Urban Institute, September 1991).

10 Devah Pager, The Mark of A Criminal Record, 108 *American Journal of Sociology* 937, 960 (2003).

11 Robert L. Kaufman, *Race, Gender, and the Labor Market: Inequalities at Work* (Lynne Rienner Publishers, 2010), examining segregation and earning gaps along race and sex and also race-sex lines. See also Francine D. Blau and Lawrence M. Kahn, The Gender Wage Gap: Extent, Trends, and Explanations, National Bureau of Economic Research (unpublished working paper, 2016), examining the persistence of an unexplained gender wage gap and evaluating possible explanations.

12 See, for example, Theodore Eisenberg and Kevin M. Clermont, Plaintiphobia in the Supreme Court, 100 *Cornell Law Review* 193 (2014), and Kevin M. Clermont and Stewart J. Schwab, Employment Discrimination Plaintiffs in Federal Court: From Bad to Worse, 3 *Harvard Law and Policy Review* 103 (2009).

13 See Laura Beth Nielsen, Robert L. Nelson, and Ryon Lancaster, Uncertain Justice: Litigating Claims of Employment Discrimination in the Contemporary United States, 7 *Journal of Empirical Legal Studies* 175 (2010). For an extensive qualitative and quantitative study on employment discrimination litigation, finding that the process tends to reinscribe workplace hierarchies, see Laura Beth Nielsen, Robert L. Nelson, and Ellen C. Berrey, *Rights on Trial: Employment Civil Rights Litigation in the US* (forthcoming, University of Chicago Press Law and Society Series) (manuscript draft on file with author).

14 A requirement that all employees be at least 6 feet tall and 175 pounds, for example, might be unlawful discrimination because of its disparate impact on women even though the requirement is applied equally to all applicants.

15 For brief historical account of the passage of the Civil Rights Act, see David B. Filvaroff and Raymond E. Wolfinger, The Origin and Enactment of the Civil Rights Act of 1964, in *Legacies of the 1964 Civil Rights Act* 9 (Bernard Grofman ed., University of Virginia Press, 2000).

16 For an account of the centrality of Title VII to women's rights, see Ruth Rosen, *The World Split Open* (Penguin Books, 2000).

17 See EEOC Charge Statistics, FY 1997 – FY 2014, available at: http://eeoc.gov/eeoc/statistics/enforcement/charges.cfm (last visited March 28, 2016).

18 For more on whether discrimination against Latinos and Latinas should be considered based on race, and the fact that Americans tend today to categorize Latinos and Latinas as nonwhite, see John Skrentny, *After Civil Rights: Racial Realism in the New American Workplace* 33–34 (Princeton University Press, 2014).

19 Age Discrimination in Employment Act, 29 U.S.C. §621 *et seq.*

20 Americans with Disabilities Act, 42 U.S.C. §12101 *et seq.*

21 I use the pseudonym "Large Company X" to refer to the organization because I am relying on a sociologist's ethnographic account in which she uses a pseudonym, "Bonhomie Corporation," or "BC." Jennifer L. Pierce, *Racing for Innocence: Whiteness, Gender, and the Backlash against Affirmative Action* (Stanford University

Press, 2012), and an earlier article, Jennifer L. Pierce, "Racing for Innocence": Whiteness, Corporate Culture, and the Backlash Against Affirmative Action, 26 *Qualitative Sociology* 53 (2003).

22 Pierce, *Racing for Innocence*, at 13 (of the forty-three attorneys in 1989, Pierce was able to interview thirty-three).

23 *Ibid.*, at 3.

24 Pierce uses pseudonyms for the people that she describes.

25 Pierce, *Racing for Innocence*, at 67.

26 *Ibid.*, at 70.

27 *Ibid.*, at 77.

28 *Ibid.*, at 78.

29 *Ibid.*

30 *Ibid.*

31 *Ibid.*

32 *Ibid.*, at 79.

33 *Ibid.*, at 76.

34 *Ibid.*, at 77.

35 *Ibid.*, at 77–78. Kingsley goes on to say that after the incident with the head of the department, "they all start acting weird, really nice, but really defensive … It's like they were all racing for innocence … And so I decided to move on." *Ibid.*, at 78.

36 See Lauren A. Rivera, *Pedigree: How Elite Students Get Elite Jobs* (Princeton University Press, 2015) for more on hiring for elite jobs, high-wage jobs in investment banks, management consulting firms, and law firms. Rivera shows that those involved in interviewing and deciding whom to hire tend to define and evaluate merit in ways and through processes that tilt the playing field in favor of socioeconomically advantaged individuals and white men.

37 See Candida G. Brush, Patricia G. Greene, Lakshmi Balachandra, and Amy E. Davis, *Diana Report. Women Entrepreneurs 2014: Bridging the Gender Gap in Venture Capital* (2014). This was down from 10 percent in the last study, conducted in 1999.

38 My description of the allegations and evidence presented in the case is compiled from Pao's complaint and various news articles, including David Streitfeld, In Ellen Pao's Suit vs. Kleiner Perkins, World of Venture Capital is Under Microscope, *New York Times*, March 5, 2015; Ellen Huet, Kleiner Perkins Trial Details Firm's All-Male Ski Trip and Dinner Party, *Forbes*, February 25, 2015; and a series of articles by Nellie Bowles and Liz Gannes in *Re/code* describing each day of evidence presented at trial. A copy of the complaint in the case is publicly available at: www.nytimes.com/interactive/2015/02/20/technology/document-pao-complaint-for-damages.html (last visited March 28, 2016).

39 Farhad Manjoo, Ellen Pao Disrupts How Silicon Valley Does Business, *New York Times*, March 27, 2015, and Kristen V. Brown, What the Ellen Pao case means for companies in Silicon Valley, *SF Gate*, March 25, 2015.

40 On the discrimination in promotion claim, the jury found for Kleiner Perkins 10–2. Pao also alleged a claim of retaliation, and failure to take all reasonable steps to prevent discrimination against her. She lost on those claims as well.

41 On statements by two jurors in the case, see Nellie Bowles and Liz Gannes, Juror Speaks About His Vote for Kleiner Perkins But Still Wants the Firm to "Be

Punished," *Re/code*, March 30, 2015, and Alexia Tsotsis, Two Jurors on Opposite Sides Share Their Pao v. Kleiner Perspectives, techcrunch.com, March 27, 2015.

42 The instructions reflect California law, the California Fair Employment and Housing Act, under which Pao sued. Federal law under Title VII differs slightly, requiring only Pao's gender to have been a "motivating factor" in the decision not to promote. 42 U.S.C. §2000e-2(m).

43 Lilly Ledbetter with Lanier Scott Isom, *Grace and Grit: My Fight for Equal Pay and Fairness at Goodyear and Beyond* (Three Rivers Press, Random House, Inc., 2012).

44 Liza Featherstone, *Selling Women Short: The Landmark Battle for Workers' Rights at Wal-Mart* 2 (Basic Books, 2005), reporting that Betty Dukes started working at Wal-Mart earning $5 per hour.

45 *Vance v. Ball State Univ.* 133 S. Ct. 2434 (2012).

46 For research showing that the drive for "diversity" in organizations can result in efforts to increase diversity selectively in higher-level jobs but not at all in lower-level jobs, see Ellen Berrey, *The Enigma of Diversity: The Language of Race and the Limits of Racial Justice* (The Chicago University Press, 2015).

1. THE THREADS OF ORGANIZATIONAL INNOCENCE

1 These three threads are specific to courts' understanding of discrimination within organizations. They operate in addition to (in several respects as part of) the over-arching social and political pressures of the time, such as neoliberalism and post-racialism, discussed in the Introduction.

2 See Herbert Hill, *Black Labor and the American Legal System: Race, Work, and the Law* (The University of Wisconsin Press, 1977).

3 42 U.S.C. §2000e-2(a)(1). It also states that it is an unlawful employment practice to "limit, segregate, or classify his employees or applicants for employment in any way which would deprive or tend to deprive any individual of employment opportunities or otherwise adversely affect his status as an employee, because of such individual's race, color, religion, sex, or national origin." §2000e-2(a)(2).

4 See, for example, *Gunn v. Layne & Bowler, Inc.*, 1 Empl. Prac. Dec. 9823 (W.D. Tenn. 1967).

5 See, for example, *Weeks v. Southern Bell Tel. & Tel. Co.*, 408 F.2d 228 (5th Cir. 1969), and *Bowe v. Colgate-Palmolive Co.*, 272 F. Supp. 332 (S.D. Ind. 1967).

6 *Griggs v. Duke Power Co.*, 401 U.S. 424 (1971).

7 For background on the case against Duke Power, see Robert K. Belton, *The Crusade for Equality in the Workplace: The Griggs v. Duke Power Story* (Stephen L. Wasby, ed., University Press of Kansas, 2014).

8 *Griggs* was decided in an era when sociologists and labor economists were emphasizing the ways in which ossified industrial practices kept women and minorities in certain careers and in lower-paying positions. The talk in these days was more about "institutional racism and sexism" than of individual biases. And the enforcement lens was also decidedly macro, with the Department of Justice and the Equal Employment Opportunities Commission (EEOC) suing not just large organizations, but whole industries. In the early 1970s, after succeeding in two suits against Bethlehem Steel and United States Steel, the Department of Justice brought suit

against nine major steel companies, representing 75 percent of the steel industry, in a single action. *United States v. Allegheny-Ludlum Indus.*, 517 F.2d 826, 834 n. 1 (5th Cir. 1975) (approving proposed consent decree). In 1974, the government sued seven major trucking companies for failing to hire minorities for higher-paying jobs and for maintaining discriminatory seniority and transfer systems. See *In re Trucking Indus. Employment Practices Litig.*, 384 F. Supp. 614 (J.P.M.L. 1974). The suit originally named a defendant class of 349 trucking companies across the country, with 7 named as representatives. See Alfred W. Blumrosen, *Modern Law: The Law Transmission System and Equal Employment Opportunity* (University of Wisconsin Press, 1993).

9 *Int'l Bhd. of Teamsters v. United States*, 431 U.S. 324 (1977).

10 *McDonnell Douglas Corp. v. Green*, 411 U.S. 792 (1972).

11 Whether he participated in the lock-in was contested. He apparently did not admit to participating, but the district court portrayed him as having done so based on his status as a leader in the group involved.

12 *McDonnell Douglas*, at 801.

13 For a description of some of Green's civil rights activities, see David B. Oppenheimer, The Story of *Green v. McDonnell Douglas*, in *Employment Discrimination Stories* 13 (Joel Wm. Friedman ed., Foundation Press, 2006).

14 *McDonnell Douglas*, at 804–5.

15 *Ibid.*, at 805 n. 19.

16 See Paul J. Wahlbeck, James F. Spriggs II, and Forest Malzman, The Burger Court Opinion-Writing Database (2011), *McDonnell Douglas v. Green*, available at http://supremecourtopinions.wustl.edu (last visited July 5, 2016).

17 *Furnco Construction Corp. v. Waters*, 438 U.S. 567 (1968).

18 Justice Marshall, Justice Brennan joining, dissented on the ground that on remand the lower courts should consider the plaintiffs' case under a disparate impact theory as well.

19 *Furnco*, at 576.

20 Or, put another way, whether his stated reason for not hiring the men – that none of their names was on his list – was a pretext for discrimination. See *McDonnell Douglas* on proving that a defendant's proffered decision was pretext for discrimination.

21 *Slack v. Havens*, No 72-59-GT, 1973 WL 339 at *1 (S.D. Cal. July 17, 1973).

22 *Price Waterhouse v. Hopkins*, 490 U.S. 228 (1989).

23 Price Waterhouse pushed hard on this point, to some success in Justice O'Connor's opinion. See Chapter 2 for further discussion.

24 Walmart, Global Statement of Ethics, at 11, available at www.walmartethics.com/uploadedFiles/Content/U.S.%20-%20English.pdf (last visited January 8, 2016). Note: For consistency, I use "Wal-Mart" throughout the book. "Wal-Mart Stores, Inc." is the company's name of incorporation, even though the company uses "Walmart" today for its logo and is often referred to as "Walmart" in the media.

25 See Walmart, Walmart Requires Diversity in its Law Firms, http://corporate.walmart.com/_news_/news-archive/2005/12/09/wal-mart-requires-diversity-in-its-law-firms (last visited January 18, 2016).

26 Lilly Ledbetter with Lanier Scott Isom, *Grace and Grit: My Fight for Equal Pay and Fairness at Goodyear and Beyond* (Three Rivers Press, Random House Inc., 2012).

27 Ledbetter's complaint stated legal claims under the Equal Pay Act and Age Discrimination in Employment Act as well as Title VII of the Civil Rights Act. Only the Title VII claim ended up before the Supreme Court.

28 In most states, plaintiffs have 300 days in which to file with the relevant state agency, if there is one, or the EEOC. In Alabama, the time frame is tighter, at 180 days.

29 For a more detailed account of the evidence, see Tristin K. Green, Insular Individualism: Employment Discrimination Law After *Ledbetter* v. *Goodyear*, 43 *Harvard Civil Rights Civil Liberties Law Review* 353, 360–62 (2008).

30 See *Ledbetter* v. *Goodyear Tire & Rubber Co.*, 550 U.S. 618, 622 and 632 n. 4 (2007). The question on which Ledbetter sought review also tended to frame the case as involving a past incident, outside of the limitations period. See *Ledbetter*, at 621, posing the question as "whether and under what circumstances a plaintiff may bring an action under title VII of the Civil Rights Act of 1964 alleging illegal pay discrimination when the disparate pay is received during the statutory limitations period, but is the result of intentionally discriminatory pay decisions that occurred outside the limitations period").

31 *Ledbetter*, at 632 n. 4. This same concern about unfairness to the organization in litigating claims involving individual employees also surfaces in *St. Mary's Honor Center* v. *Hicks*. There, in rejecting the dissent's argument that a defendant should be worse off after presenting a nondiscriminatory reason for a particular decision that is false than if it presented no reason at all, the Court explained that "in these Title VII cases, the defendant is ordinarily *not* an individual but a company, which must rely upon the statement of an employee – often a relatively low-level employee – as to the central fact; and that central fact is *not* a physical occurrence, but rather the employee's state of mind." *St. Mary's Honor Center* v. *Hicks*, 509 U.S. 502, 520 (1993). See Chapter 4 for more discussion of this case.

32 Lilly Ledbetter Fair Pay Act of 2009, Pub. L. No. 111–2, 123 Stat. 5.

33 Michael Shermer, He's a racist. So are you. So am I, *Los Angeles Times*, November 24, 2006.

34 See George A. Miller, The Cognitive Revolution: A Historical Perspective, 7 *Trends in Cognitive Sciences* 141 (2003), describing the shift from behaviorism in psychology to cognitive science.

35 Mahzarin R. Banaji and Anthony G. Greenwald, *Blindspot: The Hidden Biases of Good People* (Delacorte Press, Random House, Inc., 2013). The cognitive bias revolution goes well beyond biases involving protected status or characteristics, such as race and sex. In 2002, for example, economist Daniel Kahneman won the Nobel Prize in economic science for his work on a wide-ranging set of cognitive biases that distort our judgment of the world. For a sampling of some of this research, see Daniel Kahneman, *Thinking Fast and Slow* (Farrar, Straus and Giroux, 2011).

36 For a description of some of the early research on cognitive bias and discrimination, see Linda Hamilton Krieger, The Content of Our Categories: A Cognitive Bias Approach to Discrimination and Equal Employment Opportunity, 47 *Stanford Law Review* 1161, 1186 (1995).

37 John F. Dovidio and Samuel L. Gaertner, On the Nature of Contemporary Prejudice: The Causes, Consequences, and Challenges of Aversive Racism, in *Confronting Racism: The Problem and the Response* 5 (Jennifer L. Eberhardt and Susan T. Fiske eds., Sage Publications, 1998).

38 See Madeline E. Heilman, Caryn J. Block, Richard F. Martell, and Michael C. Simon, Has Anything Changed? Current Characterizations of Men, Women, and Managers, 74 *Journal of Applied Psychology* 935 (1989). For compelling synthesis of this and other studies and overall assessment of often unrecognized forces that contribute to the persistence of gender inequality, see Cecilia L. Ridgeway, *Framed by Gender: How Gender Inequality Persists in the Modern World* 100–05 (Oxford University Press, 2011).

39 Elizabeth H. Gorman, Gender Stereotypes, Same-Gender Preferences, and Organizational Variation in the Hiring of Women: Evidence from Law Firms, 70 *American Sociological Review* 702 (2005).

40 Because the analysis did not include the gender composition of the firms' actual applicant pools, Gorman controlled for factors that might result in variation across firms, including whether the firm had a high proportion of female associates, had an EEO policy, had a part-time work policy, or family leave policy. See *ibid.*, at 710–11, describing factors coded and controlled for.

41 *Ibid.*, at 717–18.

42 For a description of the IAT and its use to predict implicit bias, see Anthony G. Greenwald, Debbie E. McGee, and Jordan L. K. Schwartz, Measuring Individual Differences in Implicit Cognition: The Implicit Association Test, 74 *Personality & Social Psychology* 1464 (1998), and, written for a more lay audience, Chapter 3 in Banaji and Greenwald, *Blindspot.*

43 Banaji and Greenwald, *Blindspot*, at 105.

44 Malcolm Gladwell, *Blink: The Power of Thinking Without Thinking* (Back Bay Books, 2005).

45 See, for example, Krieger, The Content of Our Categories, and Rebecca A. White and Linda H. Krieger, Whose Motive Matters?: Discrimination in Multi-Actor Employment Decision Making, 61 *Louisiana Law Review* 495 (2001).

46 See, for example, Noah Zatz, Managing the Macaw: Third-Party Harassers, Accommodation, and the Disaggregation of Discriminatory Intent, 109 *Columbia Law Review* 1357, 1374 (2009), and Amy L. Wax, The Discriminating Mind: Define It; Prove It, 40 *Connecticut Law Review* 979, 984–85 (2008). For debate, see Patrick Shin, Liability for Unconscious Discrimination? A Thought Experiment in the Theory of Employment Discrimination Law, 62 *Hastings Law Journal* 67 (2010).

47 See, for example, *Ash* v. *Tyson Foods, Inc.*, 190 F. App'x 924, 926 (11th Cir. 2006), holding that a supervisor's use of the term "boy" to refer to a black employee was not evidence of discriminatory animus, that his use of the term was "conversational and … non-racial in context."

48 The Court of Appeals for the Eleventh Circuit in *Ash* v. *Tyson Foods*, for example, went on to state that the supervisor's use of the term "boy," "[e]ven if somehow construed as racial, … were ambiguous stray remarks not uttered in the context of the decisions at issue and are not sufficient circumstantial evidence of bias to provide a reasonable basis for a finding of racial discrimination in the denial of the promotion." For more discussion of this stray remarks doctrine as a hurdle for plaintiffs seeking to prove individualized discrimination, see Chapter 5.

49 This is sometimes called the "pretext" method of proving discrimination, laid out in the Supreme Court's decision in *McDonnell Douglas Corp.* v. *Green*, discussed earlier in this chapter.

50 Shermer, He's a racist. So are you. So am I.

51 Banaji and Greenwald argue as much. *Blindspot*, at 159 and Appendix 1.

52 Walmart, Global Statement of Ethics, at 11, available at www.walmartethics.com/uploadedFiles/Content/U.S.%20-%20English.pdf (last visited January 8, 2016).

53 Ellen Berrey, *The Enigma of Diversity: The Language of Race and the Limits of Racial Justice* 44 (The University of Chicago Press, 2015).

54 *Ibid.*, at 198.

55 For more on the development of diversity management generally, including Reagan-era influences on equal opportunity law and affirmative action, see Erin Kelley and Frank Dobbin, How Affirmative Action Became Diversity Management: Employer Response to Antidiscrimination Law, 1961–1996, 41 *American Behavioral Scientist* 960 (1998) and Dobbin, *Inventing Equal Opportunity*, Chapter 6 (Princeton University Press, 2009). For the rise in diversity management rhetoric in the managerial literature, see Lauren B. Edelman, Sally Riggs Fuller, and Iona Mara-Drita, Diversity Rhetoric and the Managerialization of Law, 106 *American Journal of Sociology* 1589 (2001).

56 For an example of an article appearing first in the early 1990s in the *Harvard Business Review* and arguing against affirmative action and in favor of managing diversity for competitive advantage, see R. Roosevelt Thomas, Jr., From Affirmative Action to Affirming Diversity, in *Differences that Work: Organizational Excellence through Diversity*, 27 (Mary C. Gentile ed., Harvard Business School Press, 1994).

57 *Regents of Univ. of Ca. v. Bakke*, 438 U.S. 265, 317 (1978).

58 See, for example, *Grutter v. Bollinger*, 539 U.S. 306 (2003), Amicus Brief, General Motors, at 13–14; Amicus Brief, MTV, at 2–3.

59 See discussion in Chapter 5.

60 Executive Order 11246 and Title VII. See Frank Dobbin, John R. Sutton, John W. Meyer, and Richard Scott, Equal Opportunity Law and the Construction of Internal Labor Markets, 99 *American Journal of Sociology* 396 (1993).

61 Equal Employment Opportunity Commission Guidelines 1974.

62 They initially advocated quota systems, tests designed to evaluate the qualifications of job candidates, and rules to formalize hiring and promotion, but as quota systems and tests came under fire, the personnel professionals pushed more strongly for formal evaluation and promotion systems. Dobbin *et al.*, Equal Opportunity Law.

63 See Lauren B. Edelman, Law at Work: The Endogenous Construction of Civil Rights, in *Handbook on Employment Discrimination Research: Rights and Realities* 337 (Robert L. Nelson and Laura Beth Nielsen eds., Springer Publishing, 2005).

64 Lauren B. Edelman, Linda H. Krieger, Scott R. Eliason, Catherine R. Albiston, and Virginia Mellema, When Organizations Rule: Judicial Deference to Institutionalized Employment Structures, 117 *American Journal of Sociology* 888 (2011); Linda Hamilton Krieger, Rachel Kahn Best, and Lauren B. Edelman, When "Best Practices" Win, Employees Lose: Symbolic Compliance and Judicial Inference in Federal Equal Employment Opportunity Cases, 40 *Law & Social Inquiry* 843 (2015).

65 See Lauren B. Edelman, S. R. Fuller, and I. Mara-Drita, Diversity Rhetoric and the Managerialization of Law.

66 Laure Bereni, "'Nothing To Do With the Law' vs. 'Beyond the Law': How Diversity Managers Relate to Antidiscrimination Law in the US and France," unpublished

paper presented at Law and Society Association Annual Conference, Seattle, 2015. The diversity personnel and equal opportunity personnel go to different conferences and belong to different professional associations. Diversity personnel follow different career trajectories, with diversity including director positions and at the top the Chief Diversity Officer, while equal opportunity job ladders are much shorter with career progression very limited. There is also a racial divide: blacks are over-represented in the equal opportunity jobs, while diversity and inclusion jobs are held by a wider range of races and a higher share of white women. *Ibid.*, at 10. In France, in contrast to the United States, diversity management personnel often describe their work as building on antidiscrimination law foundations. "Diversity is about 'respecting employees by not taking into account the grounds [of antidiscrimination law] in hiring and workplace decisions.'"

67 *Ibid.*, at 9.

68 See also Berrey, *The Enigma of Diversity*, at 251–52 (diversity officer describing diversity management as "your own business" and equal employment opportunity as "doing your taxes").

69 Bereni, "'Nothing To Do With the Law'" at 8.

70 Berrey, *The Enigma of Diversity*, at 238–40.

71 *Ibid.*, at 240–42.

72 *Ibid.*, at 242 ("leav[ing] whiteness unnamed while constructing a role for white people as participants in cordial, productive, workplace relationships").

73 See *ibid.*, at 8, describing the problem of selective inclusion associated with the diversity movement: "Cultural value is placed on the so-called diverse people who are most easily incorporated into a setting and who enhance institutional objectives such as prestige, distinction, or profit-making ... As it turns out, selective inclusion ... is surprisingly low risk for the high-status white people who do the managing diversity. It does not necessitate that leaders address racial inequalities throughout the organization or housing market."

74 Ellen Berrey, Steve G. Hoffman, and Laura Beth Nielsen, Situated Justice: A Contextual Analysis of Fairness and Inequality in Employment Discrimination, 46 *Law & Society Review* 1, 14–15 (2012), quoting in-house counsel for a research organization.

75 Dobbin, *Inventing Equal Opportunity*, at 92.

76 *Ibid.*, at 93.

77 *Ibid.*, at 213.

78 See Lauren B. Edelman, Howard S. Erlanger, and John Lande, Internal Dispute Resolution: The Transformation of Civil Rights in the Workplace, 27 *Law and Society Review* 497, 502–8 (1993), and Anne Donnellon and Deborah M. Kolb, Constructive for Whom? The Fate of Diversity Disputes in Organizations, in *Using Conflict in Organizations* 161 (Carsten K. W. De Dreu and Evert Van de Vliert eds., Sage Publishing, 1997).

79 For a qualitative and quantitative study of a dataset of case files made available by the Ohio Civil Rights Commission (OCRC) that shows the micro-relational nature of plaintiff descriptions of their experiences, see Vincent J. Roscigno, *The Face of Discrimination: How Race and Gender Impact Work and Home Lives* (Rowman & Littlefield Publishers, 2007).

80 *Ashcroft* v. *Iqbal*, 556 U.S. 662 (2011).

81 *Ashcroft*, at 675, discussing Iqbal's *Bivens* claims, which were based on *Bivens v. Six Unknown Named Agents of Fed. Bureau of Narcotics*, 403 U.S. 388 (1971).

82 *Ashcroft*, at 677.

83 *Ashcroft*, at 683.

2. INDIVIDUAL DISCRIMINATION: THE EMERGING LAW OF COMPLAINT AND RESPONSE

1 See, for example, Linda Hamilton Krieger, The Content of Our Categories: A Cognitive Bias Approach to Discrimination and Equal Employment Opportunity, 47 *Stanford Law Review* 1161 (1995).

2 See, for example, Katie R. Eyer, That's Not Discrimination: American Beliefs and the Limits of Anti-discrimination Law, 96 *Minnesota Law Review* 1275 (2012).

3 *Slack v. Havens*, 7 Fair Empl. Prac. Cas. (BNA) 885 (S.D. Ca. 1973).

4 *Price Waterhouse v. Hopkins*, 490 U.S. 228 (1989).

5 *Hopkins v. Price Waterhouse*, 618 F. Supp. 1109 (D.C. 1985).

6 *Ibid.*, at 1119.

7 *Hopkins v. Price Waterhouse*, 825 F.2d 458, 469 (D.C. Cir. 1987).

8 *Price Waterhouse*, 490 U.S. 228.

9 Justice O'Connor explained that in her view "[neither] stray remarks in the workplace, … [n]or statements by nondecisionmakers, [n]or statements by decisionmakers unrelated to the decisional process itself, [can] suffice to satisfy the plaintiff's burden." *Ibid.*, at 277.

10 *Watson v. Fort Worth Bank & Trust*, 487 U.S. 977, 992 (1988).

11 *Price Waterhouse*, 490 U.S. at 275.

12 Richard Thompson Ford, Bias in the Air: Rethinking Employment Discrimination Law, 66 *Stanford Law Review* 1381, 1411 (2014).

13 See, for example, *Miller v. Maxwell's Int'l*, 991 F.2d 583 (9th Cir. 1993). The Supreme Court has not ruled on the question of whether individual employees can be liable under Title VII, though most lower courts, such as the Ninth Circuit Court of Appeals in *Miller*, have held that they cannot.

14 This is unlike vicarious liability in tort, where the employer's vicarious liability serves as a back-up to individual liability, and the employer is entitled to indemnity from the individual employee. Title VII, as a statute intended to impose a non-discrimination obligation on employers, in contrast to tort law, relies exclusively on employer liability. For further explanation, see Martha Chamallas, Two Very Different Stories: Vicarious Liability under Tort and Title VII Law, 75 *Ohio State Law Journal* 1315, 1330–32 (2014).

15 This distinction between claims based on indirect liability and those based on directly liability is carried through to the Supreme Court's interpretation of when punitive damages are available under Title VII. See *Kolstad v. Am. Dental Assoc.*, 527 U.S. 526, 545 (1999), holding that an employer may not be vicariously liable for punitive damages where the individual's decisions were "contrary to an employer's good-faith efforts to comply with Title VII."

16 *Burlington Indus. v. Ellerth*, 524 U.S. 742 (1998).

17 *Faragher v. City of Boca Raton*, 524 U.S. 775 (1998).

18 *Meritor Sav. Bank, FSB v. Vinson*, 477 U.S. 57 (1986).
19 *Faragher v. City of Boca Raton*, 111 F.3d 1530, 1536 (11th Cir. 1997).
20 *Faragher*, 524 U.S. at 807, and *Burlington Indus.*, 524 U.S. at 757, stating that "[t]he harassing supervisor often acts for personal motives, motives unrelated and even antithetical to the objectives of the employer."
21 *Burlington Indus.*, 524 U.S. at 764–65.
22 Ford, Bias in the Air, at 1412.
23 *Burlington Indus.*, 524 U.S. at 760. Although the Court did not issue a holding on the standard for employer liability for co-worker harassment, it implied that employers would be liable in those cases only if they are negligent.
24 *Ibid.*, at 764.
25 The EEOC issued guidance in 1980 that included sexual harassment as discrimination. 29 C.F.R. §1640.11 (1980).
26 See, for example, *Corne v. Bausch & Lomb, Inc.*, 390 F. Supp. 161 (D. Ariz. 1975), in which the judge characterized a supervisor's repeated verbal and physical sexual advances as "satisfying a personal urge" that was not the result of a "company directed policy."
27 Leigh Ann Wheeler, *How Sex Became a Civil Liberty* (Oxford University Press, 2013).
28 *Ibid.*, at 195.
29 *Ibid.*, at 197.
30 *Ibid.*, at 198.
31 *Ibid.*
32 *Meritor Savings Bank v. Vinson*, 477 U.S. 57 (1986).
33 See 29 C.F.R. §1640.11 (1980); Brief for the United States and the Equal Employment Opportunity Commission as Amici Curiae.
34 DOJ/EEOC Brief, at 25–26.
35 *Ibid.*, at 26.
36 *Meritor*, at 62–63.
37 *Ibid.*, at 64–65.
38 DOJ/EEOC brief, at 22, citing a well-known treatise on the subject of torts, W. Prosser and R. Keeton, *Law of Torts* (1984).
39 For argument that the Court misconstrued the term "agent" as limiting and thereby broke from longstanding understanding of Title VII as a federal reform statute by drawing in common law of torts and agency, see Chamallas, Two Very Different Stories. As Chamallas explains, the Court could also have interpreted tort agency principles differently, by focusing on "predictable risk." The dominant frame of organizational innocence, however, pushes against this risk-based approach just as it leads toward a tort-like conception of discrimination.
40 *Harris v. Forklift Systems*, 510 U.S. 17 (1993).
41 *Ibid.*, at 19–20.
42 Jeffrey Rosen, for example, wrote in the *New Republic* that to find such conduct actionable as harassment would represent "the most serious threat to the First Amendment of the past decade." Jeffrey Rosen, Reasonable Women, *The New Republic*, October 31, 1993. For an account of the role that First Amendment concerns played in arguments against broad employer liability for harassment, see Wheeler, *How Sex Became a Civil Liberty*, at 204–5.

43 *Harris*, at 22.

44 *Ibid.*

45 *Jansen v. Packaging Corp. of America*, 123 F.3d 490, 511–13 (7th Cir. 1997) (Posner, C.J., concurring and dissenting).

46 *Burlington Indus.*, 524 U.S. 742, 756 (1998).

47 *Ibid.*, at 770 (Thomas, J., and Scalia, J., dissenting).

48 And more recently in *Vance v. Ball State U.*, 133 S. Ct. 2434 (2103) (narrowly defining supervisor).

49 For a description of cases involving nonsexual, sex-based harassing acts and a critique of the sexual desire-dominance paradigm in harassment law, see Vicki Schultz, Reconceptualizing Sexual Harassment, 107 *Yale Law Journal* 1683 (1998).

50 *Vance v. Ball State Univ.*, 133 S. Ct. 2434 (2012).

51 *Vance v. Ball State Univ.*, 646 F.3d 461, 470 (7th Cir. 2010).

52 *Ibid.*, at 471.

53 For further discussion, see Chapter 4.

54 *Vance v. Ball State Univ.*, 133 S. Ct. 2434 (2012).

55 Justice Ginsburg notes this in her dissent in *Vance*. See *Vance*, 133 S. Ct. at 2463–64 (Ginsburg, J., dissenting).

56 *McCormack v. Safeway Stores, Inc.*, No. CV-12-02547 (D. Ariz., February 12, 2014).

57 *EEOC v. BCI Coca-Cola Bottling Co., of Los Angeles*, 450 F.3d 476 (10th Cir. 2006), and at 484, explaining use of the term "cat's paw" to describe a situation in which a subordinate uses a formal decision maker as a "dupe" in his plan to discriminate. For further treatment of this case and the legal issues it raises, see Tristin K. Green, Insular Individualism, 43 *Harvard Civil Rights Civil Liberties Law Rev.* 353, 369–371 (2008).

58 *BCI*, at 483.

59 *Ibid.*, at 487.

60 *Staub v. Proctor Hospital*, 562 U.S. 411 (2011).

61 *Staub* leaves open a host of questions, including whether the Court would hold differently if the initial discriminatory act were taken by a co-worker rather than a supervisor. There is also the apparent inconsistency between the Court's decision in *Vance* defining a supervisor as someone with the power to take ultimate action, and the Court's description of the initial actors in *Staub* as supervisors.

62 In a footnote, the *Staub* Court stated: "We also observe that Staub took advantage of Proctor's grievance process, and we express no view as to whether Proctor would have an affirmative defense if he did not." *Staub*, 562 U.S. at 422, n. 4.

63 *Thomas v. Eastman Kodak Co.*, 183 F.3d 38 (1st Cir. 1999).

64 Several amicus briefs in *Staub*, including the brief for the government, argued that an employer should be vicariously liable for the discriminatory actions that are a proximate cause of a later adverse decision only if the earlier action was taken by someone acting with authority delegated by the employer. Employers under this view would not be vicariously liable for discriminatory actions taken by co-workers, for example.

65 See Amy Wax, Discrimination as Accident, 74 *Indiana Law Journal* 1129 (1999).

66 See, for example, David Benjamin Oppenheimer, Negligent Discrimination, 141 *University Pennsylvania Law Review* 899, 969–70 (1993), and Noah Zatz, Managing the Macaw: Third-Party Harassers, Accommodation, and the Disaggregation of

Discriminatory Intent, 109 *Columbia Law Review* 1357 (2009). For more discussion of these works, see Tristin K. Green, The Future of Systemic Disparate Treatment Law, 32 *Berkeley Journal of Employment and Labor Law* 395, 425–29 (2011).

67 Ford, Bias in the Air.

3. SYSTEMIC DISCRIMINATION: ERASING THE AGGREGATE AND ENTRENCHING A LAW OF COMPLAINT AND RESPONSE

1 *Wal-Mart Stores, Inc., v. Dukes*, 131 S. Ct. 2541 (2011).
2 Except in rare circumstances for sex-based decisions, when sex is a bona fide occupational qualification for a job. 42 U.S.C. §2000e-2(e)(1).
3 42 U.S.C. §2000e-6.
4 *Int'l Bhd. of Teamsters v. United States*, 431 U.S. 324, 336 (1977).
5 *Ibid.*, at 336.
6 *Ibid.*
7 *Ibid.*, at 337.
8 See *United Steelworkers of America v. Weber*, 443 U.S. 193 (1979) and *Johnson v. Transportation Agency, Santa Clara County*, 480 U.S. 616 (1987) for cases upholding employers' plans that included consideration of race and sex in employment decisions, but discouraging quotas as "unnecessarily trammel[ling]" the interests of the majority.
9 For an explanation of some of the mistakes that courts (and litigants) make when it comes to making sense of statistics in systemic disparate treatment cases, see Richard Lempert, Befuddled Judges: Statistical Evidence, in *Title VII Cases, Legacies of the 1964 Civil Rights Act* 263 (Bernard Grofman, ed., University Press of Virginia, 2000).
10 *Teamsters*, at 340.
11 *Ibid.*, at 359–60.
12 Sometimes this part of the Court's holding is explained as if it is based on probability, but that is not quite right. The Court did not require that the disparity be so great as to give rise to an inference that an individual was discriminated against, and indeed has cautioned against such an assumption. See *McDonnell Douglas v. Green*, discussed in Chapter 1. Instead, the Court in *Teamsters* created a legal presumption. Once systemic disparate treatment is established, the law presumes that individuals have been discriminated against.
13 The lack of minority workers in the job category is not itself evidence of discrimination. Rather, it is the comparison between the percentage in the category and the percentage in the labor pool that matters. For an explanation of this, see Lempert, Befuddled Judges, at 275, critiquing a court for assuming otherwise.
14 This is just as a random coin flipped 100 times and resulting in 100 tails and 0 heads seems suspicious. While it is not impossible to achieve this result by chance, with a fair coin and fair flips, such a result is highly unlikely.
15 The Court explained that "'if the difference between the expected value and the observed number is greater than two or three standard deviations,' then the hypothesis that teachers were hired without regard to race would be suspect," which has become known as the "2–3 standard deviation rule." The rule is often used as

a "rule of thumb," although not always justified in a particular case. See again Lempert, Befuddled Judges, at 276, cautioning against overreliance on statistical rules of thumb.

16 42 U.S.C. §2000e-5(k).

17 *Christiansburg Garment Co.* v. *EEOC*, 434 U.S. 412 (1978).

18 In 1972, Congress amended Title VII to provide the EEOC with enforcement authority. At the same time, the amendments expanded the EEOC's authority to sue to enforce private rights and to vindicate the public interest under section 706. For an account of the history of EEOC authority, see Alfred W. Blumrosen, *Modern Law: The Law Transmission System and Equal Employment Opportunity* (University of Wisconsin Press, 1993). The Attorney General retains a role in suits against state and local governments. See 42 U.S.C. § 2000e-5(5)(1).

19 See *General Telephone* v. *EEOC*, 446 U.S. 318 (1980).

20 Courts have generally been unwilling to implement organizational solutions for individual discriminatory decisions, and several have held that private plaintiffs must obtain class certification in order to obtain broader relief. See, for example, *Davis* v. *Coca-Cola Bottling Co.*, 516 F.3d 955, 965–69 (11th Cir. 2008).

21 Claims alleging systemic discrimination were considered to fall easily into class treatment in large part because they often involved injunctive relief such as changes in organizational practices that would affect a large group of people, regardless of whether each person affected had planned to sue individually.

22 See *General Telephone Co. of the Southwest* v. *Falcon*, 457 U.S. 147 (1982).

23 Some may question here why I do not include language of employer purpose or intent. I do not do so because the intentional discrimination involved in systemic disparate treatment cases occurs at the moment that bias (whether conscious or unconscious) affects the treatment of individuals, resulting in different treatment of members of one group as compared to another. This understanding is consistent with the Supreme Court's holding in *Teamsters*, and with the Court's view of the evidence presented in that case. Put another way, proof of intent on the part of the high-level executives who set the policies and practices of the organizations is not required to prove systemic disparate treatment. More on this in Chapter 5.

24 *Teamsters*, 431 U.S. 324, 338 n. 19 (1977).

25 *Hazelwood*, 433 U.S. 299, 303 (1977).

26 *Ibid.*, at 303.

27 *Leisner* v. *New York Tel. Co.*, 358 F. Supp. 359 (S.D.N.Y. 1973).

28 *Ibid.*, at 365.

29 Thirty private employment discrimination class action lawsuits were filed in federal courts in 1992. That number had more than doubled by 1997 (67 were filed in 1997, 77 in 2000, and 70 in 2001). For data on federal court filings, see Ann. Rep. of Dir. Of the Admin. Off. of the U.S. Cts., Table X-5, U.S. District Courts Class Action Civil Cases Commenced, available at www.uscourts.gov/statistics-reports/caseload-statistics-data-tables (last visited July 5, 2016).

30 For a description of some of these cases, see Tristin K. Green, Targeting Workplace Context: Title VII as a Tool for Institutional Reform, 72 *Fordham Law Review* 659, 682–89 (2003).

31 There is reason to believe that the media overstates the risk posed by employment discrimination litigation. See Laura Beth Nielsen and Aaron Beim, Media

Misrepresentation: Title VII, Print Media, and Public Perceptions of Discrimination Litigation, 15 *Stanford Law & Policy Review* 237 (2004), showing that print news outlets from 1990 to 2000 reported a plaintiff win-rate nearly three times the actual win-rate, and that the median of award and amount of settlement reported in the media were also vastly higher than the median of awards and settlement amounts in all cases.

32 See Nadya Aswad, Court Approves $65 Million Settlement of Sex Bias Suit Against Home Depot, 11 *Daily Labor Report* (BNA), at D19 (January 16, 1998).

33 See *Abdallah* v. *Coca-Cola Co.*, 133 F. Supp. 2d 1364 (N.D. Ga. 2001).

34 See Order Approving Consent Decree, *Kosen* v. *Am. Express Fin. Advisors, Inc.*, No. 1: 02CV0082 (D.C. June 16, 2002).

35 Allen R. Myerson, Home Depot Pays $87.5 Million for Not Promoting More Women, *New York Times*, September 20, 1997.

36 Plaintiffs must also show that "the class is so numerous that joinder of all members is impracticable"; that "the claims or defenses of the representative parties are typical of the claims or defenses of the class"; and that "the representative parties will fairly and adequately protect the interests of the class." Federal Rule of Civil Procedure 23(a). In addition, the court must certify the class under one of three categories listed under Rule 23(b), Federal Rule of Civil Procedure 23.

37 For accounts of this "public law" litigation model, see Owen M. Fiss, Foreword, The Forms of Justice, 93 *Harvard Law Review* 1 (1979) and Abram Chayes, The Role of the Judge in Public Law Litigation, 89 *Harvard Law Review* 1281 (1976).

38 See, for example, Michael Selmi, The Price of Discrimination: The Nature of Class Action Employment Discrimination and its Effects, 81 *Texas Law Review* 1249, 1326 (2003), describing employment discrimination litigation today as "just another form of tort." For a description of some of the differences between more recent systemic employment discrimination cases and earlier ones that may have contributed to this perception, see Green, Targeting Workplace Context, at 687–89.

39 For a description of the positions in this "war," and citation to many of the key scholarly articles, see Jeffrey W. Stempel, Class Actions and Limited Vision: Opportunities for Improvement Through a More Functional Approach to Class Treatment of Disputes, 83 *Washington University Law Quarterly* 1127 (2005). For an even more succinct description that also includes *Wal-Mart* in the arena, see Judith Resnik, Fairness in Numbers: A Comment on *AT&T* v. *Concepcion*, *Wal-Mart* v. *Dukes*, and *Turner* v. *Rogers*, 125 *Harvard Law Review* 78, 145–47 (2011).

40 A statistician hired by the plaintiffs analyzed Wal-Mart's payroll and personnel data and found that, on average, women in hourly positions made $1,000 less annually than men. In salaried management positions, the annual pay gap was $14,500. At the time, Wal-Mart had a strong policy of promoting from within, yet women comprised 67% of hourly workers and 78% of hourly department managers and only 35.7% of assistant managers, 14.3% of store managers, and 9.8% of district managers. The plaintiffs also presented evidence comparing the percentage of women in management at Wal-Mart, 35.4%, to the percentage of women in management at comparable retailers, 56.6%. Details of the evidence can be found in several judicial opinions in the case and in the parties' filings. See, for example,

Motion to Certify Class, *Dukes v. Wal-Mart Stores, Inc.*, No. C-01-2252 (N.D. Cal., April 28, 2003) (No. 99), and *Dukes v. Wal-Mart Stores, Inc.*, 222 F.R.D. 137 (N.D. Cal. 2004). For more on the statistical analyses presented, see Declaration of Richard Drogin, Ph.D. in Support of Plaintiffs' Motion for Class Certification.

41 See *Dukes*, 222 F.R.D. 137 (N. D. Cal. 2004).

42 See *Dukes v. Wal-Mart Stores, Inc.*, 509 F.3d 1168 (9th Cir. 2007).

43 *Dukes v. Wal-Mart Stores, Inc.*, 603 F.3d 571 (9th Cir. 2010) (en banc).

44 Roger Parloff, The War Over Unconscious Bias, *Fortune*, October 15, 2007.

45 Michael Orey, White Men Can't Help It, *Business Week*, May 15, 2006.

46 *Dukes*, 222. F.R.D. at 145.

47 *Ibid.*, at 149.

48 See Plaintiffs' Motion for Class Certification and Memorandum of Points and Authorities, *Dukes v. Wal-Mart Stores, Inc.*, No. C-01-2252 (N.D. Cal. 2003), at 13–14. Although Judge Jenkins cited exclusively to the plaintiffs' social science expert report by William Bielby for evidence of sex stereotyping in Wal-Mart's work culture, declarations and deposition testimony submitted by plaintiffs relayed the material above in text and also comments by male managers and executives reflecting sex stereotyping, incidents of male managers insisting on holding meetings at Hooters and attending strip clubs on business trips.

49 Richard A. Nagareda, Class Certification in the Age of Aggregate Proof, 84 *New York University Law Review* 97, 104 (2009).

50 *Ibid.*, at 155–56.

51 This is the same concern that motivated the Court to limit employer liability initially in *Faragher* and *Burlington Industries*, and later in *Vance*. See Chapter 2. If all the employer does is provide "proximity and regular contact [that] may afford a captive pool of potential victims," as the Court put it in *Burlington Industries*, then why hold it automatically responsible? See, for example, Richard A. Posner, An Economic Analysis of Sex Discrimination Laws, 56 *University of Chicago Law Review* 1311, 1318 (1989), describing harassment as a "conduit" type of discrimination "because ordinarily it is not the employer himself (more often, itself) who harasses women, but male employees … [t]he employer merely doesn't want to go to the expense of preventing harassment by its employees." See also Ford, Bias in the Air, discussed in Chapter 2.

52 See, for example, D. Theodore Rave, Governing the Anticommons in Aggregate Litigation, 66 *Vanderbilt Law Review* 1183, 1185 n. 5 (2013), including the *Wal-Mart* case in a list of mass torts, like asbestos exposure.

53 42 U.S.C. §1981a. The section also placed caps on damages based on size of employer.

54 Juries are constitutionally offered for cases at law. See Amendment VII, U.S. Constitution. Back pay under Title VII, however, was considered equitable relief, and therefore Title VII cases, not cases at law, did not fall within the jury right.

55 See Green, *Targeting Workplace Context*, at 689, n. 132. This trend was not unique to employment discrimination cases. For a discussion of the decline of public law firms and the rise of practice of public interest law in private law firms, see Debra S. Katz and Lynne Bernabei, Practicing Public Interest Law in a Private Public

Interest Law Firm: The Ideal Setting to Challenge the Power, 96 *West Virginia Law Review* 293 (1993).

56 See Nagareda, Class Certification in the Age of Aggregate Proof. Indeed, Nagareda took the analogy one step further, arguing that systemic disparate treatment claims are like claims against firearms manufacturers "for negligent marketing practices that elevate the risk of gun-related violent crime." This analogy, too, misses the mark. Discrimination is not a product that passes through different hands; it is an action (sometimes at the individual level, sometimes at the organizational level) made unlawful by federal statute.

57 *Wal-Mart Stores, Inc. v. Dukes*, 131 S. Ct. 2541 (2011).

58 Federal Rule of Civil Procedure 23.

59 *Wal-Mart*, at 2553.

60 See, for example, *ibid.*, at 2552, stating that "[t]he crux of a Title VII inquiry is 'the reason for the particular employment decision'," and "[h]ere respondents wish to sue about literally millions of employment decisions at once."

61 *Ibid.*, at 2556.

62 *Ibid.*

63 *Ibid.*, at 2554.

64 See Declaration of William T. Bielby, PhD, in Support of Plaintiffs' Motion for Class Certification, Dukes, No. C-01-CC52 (April 21, 2003).

65 *Wal-Mart*, at 2554.

66 *Ibid.*, at 2555.

67 *Ibid.*, at 2555.

68 *Ibid.*

69 *Ibid.*

70 *Ibid.*, at 2553.

71 This is the kind of evidence that would be needed if the law required proof of "common direction," *Ibid.*, at 2555, reason to believe that high-level executives directed managers to discriminate or adopt a discretionary decision-making system "really intended to keep down its female hourly employees." For further discussion, see Tristin K. Green, The Future of Systemic Disparate Treatment Law, 32 *Berkeley Journal of Employment and Labor Law* 395, 413–14 (2011).

72 Because the plaintiffs could not succeed in proving that enough managers were acting on their biases in similar ways, the Court never took the next step to consider whether the employer would be liable for discrimination.

73 This is also why the Court is mistaken as to its second holding in *Wal-Mart*, that certification was improper under Rule 23(b)(2). The law of Title VII does not give defendants a right or entitlement to individualized defense. For further explanation, see Melissa Hart, Civil Rights and Systemic Wrongs, 32 *Berkeley Journal of Employment and Labor Law* 455 (2011).

74 See Transcript of Oral Argument, *Wal-Mart Stores, Inc. v. Dukes*, 131 S. Ct. 2541 (2011) (No. 10–277). For quotes from the transcript and further discussion, see Tristin K. Green, On Employment Discrimination and Police Misconduct: Title VII and The Mirage of The "*Monell* Analogue," 95 *Boston University Law Review* 1077, 1082–83 (2015).

75 In theory, it is possible for a deliberate indifference standard to apply to something other than complaints, like knowledge of pay and promotion disparities, but that is

not how it has generally applied. Indeed, Justice Ginsburg and Justice Breyer seem to contemplate this broader possibility in their questioning, though neither refers to the standard of deliberate indifference. See Transcript of Oral Argument, at 6–7, and 36.

76 *Monell v. New York City Dept. of Soc. Serv.*, 436 U.S. 658 (1978). In the case of Title IX, the Court relied on statutory language for this holding, that the statute, unlike Title VII, does not include the term "agent." *Gebser v. Lago Vista Indep. School Dist.*, 524 U.S. 274, 283 (1998).

77 See *City of Canton v. Harris*, 489 U.S. 378 (1989) (O'Connor, J., concurring in part and dissenting in part).

78 See Transcript of Oral Argument, at 4. Justice Kennedy refers there specifically to the Court's section 1983 decision in *Monell*, and says "A city is not liable … for a constitutional violation unless it has a policy. Would you think that we could use that as an analogue to determine whether or not there is a common question here?"

79 Transcript of Oral Argument, at 39–40.

80 The government is authorized by statute to bring claims against entities, such as a police department or city, alleging a "pattern or practice" of police brutality, a "pattern or practice" of conduct that deprives persons of constitutional rights. If the government is successful in proving liability, it can obtain generalized injunctive relief, measures that change departments, which is relief that individuals bringing challenges on their own have difficulty obtaining. The Department of Justice has yet to litigate a "pattern or practice" claim, but some courts have held that it would have to meet the same standards as an individual plaintiff, which means that it would have to show deliberate indifference to repeated violations of constitutional rights.

81 See Craig G. Futterman, H. Melissa Mather, and Melanie Miles, The Use of Statistical Evidence to Address Police Supervisory and Disciplinary Practices: The Chicago Police Department's Broken System, 1 *DePaul Journal for Social Justice* 251 (2008).

82 See *ibid.*, at 259–79, describing statistics gathered and statistical analyses conducted for a case against the City of Chicago.

83 Transcript of Oral Argument, at 4–5. Justice Roberts's question does allow for an organizational solution, revisiting subjectivity in decision making, but presumably as a means of better insulating decisions against biases of individual, rogue actors.

4. CLASS, CULTURE, AND LIMITING THE PURVIEW OF TITLE VII

1 *St. Mary's Honor Cntr. v. Hicks*, 509 U.S. 502 (1993).

2 *Hicks v. St. Mary's Honor Cntr.*, 756 F. Supp. 1244 (E.D. Mo. 1991).

3 *Ibid.*, at 1252.

4 *St. Mary's Honor Cntr.*, 509 U.S. at 510–11.

5 For further discussion of these cases and other ways in which courts close racial emotion out of antidiscrimination concern, see Tristin K. Green, Racial Emotion in the Workplace, 86 *Southern California Law Review* 959 (2013).

6 *Sweezer v. Mich. Dep't of Corr.*, 229 F.3d 1154 (6th Cir. 2000) (per curium, unpublished opinion), available at 2000 WL 1175644 (Thomson Reuters Westlaw Database).

7 *Ibid.*, at *3.

8   *Ibid.*, at *4.
9   See *Harris v. Forklift Systems*, 510 U.S. 17, 22 (1993). For discussion of *Harris*, see Chapter 2.
10 *Pratt v. Austal*, U.S.A., L.L.C., No. 08-00155-KD-N (S.D. Ala., July 27, 2011).
11 *White v. Government Employees Ins. Co.*, 457 Fed. Appx. 374 (5th Cir. 2012).
12 *Ibid.*, at 381.
13 *Ibid.*
14 See *Vance v. Ball State Univ.*, 133 S. Ct. 2434 (2012), discussed in Chapter 2.
15 See, for example, Vicki Schultz, Reconceptualizing Sexual Harassment, 107 *Yale Law Journal* 1683 (1998).
16 *EEOC v. Boh Brothers Construction Co.*, 731 F.3d 444 (5th Cir. 2013) (en banc). The EEOC actually brought the case on Woods's behalf.
17 *Ibid.*, at 249–50.
18 The panel suggested harassment "because of sex" might not include stereotyping, which was rejected en banc.
19 *Boh Brothers*, at 456.
20 *Ibid.*, at 456–60.
21 *Ibid.*, at 470–76 (Jolly, J., dissenting), and at 475 (Jones, J., dissenting).
22 This concern seems thin given that the judges suggest that a woman in Woods's position, with the same evidence, would have a provable claim. We would expect that most women in that workplace would have a claim as well.
23 *Boh Brothers*, at 470.
24 *EEOC v. Boh Bothers Construction Co.*, 689 F.3d 458, 459 (5th Cir. 2012).
25 *Boh Brothers*, 731 F.3d 444, 475 (5th Cir. 2013) (en banc).
26 *Ibid.*, at 475 n. 2.
27 *Ibid.*, at 475 (stating that the judgment "portends a government-compelled workplace speech code").
28 *Ibid.*, at 473.
29 *DeClue v. Central Illinois Light Co.*, 223 F.3d 434 (7th Cir. 2000).
30 *Ibid.*, at 439 n. 2 (Rovner, J., dissenting)
31 *Ibid.*, at 434.
32 *Ibid.*, at 438.
33 *Ibid.*, at 439 n. 2.
34 *Ibid.*, at 437.
35 And plays up a "women are from Venus; men from Mars" mentality. See *Boh Brothers*, 731 F.3d at 436, stating that "Women are more reticent about urinating in public than men."
36 It is possible that Audrey DeClue really saw her case in the neutral disparate impact frame that Posner pushes. See Mary Ann Case, All the World's the Men's Room, 74 *University of Chicago Law Review* 1655, 1660 n. 18 (2007), relaying DeClue's description of her discomfort from deposition testimony.
37 See, for example, *Williams v. City of Chicago*, 325 F. Supp. 2d 867, 876 n. 18 (N.D. Ill. 2004), suggesting that disparate impact theory applies to pornography not targeted at the plaintiff because she is a woman, citing to *DeClue*.
38 See *Robinson v. Jacksonville Shipyards Inc.*, 760 F. Supp. 1486, 1498 (M.D. Fla. 1991), involving "men only" painted on a trailer after the plaintiff complained about calendar depicting scantily clad women in sexually suggestive positions; comments

of a sexual nature, including a welder telling the plaintiff he wished her skirt would blow over head so he could look and another telling her he wished she would wear a tighter shirt because it would be sexier; a foreman asking her to come "sit on his lap"; being called "honey," "baby," and "sugar"; statements that "women are only fit company for something that howls" and "there's nothing worse than having to work around women," among others.

39 Although sometimes courts point this out as a way of distinguishing cases involving "the mere presence of visible pornography" from cases in which plaintiffs have established a hostile work environment. See, for example, *Williams v. CSX Transp. Co., Inc.*, 533 Fed. Appx. 637, 641–42 (6th Cir. 2013).

40 *Ocheltree v. Scollon Prod., Inc.*, 335 F. 3d 325, 332 (4th Cir. 2003) (en banc).

41 *Ibid.*, at 332.

42 *Ibid.*, at 332–33, explaining that "a reasonable jury could find that Ocheltree was the individual target of harassment because of her sex"; and at 341 (Williams, J., dissenting in part and concurring in part). Some courts have rejected such a requirement. See, for example, *Reeves v. C.H. Robinson Worldwide, Inc.*, 594 F.3d 798 (11th Cir. 2010) (en banc). For other cases holding nontargeted action is insufficient, see *Ellett v. Big Red Keno, Inc.*, 221 F.3d 1342, at *1 (8th Cir. July 21, 2000) (unpublished table decision) ("A dually offensive sexual atmosphere [including pornography] in the workplace, no matter how offensive, is not unlawful discrimination unless one gender is treated differently than the other."); *Scott-Riley v. Mullins Food Prods., Inc.*, 391 F. Supp. 2d 707, 718 (N.D. Ill. 2005) ("[P]ornographic pictures not directed at a plaintiff (i.e., so called 'second-hand harassment') may not constitute a hostile environment"). For more discussion, see L. Camille Hébert, Sexual Harassment as Discrimination "Because of … Sex": Have We Come Full Circle?, 27 *Ohio Northern University Law Review* 439 (2001).

43 *Robinson v. Jacksonville Shipyards, Inc.*, 760 F. Supp. 1486 (M.D. Fla. 1991).

44 Leigh Ann Wheeler, *How Sex Became a Civil Liberty* 200 (Oxford University Press, 2013), quoting the executive director of the Florida affiliate of the ACLU at the time that the district judge in the Robinson case ruled in Robinson's favor and ordered Jacksonville Shipyards to take down the pornographic pictures of women.

45 *McReynolds v. Merrill Lynch, Pierce, Fenner, & Smith, Inc.*, 672 F.3d 482 (7th Cir. 2012).

46 Katherine E. Lamm, Work in Progress: Civil Rights Class Actions After *Wal-Mart v. Dukes*, 50 *Harvard Civil Rights Civil Liberties Law Review* 153, 169 (2015).

47 The case settled in 2013, with Bank of America (which had bought Merrill Lynch) agreeing to pay $160 million and to undertake organizational assessment and change. See Settlement Agreement and Release, *McReynolds v. Merrill Lynch, Pierce, Fenner, & Smith, Inc.*, No. 05-CV-06583 (N.D. Ill. August 23, 2013). For more discussion of the settlement, see Chapter 7.

48 *McReynolds*, 672 F.3d at 489: "The teams, they say, are little fraternities (our term but their meaning), and as in fraternities the brokers choose as team members people who are like themselves. If they are white, they, or some of them anyway, are more comfortable teaming with other white brokers. Obviously they have their eyes on the bottom line; they will join a team only if they think it will result in their getting paid more, and they would doubtless ask a superstar broker to join their team regardless of his or her race. But there is bound to be uncertainty about who

will be effective in bringing and keeping shared clients; and when there is uncertainty people tend to base decisions on emotions and preconceptions, for want of objective criteria."

49 Plaintiffs alleged claims using both systemic disparate treatment theory and disparate impact theory, but the court of appeals rejected the systemic disparate treatment claims without substantial analysis, assuming that a systemic disparate treatment claim would require evidence that high-level executives wanted to discriminate: "There is no indication that the corporate level of Merrill Lynch (or its parent, Bank of America) *wants* to discriminate against black brokers. Probably it just wants to maximize profits. But in a disparate impact case the presence or absence of discriminatory intent is irrelevant; and permitting brokers to form their own teams and prescribing criteria for account distributions that favor the already successful – those who may owe their success to having been invited to join a successful or promising team – are practices of Merrill Lynch." *McReynolds*, 672 F.3d at 490.

50 The *Wal-Mart* Court states: "In the landmark case of ours which held that giving discretion to lower-level supervisors can be the basis for Title VII liability under a disparate-impact theory, the plurality opinion *conditioned* that holding on the corollary that merely proving that the discretionary system has produced a racial or sexual disparity *is not enough.* '[T]he plaintiff must begin by identifying the specific employment practice that is challenged.'" 131 S. Ct. at 2555. The Court cites *Wards Cove Packing Co., Inc. v. Atonio*, 490 U.S. 642 (1989), a case which the Court acknowledges was "superseded by statute" in the 1991 Civil Rights Act amendments to Title VII. Congress was responding in the 1991 Civil Rights Act in part specifically to the Court's decision in *Wards Cove*. What the *Wal-Mart* Court does not acknowledge in its statement is that Title VII as amended by the 1991 Civil Rights Act provides that if individual practices "are not capable of separation for review," then they can be challenged together. Moreover, nothing in the 1991 Act states that proof that a subjective decision-making system has a disparate impact cannot lead to employer liability, that there must be some other "specific employment practice" that is isolated for analysis. 42 U.S.C. §2000e-2(k).

51 *EEOC v. Boh Brothers Constr., Co. LLC*, 731 F.3d, 444, 472 (5th Cir. 2013) (en banc) (Jolly, J., dissenting).

52 For data showing, the difficulty that working parents face from increased employer-controlled variable schedules, see Elaine McCrate, Parents' Work Time in Rural America: The Growth of Irregular Schedules, in *Economic Restructuring and Family Well-Being in Rural America* 177 (Kristin E. Smith and Ann R. Tickamyer eds., Pennsylvania State University Press, 2011). For more on using the law to increase working options for working families, see Tristin K. Green, Civil Rights Lemonade: Title VII, Gender, and Working Options for Working Families, 10 *Stanford Journal of Civil Rights & Civil Liberties* 191 (2014).

5. THE LAUNDERED WORKPLACE

1 My point here is not a causal one, that the law has led to the current organizational approach to discrimination. Indeed, evidence suggests quite the opposite, that organizations and the diversity profession have played a substantial role in shaping

the law. See Frank Dobbin, *Investing in Equal Opportunity* (Princeton University Press, 2009). It is important to see, nonetheless, that organizations are doing exactly what we would expect under the current legal regime, a regime that draws a very narrow realm of employer liability that maps on to a sense within organizations that discrimination is rare, is carried out by rogue actors, and is being adequately addressed through complaint, investigation, and discipline.

2 Prominent sociologist Erving Goffman described the relational component in his work, Erving Goffman, *Interaction Ritual: Essays on Face-to-Face Behavior* 3 (Pantheon Books, 1967). For a brief discussion and reference to more recent studies, see Tristin K. Green and Alexandra Kalev, Discrimination-Reducing Measures at the Relational Level, 59 *Hastings Law Journal* 1435 (2008).

3 Barbara F. Reskin, The Proximate Causes of Employment Discrimination, 29 *Contemporary Sociology* 319, 320 (2000).

4 See John F. Dovidio and Samuel L. Gaertner, Stereotypes and Evaluative Intergroup Bias, in *Affect, Cognition, and Stereotyping: Interactive Processes in Group Perception* 167 (Diane M. Mackie and David L. Hamilton, eds., Academic Press Inc., 1993). For a review of some of the earlier research on in-group favoritism, see Linda Hamilton Krieger, Civil Rights Perestroika: Intergroup Relations After Affirmative Action, 86 *California Law Review* 1251, 1318–27 (1998). For recent research based on interviews with whites showing substantial privilege and reliance on social capital in obtaining and succeeding in jobs, and yet denial of that privilege through an emphasis on individualism, see Nancy DiTomaso, *The American Non-Dilemma: Racial Inequality without Racism* (Russell Sage Foundation, 2013).

5 Claude M. Steele, *Whistling Vivaldi: How Stereotypes Affect Us and What We Can Do* (W. W. Norton & Co., 2010).

6 *Ibid.*, at 51. And this is true particularly when a person's social identity is strongly tied to performance. Students who considered themselves "good" students, those who wanted to achieve in school, were more likely to be fazed by stereotype threat than those who did not care much about achieving in school. *Ibid.*, at 57.

7 *Ibid.*, at 200–6.

8 In addition to Steele, above, see Phillip Atiba Goff, Claude M. Steele, and Paul G. Davies, The Space Between Us: Stereotype Threat and Distance in Interracial Contexts, 94 *Journal of Personality & Social Psychology* 91 (2008).

9 See John F. Dovidio, Kerry Kawakami, and Samuel L. Gaertner, Implicit and Explicit Prejudice and Interracial Interaction, 82 *Journal of Personality & Social Psychology* 62 (2002).

10 See E. Ashby Plant and David A. Butz, *The Causes and Consequences of an Avoidance-Focus for Interracial Interactions*, 32 *Personality & Social Psychological Bulletin* 833 (2006). See also Carl O. Word, Mark P. Zanna, and Joel Cooper, The Nonverbal Mediation of Self-Fulfilling Prophecies in Interracial Interaction, 10 *Journal of Experimental Social Psychology* 109 (1974). Some behaviors that whites adopt as strategies for what they think will be improved interracial interactions, such as avoiding mention of race, can actually result in nonverbal behaviors that are less friendly and can result in greater perceptions of racial prejudice by black interactional partners. See Evan P. Apfelbaum, Samuel R. Sommers, and Michael I. Norton, Seeing Race and Seeming Racist? Evaluating Strategic Colorblindness in Social Interaction, 95 *Journal of Personality & Social Psychology* 918 (2008).

11 Nellie Bowles and Liz Gannes, Performance Review Rewrites and Pao's Genetic Makeup: Pao v. Kleiner Perkins Trial Day 4, *Re/Code*, February 27, 2015.

12 Davey Alba, How Ellen Pao's Case Stacks Up Against Kleiner, *Wired*, March 1, 2015.

13 Nellie Bowles and Liz Gannes, A Juror Speaks About his Vote for Kleiner Perkins but Still Wants the Firm to "Be Punished," *Re/Code*, March 30, 2015.

14 See Chapter 2 for discussion of this requirement. Courts basically say that a plaintiff must experience an "adverse" or "material" or, as some courts put it, "ultimate" action, such as a rejection in hiring, a discharge, a pay disparity, or a promotion denial before a claim of discrimination is legally actionable. See, for example, *Ledergerber v. Stangler*, 122 F.3d 1142, 1144 (8th Cir. 1997), stating that while the lateral transfer complained of "may have had a tangential effect on [the plaintiff's] employment, it did not rise to the level of an ultimate employment decision intended to be actionable under Title VII."

15 In *Sprint/United Management Co. v. Mendelsohn*, 552 U.S. 379 (2008), the Supreme Court by unanimous, per curiam opinion held that such evidence is "neither per se admissible nor per se inadmissible," leaving the decision whether to exclude or admit the evidence to the discretion of the trial court.

16 For a description of some of the cases relying on the "stray remark" label, to various ends, see Kerri Lynn Stone, Taking in Strays: A Critique of the Stray Comment Doctrine in Employment Discrimination Law, 77 *Missouri Law Review* 149 (2012).

17 In some cases, the rules do seem to be applied too strictly, for example, in *Simmons v. Océ-USA, Inc.*, 174 F.3d 913 (8th Cir. 1999), where the court held that racially derogatory comments made by the plaintiff's supervisor two years before a decision terminating the plaintiff's employment were "unrelated to the decisional process" even though the supervisor also conducted low performance ratings of the plaintiff during the time of the comments. But this does not necessarily mean that the rules themselves are unwarranted.

18 Hostile work environment law eases the harshness of this reality a little by allowing individuals to sue for discriminatory conditions that are severe or pervasive enough so as to alter the terms and conditions of work. A woman who is kept out of golf games, for example, might successfully sue under a hostile work environment theory. Similarly, a man like Randall Kingsley might sue if he is being denied help (when his white colleagues are not). This said, hostile work environment law requires that conduct be severe or pervasive before it will violate Title VII.

19 *Int'l Bhd. of Teamsters v. United States*, 431 U.S. 324 (1977).

20 Nor do they create an "inference" of discrimination in individual instances, as Nagareda insists. Instead, the Court in *Teamsters* created a legal presumption that individuals in the group experienced discrimination. See Chapter 3.

21 See *Teamsters*, at 338 n. 18.

22 On measures sought by the EEOC in consent decrees, see Margo Schlanger and Pauline Kim, The Equal Employment Opportunity Commission and Structural Reform of the American Workplace, 91 *Washington University Law Review* 1519 (2014). Again, I do not attempt a causal claim here, only to show that the law is matching up with organizational measures being taken, and even remedies sought by plaintiffs and the EEOC, all of which tend to focus on individuals as described in this chapter.

23 *Wal-Mart*, 131 S. Ct. at 2553.

24 See John W. Meyer and Brian Rowan, Institutionalized Organizations: Formal Structure as Myth and Ceremony, 83 *American Journal of Sociology* 340 (1977), describing decoupling wherein executives embrace policies/innovations that symbolize commitment, yet organizational participants may sustain entrenched routines at odds with those policies/innovations.

25 See, for example, Brenda Major and Pamela J. Sawyer, Attributions to Discrimination: Antecedents and Consequences, in *Handbook of Prejudice, Stereotyping, and Discrimination* 89, 91 (Todd D. Nelson ed., Psychology Press, 2009), and also Beth A. Quinn, The Paradox of Complaining: Law, Humor, and Harassment in the Everyday Work World, 25 *Law & Social Inquiry* 1151 (2000).

26 Because whites, in contrast to blacks and other racial minorities, tend to believe that discrimination is not prevalent and to define discrimination narrowly as incidents involving overt expressions of racial hostility, they are likely to experience exasperation or frustration when blacks or other racial minorities raise concerns about discrimination. For more discussion of this tendency, see Russell K. Robinson, Perceptual Segregation, 108 *Columbia Law Review* 1093, 1109–10 (2008).

27 See, for example, *Clark Cnty Sch. Dist. v. Breeden*, 532 U.S. 268 (2001), involving a plaintiff who complained about a comment made by her supervisor, which the Court held "no reasonable person could have believed … violated Title VII's standard." For a thorough review and critique of the law of retaliation, see Deborah L. Brake, Retaliation in an EEO World, 89 *Indiana Law Journal* 115 (2014).

28 Ellen Berrey, Steve G. Hoffman, and Laura Beth Nielsen, Situated Justice: A Contextual Analysis of Fairness and Inequality in Employment Discrimination Litigation, 46 *Law & Society Review* 1, 14 (2012).

29 See, for example, Vicki Schultz, The Sanitized Workplace, 112 *Yale Law Journal* 2061 (2003).

30 Timothy D. Wilson and Nancy Brekke, Mental Contamination and Mental Correction: Unwanted Influences on Judgments and Evaluations, 116 *Psychological Bulletin* 117, 119–20 (1994).

31 Frank Dobbin, Daniel Schrage, and Alexandra Kalev, Rage against the Iron Cage: The Varied Effects of Bureaucratic Personnel Reforms on Diversity, 80 *American Sociological Review* 1014, 1026 (2015).

32 See, for example, E. Ashby Plant and Patricia G. Devine, The Antecedents and Implications of Interracial Anxiety, 29 *Personality & Social Psychology Bulletin* 790 (2003).

33 See Schultz, The Sanitized Workplace.

34 For an overview of some of the changes in rhetoric and in specific measures adopted by organizations to manage diversity (and sometimes to reduce discrimination) over the past several decades, see Dobbin, *Inventing Equal Opportunity*, and also on measures undertaken by organizations, see Soohan Kim, Alexandra Kalev, and Frank Dobbin, Progressive Corporations at Work: The Case of Diversity Programs, 36 *New York University Review of Law & Social Change* 171 (2012).

35 On wide adoption, see Alexandra Kalev, Frank Dobbin, and Erin Kelly, Best Practices or Best Guesses? Assessing the Efficacy of Corporate Affirmative Action and Diversity Policies, 71 *American Sociological Review* 589, 599 (2006) (39 percent of establishments studied); and on earlier adoption, Mark J. Bendick,

Mary Lou Egan, and S. M. Lofhjelm, *The Documentation and Evaluation of Antidiscrimination Training in the United States* (Russell Sage Foundation, 1998).

36 See Ellen Berrey, *The Enigma of Diversity: The Language of Race and the Limits of Racial Justice* 241 (University of Chicago Press, 2015), describing diversity training at one large firm. See also Susan T. Fiske, Stereotyping, Prejudice, and Discrimination, in *Handbook of Social Psychology* II, 357 (Daniel T. Gilbert , Susan T. Fiske, and Gardner Lindzey, eds., Sage Publishing, 4th ed. 1998); Thomas E. Nelson, Michelle Acker, and Melvin Manis, Irrepressible Stereotypes, 32 *Journal of Experimental Social Psychology* 13 (1996), and Lauren B. Edelman, Sally Riggs Fuller, and Iona Mara-Drita, Diversity Rhetoric and the Managerialization of Law, 106 *American Journal of Sociology* 1589, 1616–18 (2001), surveying diversity rhetoric in business literature for definitions of diversity, which are often quite broad, including "all the ways in which we differ."

37 Kalev, Dobbin, and Kelly, Best Practices or Best Guesses?

38 Justine E. Tinkler, Resisting the Enforcement of Sexual Harassment Law, 37 *Law & Social Inquiry* 1 (2012), describing participant reactions to diversity training. See also Deborah L. Kidder, Melenie J. Lankau, Donna Chobrot-Mason, Kelly A. Mollica, and Raymond A. Friedman, Backlash Toward Diversity Initiatives: Examining the Impact of Diversity Program Justification, Personal and Group Outcomes, 15 *International Journal of Conflict Management* 77, 91 (2004).

39 Tinkler, Resisting the Enforcement of Sexual Harassment Law, at 18.

40 See Ellen Huet, Rise of the Bias Busters: How Unconscious Bias Became Silicon Valley's Newest Target, *Forbes Tech*, November 2, 2015.

41 See Fiske, Stereotyping, Prejudice, and Discrimination.

42 One of the things the Google workshop does is ask individuals to hold each other accountable for unconscious biases. Google uploaded a presentation by Welle to YouTube: www.youtube.com/watch?v=nLjFTHTgEVU (last visited July 4, 2016).

43 Dobbin, *Inventing Equal Opportunity*.

44 Barbara F. Reskin and Debra Branch McBrier, Why Not Ascription? Organizations' Employment of Male and Female Managers, 65 *American Sociological Review* 220 (2000).

45 Eric Lewis Uhlmann and Geoffrey L. Cohen, Constructed Criteria: Redefining Merit to Justify Discrimination, 16 *Psychological Science* 474 (2005).

46 Removing all indicators of race and sex from resumés is also helpful, as well-known research by Claudia Goldin and Cecilia Rouse on the effects of "blind" auditions suggests (more women were hired into an orchestra when they auditioned behind a screen). Claudia Goldin and Cecilia Rouse, Orchestrating Impartiality: The Impact of "Blind" Auditions on Female Musicians, 90 *American Economic Review* 715 (2000). Several startups have emerged that will do resume stripping for companies seeking to reduce bias in hiring, and algorithms are also increasingly used to identify good candidates, but this and similar blinding or automated techniques are much less helpful once a person has been hired. Algorithms, moreover, may rely on factors that are themselves biased or result in a disparate impact on particular groups. For articles in the mainstream press on blind hiring as it is being used by some businesses today, see Rachel Feintzeig, Careers: Why Bosses are Turning to Blind Hiring, *Wall Street Journal*, January 6, 2016, and on algorithms, see Bourree

Lam, For More Workplace Diversity, Should Algorithms Make Hiring Decisions?, *The Atlantic*, June 22, 2015.

47 See Philip E. Tetlock, Accountability: A Social Check on the Fundamental Attribution Error, 48 *Social Psychology Quarterly* 227 (1985).

48 Robert L. Nelson and William P. Bridges, *Legalizing Gender Inequality: Courts, Markets and Unequal Pay for Women in America* (Cambridge University Press, 1999); Reskin and McBrier, Why Not Ascription?

49 See Dobbin, Schrage, and Kalev, Rage Against the Iron Cage, at 1014.

50 Emilio J. Castilla and Stephen Benard, The Paradox of Meritocracy in Organizations, 55 *Administrative Science Quarterly* 543 (2010).

6. HOW ORGANIZATIONS DISCRIMINATE – AND WHAT THEY CAN DO TO STOP

1 For a description of some of the allegations in the case, see www.naacpldf. org/case-issue/cogdell-v-wet-seal and CNN story, including an interview with Cogdell, at: www.naacpldf.org/update/cogdell-v-wet-seal-plaintiff-discusses-her-case-cnn (both last visited July 4, 2016).

2 Cogdell, CNN.

3 John D. Skrentny, *After Civil Rights: Racial Realism in the New American Workplace* (Princeton University Press, 2014).

4 *Ibid.*, at 5–13.

5 For a compelling history of race management in the United States, see David R. Roediger and Elizabeth D. Esch, *The Production of Difference: Race and the Management of Labor in U.S. History* (Oxford University Press, 2012).

6 Skrentny, *After Civil Rights*, at 230–31, citing the López-Sanders study. Laura López-Sanders, Trapped at the Bottom: Racialized and Gendered Labor Queues in New Immigrant Destinations, Working Paper 176, Center for Comparative Immigration Studies, University of California, San Diego, 2009.

7 Kevin Stainback and Donald Tomaskovic-Devey, *Documenting Desegregation: Racial and Gender Segregation in Private-Sector Employment Since the Civil Rights Act* 213 (Russell Sage Foundation, 2012). See also Tiffany Taylor, Supply, Demand, and Organizational Processes: Changes in Women's Share of Management in United States Workplaces, 1966–2000, in *Interactions and Intersection of Gendered Bodies at Work, at Home, and at Play* 116 (Marcia Texler Segal, ed., Advances in Gender Research Vol. XIV, Emerald Group Publishing Ltd., 2010).

8 Margaret M. Chin, *Sewing Women: Immigrants and the New York City Garment Industry* (Columbia University Press, 2005).

9 In 2005, an investigation in New York revealed that domestic worker employment agencies sorted workers by race and nationality and sent them to potential employers based on such requests. According to one report, a client looking for a housekeeper requested: "No black. Must not have pet allergies." See Jennifer Steinhauer, Domestic Workers Face Blatant Discrimination, Investigation Reveals, *New York Times*, June 1, 2005.

10 Sarah Maslin Nir, The Price of Nice Nails, *New York Times*, May 7, 2015.

11 A similar brand issue arose with Abercrombie and Fitch in the early 2000s. African Americans did not fit the "A & F look," at least not in great numbers. Steven Greenhouse, Going for the Look, but Risking Discrimination, *New York Times*, July 13, 2003.

12 Philip Moss and Chris Tilly, *Stories Employers Tell: Race, Skill, and Hiring in America* 105 (Russell Sage Foundation, 2001).

13 For more on the business case for diversity, see Chapter 1.

14 Amicus Curiae Brief of MTV Networks, *Grutter v. Bollinger*, 549 U.S. 306 (2003).

15 See, for example, Google's emphasis on the need to have an employee base that reflects "our user base" in its explanation of why it cares about hiring and promoting more women. Farhad Manjoo, The Business Case for Diversity in the Tech Industry, *New York Times*, September 26, 2014. There is nothing wrong, of course, with acknowledging that those who innovate and make new products will set the standard that may exclude segments of the population that were not part of the design team. Indeed, it is a good reason for integrating more women and racial minorities into powerful positions across the workforce, not just in product innovation. But focusing on the user market for products as the sole case for diversity risks race- and gender-matching that can be in tension with nondiscrimination goals.

16 See Jannette L. Dates, Advertising, in *Split Image: African Americans in the Mass Media*, 421, 438–44 (Jannette L. Dates and William Barlow, eds., Howard University Press, 1990).

17 See Taylor, Supply, Demand, and Organizational Processes, at 167, arguing that "women's progress is largely the result of demand created by economic restructuring" and that "women have simply added paid work providing services to strangers to their unpaid work providing services for families."

18 For more on segregation and the effects on interaction, see Donald Tomaskovic-Devey, *Gender and Racial Inequality at Work: The Sources and Consequences of Job Segregation* (Cornell University, 1993); Barbara Reskin, Sex Segregation in the Workplace, 19 *Annual Review of Sociology* 241 (1993); and Cecilia L. Ridgeway and Lynn Smith-Lovin, The Gender System and Interaction, 25 *Annual Review of Sociology* 191 (1999).

19 Barbara Rose, Diversity Goals, Bias Can Collide, *Chicago Tribune*, March 19, 2007, stating that according to a Walgreens spokesman, 17 percent of the company's store and district managers are African American, compared to 9 percent average for the retail drugstore industry. For a brief description of the Walgreens case, see Skrentny, *After Civil Rights*, at 87.

20 See Rose, Diversity Goals, Bias Can Collide.

21 See David B. Wilkins, "From Separate to Inherently Unequal" to "Diversity is Good for Business": The Rise of Market-Based Diversity Arguments and the Fate of the Black Corporate Bar, 117 *Harvard Law Review* 1548 (2004).

22 *Ibid.*, at 1595. A similar pattern emerged in Wall Street firms studied by sociologist Louise Marie Roth. Louise Marie Roth, *Selling Women Short: Gender Inequality on Wall Street* 110 (Princeton University Press, 2006).

23 Rose, Diversity Goals, Bias Can Collide.

24 See EEOC press release, Walgreens Sued for Job Bias Against Blacks, March 7, 2007.

25 See www.naacpldf.org/case-issue/cogdell-v-wet-seal for a description of some of the settlement terms.

26 See Valerie Purdie-Vaughns, Claude M. Steele, Paul G. Davies, Ruth Ditlmann, and Jennifer Randall Crosby, Social Identity Contingencies: How Diversity Cues Signal Threat or Safety for African Americans in Mainstream Institutions, 94 *Journal of Personality & Social Psychology* 615 (2008).

27 See Devon W. Carbado and Mitu Gulati, Working Identity, 85 *Cornell Law Review* 259 (2000). See also Devon W. Carbado and Mitu Gulati, *Acting White? Rethinking Race in "Post-Racial" America* (Oxford University Press, 2013).

28 See David Streitfeld, In Ellen Pao's Suit vs. Kleiner Perkins, World of Venture Capital is Under Microscope, *New York Times*, March 5, 2015.

29 See Davey Alba, How to Succeed in Venture Capital the John Doerr Way, *Wired*, March 4, 2015.

30 Liz Gannes and Nellie Bowles, Kleiner Perkins Wrote an Employment Policy After Female Partner Complaints, *Re/code*, March 12, 2015.

31 Nellie Bowles and Liz Gannes, Juror Speaks About his Vote for Kleiner Perkins but Still Wants the Firm to "Be Punished," *Re/code*, March 30, 2015.

32 Streitfeld, Ellen Pao's Suit vs. Kleiner Perkins.

33 Title VII exempts from coverage employers with fewer than fifteen employees. 42 U.S.C. §2000e(b).

34 See, for example, Susan T. Fiske, Monica Lin, and Steven L. Neuberg, The Continuum Model: Ten Years Later, in *Dual Process Theories in Social Psychology* 231–53 (Shelly Chaiken and Yaacov Trope eds., The Guilford Press, 1999), describing a study finding that men who were primed with stereotypic statements about women were more likely to ask a female job applicant "sexist" questions, and Gretchen B. Sechrist and Charles Stangor, Perceived Consensus Influences Intergroup Behavior and Stereotype Accessibility, 80 *Journal of Personality & Social Psychology* 645 (2001), finding that individuals who believed that they were "out of step" with their peers in racial stereotyping exhibited lower levels of automatic race stereotypes than individuals who believed that their racial beliefs were congruent with those of their peers.

35 Rosabeth Moss Kanter, *Men and Women of the Corporation* (Basic Books, 1977).

36 See, for example, Cecilia L. Ridgeway and Lynn Smith-Lovin, The Gender System and Interaction, 25 *Annual Review of Sociology* 191 (1999), explaining expectation states theory, which posits that when men and women interact within a structurally unequal context, status beliefs are perpetuated, leading them to recreate the gender system in everyday interaction.

37 See Cecilia L. Ridgeway, Linking Social Structure and Interpersonal Behavior: A Theoretical Perspective on Cultural Schemas and Social Relations, 69 *Social Psychology Quarterly* 5 (2006).

38 Ridgeway and Smith-Lovin, The Gender System and Interaction, at 202. Studies suggest similar dynamics in mixed-race interactions. See Mark Chen and John A. Bargh, Nonconscious Behavioral Confirmation Processes: The Self-Fulfilling Consequences of Automatic Stereotype Activation, 33 *Journal of Experimental Social Psychology* 541 (1997).

39 See, for example, Claude M. Steele, *Whistling Vivaldi: How Stereotypes Affect Us and What We Can Do* (W. W. Norton & Co., 2010), at 146, describing a study showing that black applicants trusted a firm with balanced demographics and

also a firm with skewed demographics where the firm espoused a valuing-diversity policy over a color-blind one.

40 Gerhard Daday and Beverly Burris, Technocratic Teamwork: Mitigating Polarization and Cultural Marginalization in an Engineering Firm, in *Research in the Sociology of Work* 241, 257 (Stephen Vallas, ed., vol. X, Emerald Group Pub. Ltd., 2001).

41 Laurel Smith-Doerr, *Women's Work: Gender Equality vs. Hierarchy in the Life Sciences* (Lynne Rienner Publishers, 2004).

42 Alexandra Kalev, Cracking the Glass Cages? Restructuring and Ascriptive Inequality at Work, 114 *American Journal of Sociology* 1591 (2009).

43 Culture is usually explained in the sociological literature as a process of developing shared meanings of experience through ongoing, day-to-day social interaction. In this sense, culture is a form of "'impression management': we act in a way that creates an impression in others that we are adhering to a set of values." Judith S. McIlwee and J. Gregg Robinson, *Women in Engineering: Gender, Power, and Workplace Culture* 17 (Suny Press, 1992). This understanding of culture as a process of impression management builds directly on the work of sociologist Erving Goffman. See Erving Goffman, *The Presentation of Self in Everyday Life* (Random House, 1959). For more discussion of work culture and its relationships to discrimination, see Tristin K. Green, Work Culture and Discrimination, 93 *California Law Review* 623 (2005).

44 See, for example, Gideon Kunda, *Engineering Culture: Control and Commitment in a High-Tech Corporation* 205–13 (Temple University Press, 1992), describing different work cultures in a high-tech engineering firm.

45 McIlwee and Robinson, *Women in Engineering*.

46 *Ibid.*, at 139. The authors explain: "The culture of engineering involves a preoccupation with tinkering that goes beyond the requirements of the job. Vocation becomes avocation, and, in turn, devotion. It is not enough to be competent in the hands-on aspects of engineering; one should be obsessed with them. It is not enough to know the difference between a rod and a piston; one should take obvious joy in this knowledge. The engineer must be ready not only to engage in technical exchanges during work periods, but interested in participating in them during breaks as well. To be seen as a competent engineer means throwing one's self into these rituals of tinkering."

47 *Ibid.*, at 123.

48 See Jessica Leber, A Startup that Scores Job Seekers, Whether They Know It or Not, *MIT Technology Review*, March 7, 2013.

49 See Gene Demby, Why Isn't Open Source a Gateway for Coders of Color?, *National Public Radio*, December 5, 2013.

50 For research on this point, see Marilynn B. Brewer, William von Hippel, and Martin P. Goodman, Diversity and Organizational Identity: The Problem of Entrée after Entry, in *Cultural Divides: Understanding and Overcoming Intergroup Conflict* 337 (Deborah A. Prentice and Dale T. Miller, eds., Russell Sage Foundation, 1999).

51 See also Roth, *Selling Women Short*, at 90, quoting a woman who explained that "clients always assume that I am a junior person," and another who mentioned in an exchange with a male colleague that she was in asset-backed securities, and his response was, "Oh, are you comfortable with numbers?".

52 Class and cultural homophily are also likely to be inextricably intertwined with race and gender. For research emphasizing the effects of work cultures on the decisions (and behaviors) of racial minorities working in law firms and an argument that disparities that result from these decisions might be the product of cultural homophily rather than racial bias, see Kevin Woodson, Derivative Racial Discrimination (unpublished manuscript on file with author).

53 On social closure, see Vincent J. Roscigno, Lisette M. Garcia, and Donna Bobbit-Zeher, Social Closure and Processes of Race/Sex Employment Discrimination, 609 *The Annals of the American Academy of Political and Social Science* 16 (2007).

54 The double bind was recognized by the Supreme Court in *Price Waterhouse v. Hopkins*, 490 U.S. 228, 251 (1989), stating: "An employer who objects to aggressiveness in women but whose positions require this trait places women in an intolerable and impermissible catch-22; out of a job if they behave aggressively and out of a job if they do not."

55 Catherine J. Turco, Cultural Foundations of Tokenism: Evidence from the Leveraged Buyout Industry, 75 *American Sociological Review* 894 (2010).

56 Twenty-five women and six African American men independently raised sports in their interviews as a crucial dimension of bonding within LBO firms. While all six of the African American men said that sports eased their integration into firm life, twenty-one women described sports as alienating and exclusionary. The perceived exclusion included not just conversations about sports, but also being excluded from extra-office sports events. *Ibid.*, at 901.

57 *Ibid.*, at 903.

58 *Ibid.*, at 902. For similar findings in investment banking, see Roth, *Selling Women Short*, at 139, finding that mothers' willingness to work according to a workaholic norm was suspect. Fathers earned more than mothers and also more than childless men, despite working fewer hours than the childless men.

59 See, for example, Shelley J. Correll, Stephen Benard, and In Paik, Getting a Job: Is There a Motherhood Penalty?, 112 *American Journal of Sociology* 1297 (2007).

60 Erin Reid, Embracing, Passing, Revealing, and the Ideal Worker Image: How People Navigate Expected and Experienced Personal Identities, 26 *Organizational Science* 997 (2015).

61 *Ibid.*, at 1011. For a rich, institution-oriented study of rights mobilization involving the Family and Medical Leave Act (FMLA), which mandates an opportunity for up to twelve weeks of unpaid time off for some workers (those who have worked for their employer for at least a year and who work in companies with at least fifty employees) for care for a sick child, parent, or spouse, pregnancy disability, and bonding after the birth of a child, see Catherine R. Albiston, *Institutional Inequality and the Mobilization of the Family and Medical Leave Act: Rights on Leave* (Cambridge University Press, 2010).

62 For a sophisticated treatment of the relationship between citizenship and perceptions around work and work ethic, see Jennifer Gordon and R. A. Lenhardt, Rethinking Work and Citizenship, 55 *UCLA Law Review* 1161 (2008).

63 William T. Bielby, Minority Vulnerability in Privileged Occupations: Why Do African American Financial Advisors Earn Less than Whites in a Large Financial Services Firm?, 639 *The Annals of the American Academy of Political and Social Science* 13 (2012). Class certification was granted in late 2012, and the case settled in 2013.

64 *Ibid.*, at 17.
65 *Ibid.*, at 21–22.
66 *Ibid.*, at 22.
67 *Ibid.*, at 29.
68 *Ibid.*, at 24.
69 *Ibid.*, at 25.
70 Additional research, beyond Merrill Lynch, shows that an organization's culture for professional development of junior employees can similarly affect who gets attention and ultimately succeeds in obtaining higher levels of authority within a firm. In recent research on law firms, sociologists Fiona Kay and Elizabeth Gorman found that an organizational culture fostering and taking responsibility for employees' professional development had a negative effect on the proportion of racial minorities in management. Moreover, the negative effect is stronger as a greater share of junior positions is filled by minorities. Fiona M. Kay and Elizabeth H. Gorman, Developmental Practices, Organizational Culture, and Minority Representation in Organizational Leadership: The Case of Partners in Large U.S. Law Firms, 639 *The Annals of the American Academy of Political and Social Science* 91, 108 (2012).
71 See pitch for book, Linda A. Hill, Greg Brandeau, Emily Truelove, and Kent Lineback, *Collective Genius: The Art and Practice of Leading Innovation* (2014), available at: http://collectivegeniusbook.com/ (last visited July 4, 2016).
72 Jon R. Katzenbach, Ilona Steffan, and Caroline Kronley, Cultural Change that Sticks: Start With What's Already Working, 90 *Harvard Business Review* 110 (July–August 2012).
73 *Ibid.*, at 113.
74 *Ibid.*, at 116.
75 For a sample from Los Angeles, see www.youtube.com/watch?v=mk7qF2eXkgQ (last visited July 4, 2016).
76 See Brian Grow, Diane Brady, and Michael Arndt, Renovating Home Depot, *Business Week*, March 5, 2006.
77 For discussion of this and other reforms made pursuant to the decree, see Susan Sturm, Second Generation Employment Discrimination: A Structural Approach, 101 *Columbia Law Review* 458, 509–19 (2001). The consent decree was lifted in 2002.
78 Alexandra Kalev, Frank Dobbin, and Erin Kelly, Best Practices or Best Guesses?, Assessing the Efficacy of Corporate Affirmative Action and Diversity Policies, 71 *American Sociological Review* 589 (2006).
79 Frank Dobbin, Daniel Schrage, and Alexandra Kalev, Rage Against the Iron Cage: The Varied Effects of Bureaucratic Personnel Reforms on Diversity, 80 *American Sociological Review* 1014 (2015).
80 See, for example, Emilio J. Castilla, Gender, Race, and Meritocracy in Organizational Careers, 113 *American Journal of Sociology* 1479 (2008).
81 Smith-Doerr, *Women's Work*.
82 Kalev, Cracking the Glass Cages?
83 A colorblindness narrative is often perceived as exclusionary by racial minorities and is also associated with higher levels of racial bias on the part of whites. Multiculturalism narratives, while generally associated with lower racial and gender bias and greater acceptance of others than a colorblindness narrative, can lead

to increased stereotyping, and are often met with resistance by white men, who feel excluded. For more on the integration-and-learning perspective, see Robin J. Ely and David A. Thomas, Cultural Diversity at Work: The Effects of Diversity Perspectives on Work Group Processes and Outcomes, 46 *Administrative Science Quarterly* 229 (2001). Researchers sometimes use different language to describe a similar approach. See, for example, Flannery G. Stevens, Victoria C. Plaut, and Jeffrey Sanchez-Burks, Unlocking the Benefits of Diversity: All-Inclusive Multiculturalism and Positive Organizational Change, 44 *Journal of Applied Behavioral Science* 116 (2009).

84 Susan Sturm's work sketches some of these stories, and through the Center for Institutional and Social Change, Sturm continues to generate pathways for organizations to undertake meaningful change.

85 See Jefferson P. Marquis, Nelson Lim, Lynn M. Scott, Margaret C. Harrell, and Jennifer Kavanagh, *Managing Diversity in Corporate America: An Exploratory Analysis* (RAND, 2008).

86 Details here were drawn from two *Harvard Business Review* case studies. See Rosabeth Moss Kanter and Jane Roessner, Deloitte & Touche (A): Hole in the Pipeline, No. 9-300-012, Harvard Business School, May 2, 2003, and Rosabeth Moss Kanter and Jane Roessner, Deloitte & Touche (B): Changing the Workplace, No. 9-300-013, Harvard Business School. See also Sturm, Second Generation Discrimination.

87 Deloitte & Touche (B), at 3.

88 *Ibid.*, at 4–5.

89 *Ibid.*, at 8.

90 See Murray Jacobsen, Google Finally Discloses its Diversity Data, and It's Not Good, PBS Newshour, at www.pbs.org/newshour/updates/google-discloses-workforce-diversity-data-good/ (last visited July 4, 2016).

91 For a link to the video, see Drake Baer, Here's What Google Teaches Employees in its Course on Unconscious Bias, Business Insider, September 24, 2014, www.businessinsider.com/google-course-on-unconscious-bias-2014-9 (last visited July 5, 2016).

7. REVERSING DISCRIMINATION LAUNDERING

1 See Russell K. Robinson, Perceptual Segregation, 108 *Columbia Law Review* 1093 (2008).

2 See Eden B. King, D. Dunleavy, E. Dunleavy *et al.*, Discrimination in the 21st Century: Are Science and the Law Aligned?, 17 *Psychology, Public Policy, & Law*, 54, 56–57 (2011). For a description of some of these and other racial "microaggressions," see Derald Wing Sue, Christina M. Capodilupo, Gina C. Torino *et al.*, Racial Microaggressions in Everyday Life: Implications for Clinical Practice, 62 *American Psychologist* 271 (2007).

3 See Margo Schlanger and Pauline Kim, The Equal Employment Opportunity Commission and Structural Reform of the American Workplace, 91 *Washington University Law Review* 1519 (2014), describing data on EEOC litigation and injunctive relief obtained. The authors of another recent study of employment discrimination litigation concluded that "Employment discrimination litigation is

not so much an engine for social change, or even a forum for carefully judging the merits of claims of discrimination, as it is a mechanism for channeling and deflecting individual claims of workplace justice." Laura Beth Nielsen, Robert L. Nelson, and Ryon Lancaster, Individual Justice or Collective Legal Mobilization? Employment Discrimination Litigation in the Post-Civil Rights United States, 7 *Journal of Empirical Legal Studies* 175, 196 (2010).

4 Patricia G. Devine and Kristin A. Vasquez, The Rocky Road to Positive Intergroup Relations, in *Confronting Racism: The Problem and the Response* 234, 261–62 (Jennifer L. Eberhardt and Susan T. Fiske, eds., Sage Publications, Inc., 1998). For more on the need for conversation and positive emotion in intergroup interactions, see Tristin K. Green, Racial Emotion in the Workplace, 86 *Southern California Law Review* 959, 1015–1018 (2013).

5 Jeffrey C. Connor, It Wasn't About Race. Or Was It?, 78 *Harvard Business Review* 37 (September/October 2000).

6 *Ibid.*, at 42.

7 *Ibid.*

8 The organization is seen under this model as "not only a collection of people who shape it and activate it, but also a set of attitudes and positions, which influence, constrain, and at times even define the modes of thinking and behavior of the people who populate it." Eli Lederman, Models for Imposing Corporate Criminal Liability: From Adaptation and Imitation Toward Aggregation and the Search for Self-Identity, 4 *Buffalo Criminal Law Review* 641, 686 (2000). For more on a context-based model in other areas of law, see Tristin K. Green, The Future of Systemic Disparate Treatment Law, 32 *Berkeley Journal of Employment & Labor Law* 395, 434–40 (2011).

9 This is true even as the law of section 1983 of the Civil Rights Act of 1866 focuses on individual moments. See Chapter 3. Employment discrimination law in fact holds even more potential through systemic disparate treatment theory to incorporate (or return to) a situationist story like that emphasized recently in some of the reviews of widespread police misconduct.

10 Erwin Chemerinsky, An Independent Analysis of the Los Angeles Police Department's Board of Inquiry Report on the Rampart Scandal, 34 *Loyola Los Angeles Law Review* 545 (2001).

11 Samuel Walker, The New Paradigm of Police Accountability: The U.S. Justice Department "Pattern or Practice" Suits in Context, 22 *St. Louis University Public Law Review* 3, 7 (2003).

12 United States Department of Justice, Civil Rights Division, Investigation of the Ferguson Police Department (March 4, 2015), available at: www.justice.gov/sites/default/files/opa/press-releases/attachments/2015/03/04/ferguson_police_department_report.pdf (last visited July 4, 2016).

13 *Ibid.*, at 2. See also at 12, stating that "enough officers – at all ranks – have internalized this message that a culture of reflexive enforcement action, unconcerned with whether the police action actually promotes public safety, and unconcerned with the impact the decision has on individual lives or community trust as a whole, has taken hold within FPD."

14 *Ibid.*, at 90–96.

15 *Ibid.*, at 96–102. Advocates and scholars have struggled to make similar headway in the area of sex-based harassment in educational institutions. See, for example, Katharine B. Silbaugh, Reactive to Proactive: Title IX's Unrealized Capacity to Prevent Campus Assault, 95 *Boston University Law Review* 1049 (2015), arguing in favor of a public health model for Title IX enforcement. A public health model would expand the frame of causation, though it risks leaving institutions framed as innocent.

16 EEOC Press Release, Potato Packing Companies to Pay $450,000 to Settle EEOC Suit for Sex Harassment and Retaliation.

17 See Southern Poverty Law Center, *Injustice on Our Plates* (2010) n. 6. See also Maria L. Ontiveros, Lessons From the Fields, Female Farmworkers and the Law, 53 *Maine Law Review* 157 (2002), detailing some of the data on farmworkers in the United States and some of the ways in which farmworkers have tried to use the law to fight discrimination and other illegal practices.

18 Indeed, the Court justified the affirmative defense by stating that it served two important policies: encouraging employers to adopt measures that prevent, and do not merely compensate for, discrimination; and encouraging employees to mitigate damages by reporting incidences of harassment. As one commentator recently put it, "[E]xperience shows that the *Faragher/Ellerth* defense has not served those interests in practice." Samuel R. Bagenstos, Formalism and Employer Liability under Title VII, 145 University of Chicago Legal Forum 171 (2014).

19 See, for example, Ellen Berrey, Steve G. Hoffman, and Laura Beth Nielsen, Situated Justice: A Contextual Analysis of Fairness and Inequality in Employment Discrimination Litigation, 46 *Law & Society Review* 1 (2012), studying perceived fairness by litigants in employment discrimination litigation and demonstrating structural asymmetries that "profoundly benefit employers in employment discrimination lawsuits."

20 Lilly Ledbetter with Lanier Scott Isom, *Grace and Grit: My Fight for Equal Pay and Fairness at Goodyear and Beyond* 200 (Three Rivers Press, Random House, Inc., 2012).

21 For recent work showing that individual discrimination claims today tend to reinscribe hierarchy rather than disrupt it, see Ellen Berrey, Robert L. Nelson, and Laura Beth Nielsen, *Rights on Trial: Employment Civil Rights in the Workplace and in Context* (forthcoming University of Chicago Press Law and Society Series) (manuscript draft on file with author). On rates of success, see Nielsen, Nelson, and Lancaster, Individual Justice or Collective Legal Mobilization? and on litigant perceptions, see Ellen Berrey, Steve G. Hoffman, and Laura Beth Nielsen, Situated Justice: A Contextual Analysis of Fairness and Inequality in Employment Discrimination Litigation, 46 *Law & Society Review* 1 (2012).

22 For more on the relationship between law and social science in systemic employment discrimination litigation, see Tristin K. Green, "It's Not You, It's Me": Assessing an Emerging Relationship Between Law and Social Science, 46 *Connecticut Law Review* 287 (2013).

23 Proposed Preliminary Approval of Class Settlement, *McReynolds v. Merrill Lynch, & Co., Inc.*, Case No. 05-CV-06583 (N.D. Il., August. 28, 2013), at 3, stating that: "Plaintiffs agree with Merrill Lynch that teaming and pooling are advantageous business practices and do not seek to eliminate them. The parties agree that

a desirable outcome of this Settlement would be to increase African American participation in pools and teams and eliminate teams or pools that are formed for improper reasons." See also Settlement Agreement and Release, at 47, describing proposed "programmatic relief" that retains teaming practices, including substantial discretion in selecting teammates.

24 In addition to the declarations involving senior managers calling female store managers "Janie Qs" and "girls" and the company newsletter featuring an executive at a company event sitting in a giant leopard-skin stiletto surrounded by dancing women (see Chapter 3), declarations submitted by plaintiffs recited multiple incidents where male managers responded to women's requests for transfers to departments like Hardware or Guns with sex-stereotyped refusals, including statements like "[y]]ou're a girl, why do you want to be in Hardware?" and "[y]ou don't want to work with guns." Again, my point is not that this evidence should be used to argue that all or even most male managers were operating under sex-based stereotypes, but rather that the organizational culture – and culture within stores – is one mechanism for discrimination and accordingly for an organization's effort to minimize discrimination as well. Indeed, the annual quail hunt, a corporate retreat for executives and senior management, might also signal that the once all-male bastion of executives (the hunt was started by founder Sam Walton and held for many years on his property in Texas) is less welcoming of women into its fold than it claims to be. See Plaintiffs' Motion for Class Certification and Memorandum of Points and Authorities, *Dukes* v. *Wal-Mart*, Case No. 3:01-CV-02252 (N.D. Cal., July 25, 2003), at 12, 14, describing executives' rejection of proposals to change the quail hunt to a skiing or river-rafting trip.

25 Melissa Hart, The Possibility of Avoiding Discrimination: Considering Compliance and Liability, 39 *Connecticut Law Review* 1623 (2007).

26 Richard Thompson Ford, Beyond Good and Evil in Civil Rights Law: The Case of *Wal-Mart* v. *Dukes*, 32 *Berkeley Journal of Employment and Labor Law* 513, 528 (2011).

27 On decoupling generally, see John W. Meyer and Brian Rowan, Institutionalized Organizations: Formal Structure as Myth and Ceremony, 83 *American Journal of Sociology* 340 (1977), and Patricia Bromley and Walter W. Powell, From Smoke and Mirrors to Walking the Talk: Decoupling in the Contemporary World, 36 *The Annals of the Academy of Management* 1 (2012). For a recent study analyzing practices of firms named on Fortune's "50 Best Companies for Minorities" and finding that "the path to diversity success varies according to a company's history, culture, and mission," see Jefferson P. Marquis, Nelson Lim, Lynn M. Scott, Margaret C. Harrell, and Jennifer Kavanagh, Managing Diversity in Corporate America: An Exploratory Analysis, 24 (RAND Labor and Population, 2008). The study also suggests that characteristics of a company may also influence its success with diversity. *Ibid.*, at 23–24.

28 See Lauren B. Edelman Linda H. Krieger, Scott R. Eliason, Catherine R. Albiston, and Virginia Mellema, When Organizations Rule: Judicial Deference to Institutionalized Employment Structures, 117 *American Journal of Sociology* 888 (2011), and Linda Hamilton Krieger, Rachel Kahn Best, and Lauren B. Edelman, When "Best Practices" Win, Employees Lose: Symbolic Compliance and Judicial Inference in Federal Equal Employment Opportunity Cases, 40 *Law & Social*

Inquiry 843 (2015). Recent research suggests that a focus on procedure and information production rather than directly on ultimate goals results in means-end decoupling, where organizations pursue activities, like diversity training, that are weakly linked to success in intended goals. See Bromley and Powell, From Smoke and Mirrors to Walking the Talk, at 26.

29 And "when judges defer to organizational structures – treating their mere presence as evidence of nondiscrimination while failing to scrutinize their effectiveness – employers benefit," meaning that employers are winning legal cases simply because they have the structures in place, and not because they are actually minimizing discrimination. Krieger, Best, and Edelman, When "Best Practices" Win, at 861.

30 Richard Thompson Ford, Civil Rights 2.0: Encouraging Innovation to Tackle Silicon Valley's Diversity Deficit, 11 *Stanford Journal of Civil Rights & Civil Liberties* 155, 158, 176 (2015).

31 The law does not require proportional representation; nor does it require that employers eliminate all discrimination. To avoid liability under systemic disparate treatment law, employers must minimize disparate treatment (refrain from inciting disparate treatment) to the point that it is not a regular, widespread practice.

32 Title VII is generally understood to prohibit quotas, even as it allows consideration of protected status in some circumstances. For discussion of appropriate limits and potential, see Tristin K. Green, Race and Sex in Organizing Work, "Diversity," Discrimination, and Integration, 59 *Emory Law Journal* 585 (2010). Professor Ford, in contrast, argues that employers should be freed from all Title VII constraints. See Ford, Civil Rights 2.0, at 177–78.

33 For an argument that Title VII does not permit employers to make race- or sex-based decisions for business reasons alone, but that it does and should permit race- and sex-based decisions to further the goal of reducing workplace discrimination, see Green, Race and Sex in Organizing Work.

34 As Ford sees it, "Employers with unwelcoming workplace cultures don't know how to change those cultures without risking the environment that has made them successful." Ford, Civil Rights 2.0, at 157.

35 These projects are sometimes disseminated through case studies and books written by professors in business schools. See, for example, David A. Thomas and Stephanie J. Creary, Shifting the Diversity Climate: The Sodexo Solution, Harvard Business School Case Study No. 9-412-020 (2011). Business schools might do more to emphasize the need to minimize discrimination, and undertake projects aimed at learning and practicing how to assess and implement change around diversity. See, for example, Case Study of Denny's Restaurant, IBS Research Center Study No. 408-074-1 (2009), and Robin Ely, Managing Diversity at Spencer Owens & Co., Harvard Business School Case Study No. 9-405-048 (2006). Business schools and law schools might also collaborate to bring equal opportunity law together with diversity management.

36 Indeed, it may be that organizational leaders feel hampered in devising solutions precisely because they leave gendered and racial work cultures entirely off the table when thinking about measures to reduce discrimination. See Ellen Berrey, *The Enigma of Diversity: The Language of Race and the Limits of Racial Justice* 8 (University of Chicago Press, 2015), describing the selective inclusivity of the

diversity movement whereby "[c]ultural value is placed on the so-called diverse poeple who are most easily incorporated into a setting and who enhance institutional objectives such as prestige, distinction, or profit-making." Through selective inclusion, diversity becomes "surprisingly low risk for the high-status white people who do the managing of diversity."

37 *McDonnell Douglas Corp.* v. *Green*, 411 U.S. 792, 805 n. 19 (1972). See discussion of *McDonnell Douglas* in Chapter 1.

38 The Court in *Wal-Mart* was wrong to think that defendants have a right to individualized defenses in a systemic disparate treatment case, see Melissa Hart, Civil Rights and Systemic Wrongs, 32 *Berkeley Journal of Employment and Labor Law* 455 (2011), which Congress might also correct by statute.

39 *Chen-Oster* v. *Goldman, Sachs & Co.*, No. 10 Civ. 6950 (LBS)(JCF), 2011 WL 2671813 at *4 (July 7, 2011). See also at *3, stating that "the right at the center of this case is not the right to proceed on a class basis but the substantive right under Title VII to bring a pattern or practice claim under Title VII." Courts in the district had held that individuals could not pursue pattern or practice claims; they must be pursued as a class. This made class action treatment crucial to vindicating the substantive pattern or practice claim. See *Chen-Oster* v. *Goldman, Sachs & Co.*, 785 F. Supp. 2d 394, 409 (S.D.N.Y. 2011).

40 See, for example, Kevin Stainback and Donald Tomaskovic-Devey, *Documenting Desegregation: Racial and Gender Segregation in Private-Sector Employment Since the Civil Rights Act xxxiv* (Russell Sage Foundation, 2012).

41 See C. Elizabeth Hirsh, The Strength of Weak Enforcement: The Impact of Discrimination Charges, Legal Environments, and Organizational Conditions on Workplace Segregation, 74 *American Sociological Review* 245 (2009), suggesting also at 268 that "enforcement agencies could buttress the case-by-case remedial approach by proactively identifying systematic discrimination and drawing attention to enforcement efforts."

42 See Department of Justice, Clarification of Intercollegiate Athletics Policy Guidance: The Three-Part Test, describing Part Two of the test, available at: www2. ed.gov/about/offices/list/ocr/docs/clarific.html#two (last visited July 4, 2016). I thank David Cohen for reminding me of the Title IX standard and the potential usefulness of something similar as organizations put nondiscrimination on the table and engage in organizational change aimed at minimizing discrimination in their workplaces.

Index

Age Discrimination in Employment Act
(ADEA), 9
American Civil Liberties Union (ACLU)
harassment policy, 53
on pornography, 95
Americans with Disabilities Act (ADA), 9
Ashcroft v. Iqbal, 41

Bagenstos, Samuel, 76
Banaji, Mahzarin & Greenwald, Anthony,
Blindspot, 34
Bielby, William, 79, 132
Burlington Industries v. Ellerth, 50, 55, 151
business case for diversity, *see* diversity
management

Catalyst, 139
Chemerinsky, Erwin, 148
Civil Rights Act of 1866, section 1983, 82
Civil Rights Act of 1964, 8
1991 Amendments, 77
Title IX, 82
Title VII, 8
class actions, 72
definition of employer, 21
disrupting racialized and gendered
cultures, 158
express discriminatory policies, 67
government enforcement, 71
private enforcement, 71
text, 21
class actions
controversy over, 73–74
cognitive bias, 30
aversive racism, 30
categorization, 30
effect on organizational innocence, 40–42

effect on proving discrimination, 32–33
Implicit Attitudes Test (IAT), 31
as relational, 102
and *Wal-Mart v. Dukes*, 75
complaint and grievance systems, 38
concern about over-policing, 47
effect on organizational innocence, 39
emergence of and popularity, 38–39
problems with, 110–12
Connor, Eugene "Bull," 8
context and bias
demographics, 125–26
organizing work, 126–27
racist and sexist enviroments, 124
work culture, 127–28
commitment, 130–31
engineering, 128–29
leverage buyout firms, 129–30
Merrill Lynch, 132–34
organizations shaping, 134–36
Cook, Mike, 139

DeClue v. Central Illinois Light, 92–93
deliberate indifference standard, 81
contrasting Title VII, 83
and organizational innocence, 82
and proving pattern or practice in Title IX
or section 1983, 82
Deloitte & Touche, Women's Initiative, 138–40
discrimination
difficulty detecting, 104
meaning, 7–8
over time, 101
perceptions of, 145–46
as relational, 102–04
discrimination laundering
meaning, 1

disparate impact
  employer liability, 67
  Griggs v. *Duke Power*, 21–22, 67
diversity management
  effect on organizational innocence, 36–37
  rhetoric, 3, 35, 118–19
diversity narratives
  colorblindness, 138
  integration and learning, 138
  meaning, 138
  multiculturalism, 138
diversity training
  new wave, 113
  prevalence of, 112
  problems with, 113
diversity work, 121
Dobbin, Frank, 112

Edelman, Lauren, 36
EEOC v. *BCI Coca-Cola Bottling*, 59–60
EEOC v. *Boh Brothers Construction*, 90–92
EEOC v. *Walgreens*, 120
Ely, Robin, 147
Equal Employment Opportunity Commission
    (EEOC)
  continued role, 157
  filing requirement, 61
  harassment guidance, 53
  harassment in agriculture, 149

Faragher v. *City of Boca Raton*, 50, 51, 55, 151
Federal Rule of Civil Procedure 23, 72
Ferguson, Missouri, Michael Brown
    shooting, 149
  US Dept. of Justice Report, 149
Ford, Richard, 157
formalization of criteria and job ratings
  benefits, 113
  problems with, 114
Furnco Construction v. *Waters*, 24–25

Gladwell, Malcolm, *Blink*, 31
Google, diversity initiatives, 113, 140
  Welle, Brian, unconscious bias
      workshop, 113
Gorman, Elizabeth, 30
Greenwald, Anthony, 31

Harris v. *Forklift Systems, Inc.*, 54–55
Harvard Business Review, 3, 134, 147
Havard Business School, 134
Hazelwood School District v. *United States*, 70

Hill, Linda, 134
Home Depot
  changing culture, 134–36
hostile work environment, 50
  harassment
    all-male environments, 89–92
    employer liability, 50, 51
    personalized, 52

implicit bias, *see* cognitive bias
individual disparate treatment
  acknowledging limits of, 151–52
  adverse action requirement, 61
  employer vicarious liability, 48–49
  proving, 33, 105–06
integrated work teams, 137
International Brotherhood of Teamsters v.
    United States, 22, 68–69, 107

Kalev, Alexandra, 112, 126, 137
Kanter, Rosabeth Moss, 125
Kingsley, Randall, 11–15

Ledbetter v. *Goodyear Tire*, 27–29
Ledbetter, Lilly, *Grace and Grit*, 18, 27, 152
legal endogeneity, 36
Leisner v. *New York Telephone Company*, 73
looking to the aggregate, 106
Lopéz-Sanders, Laura, 117
Los Angeles Police Department
    (LAPD), 148

McCormack v. *Safeway Stores*, 58
McDonnell Douglas v. *Green*, 23–24
McIlwee, Judith, 128
McReynolds v. *Merrill Lynch*, 95–96, 132–34
Meritor Savings Bank v. *Vinson*, 53–54

NAACP v. *Wet Seal*, 117
Nagareda, Richard, 76, 77
neo-liberalism, 2
nondiscrimination policies, 110

Ocheltree v. *Scollon Productions*, 94
organizational accountability, 137
organizational innocence
  conceptual components, 40–42
  effect on employer liability, 59
  effect on systemic disparate treatment, 66

Pao v. *Kleiner Perkins*, 15–18, 33, 38, 103,
    104–05, 121–23

pattern or practice of discrimination, *see* systemic disparate treatment
personalizing discrimination disaggregation, 89
personalizing racialized interaction, 86–87
    reasonableness and racial offense, 87–89
Pierce, Jennifer, 12
police brutality and context, 148–49
Posner, Richard
    on employer liability for harassment, 55
    and the theory switch, 92–94, 95–96
post-racialism, 2
Pratt v. Austal, 87
Price Waterhouse v. Hopkins, 25, 45, 60

quotas, 157–58

race- and sex-matching, 119
    problems with, 120
racial realism, *see* Skrentny, John, *After Civil Rights*
recruitment and outreach, 137
Regents of the University of California v. Bakke, 35
Reid, Erin, 130
relationship between law and social science, 154–55
Reskin, Barbara, 102
Robinson v. Jacksonville Shipyards, 94
Robinson, Gregg, 128

Schrage, Daniel, 112
Skrentny, John, *After Civil Rights*, 117
Slack v. Havens, 25, 45, 60
Smith-Doerr, Laurel, 126, 137
St. Mary's Honor Center v. Hicks, 86
Staub v. Proctor Hospital, 60
Steele, Claude, 103
stereotype threat, 103
stratification and segregation, 4–5
subjective decision-making cases, 72–73
Sweezer v. Michigan Department of Corrections, 86–87
systemic disparate treatment, 22–23
    anecdotal testimony, 71

a context model, 152–53
    social science experts, 107–08
contrasting disparate impact, 153–54
    organizational control over solutions, 155
employer as conduit, 75–76
employer liability, 67
pattern or practice of discrimination defense, 155–56
    proving widespread discrimination, 81
    social science experts, 71
    use of statistics, 107
proving widespread discrimination, 68
rough justice for individuals, 159
seen as mass tort, 76–77
use of statistics, 68–69

the theory switch, 92–94, 95–97
    resisting the switch, 153–54
Thomas v. Eastman Kodak, 62
Thomas, R. Roosevelt, 35
Thomas-Hill hearings, 55
Tinkler, Justine, 113
Title VII, *see* Civil Rights Act of 1964, Title VII
transparency, 137
Turco, Catherine, 129

Uniformed Services Employment and Reemployment Rights Act (USERRA), 60

Vance v. Ball State University, 56–58
Vance, Maetta, 19

Walker, Samuel, 149
Wal-Mart v. Dukes, 74–75
    deliberate indifference, 81
    Dukes, Betty, 19
    and organizational innocence, 77–80
    viewed in aggregate, 107, 108–09
    Wal-Mart's nondiscrimination policy, 26
Wheeler, Leigh Ann, 52
White v. Government Employees Insurance Company, 88–89
Wilkins, David, 120
Winfrey, Oprah, 31